PROPHET IN THE WILDERNESS

The Works of Ezequiel Martínez Estrada

THE TEXAS PAN AMERICAN SERIES

PROPHET
IN THE WILDERNESS

The Works of Ezequiel Martínez Estrada

by Peter G. Earle

UNIVERSITY OF TEXAS PRESS · AUSTIN & LONDON

Frontispiece photograph by Alejandro Wolk

The Texas Pan American Series is published with the assistance
of a revolving publication fund established by the Pan American
Sulphur Company and other friends of Latin America in Texas.

International Standard Book Number 0-292-70107-1
Library of Congress Catalog Card Number 78-165907
© 1971 by Peter G. Earle
Printed by The University of Texas Printing Division, Austin
Bound by Universal Bookbindery Inc., San Antonio

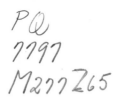
To the memory of Victor M. Earle

CONTENTS

PREFACE

This book has two purposes: to analyze the principal works of Ezequiel Martínez Estrada and to interpret his role in Argentine intellectual history. Although he is Argentina's most important essayist of the twentieth century, he is not well known outside the Hispanic world. Even in his own country relatively little has been written specifically about his work.

Nevertheless, his influence has been deep. In Argentina the intellectual community and the great majority of well-read men and women know who Martínez Estrada was, what he wrote, and what he stood for. His work is recognized now as more significant than it was at the time he wrote it. Like his greatest Hispanic American contemporaries—Jorge Luis Borges, Pablo Neruda, Miguel Angel Asturias, and Octavio Paz—Martínez Estrada extended his concern for national problems to a broad vision of universal proportions. In due time he will be recognized as one of the most powerful and sensitive writers of our time.

His central theme, repeated with variations in essays, poetry, and fiction, might be summed up as follows. All men have an ironic quality in common, their solitude. This solitude is not only personal but historical, the logical result of an age that has lost faith in progress and has reconstructed its thinking so as to consider man a victim of his own existence rather than, as formerly, the persistent adventurer in a mysterious world.

Like most prophets, Martínez Estrada was born too late to play the additional role of the reformer, a circumstance that helps explain his isolation among his compatriots. He excoriated them for what he thought to be their self-deluding view of Argentine history. Not all, naturally, were pleased by his attacks, but most were impressed, and the more conscientious were incited to begin a reevaluation of the Argentine past and of Hispanic American institutions. His literary mission was to recapitulate the hopes and disappointments of many preceding generations, of imaginative men who from the earliest colonial times to the twentieth century had sought adventure, contentment, and beauty in the open spaces of South America. The disillusionment, violence, and loneliness they found instead, he concludes, produced a collective attitude of permanent resignation. Argentine political life, in steady decline since 1930, and the foreboding spirit that has permeated Argentine literature over the same period do indeed reflect that attitude—notwithstanding the fact that around 1880 Argentina began a substantial rise to prosperity that was to make it the most affluent Hispanic American nation.

But I have no intention of portraying Martínez Estrada as a historian or sociologist. First and last, he was a writer. His numerous readings in history, sociology, anthropology, and philosophy did not diminish his poetic power. Rather, they added substance and energy to his apocalyptic vision. The author of *X-Ray of the Pampa* has joined a distinguished association of intellectual misfits that includes Montaigne, Schopenhauer, Thoreau, Nietzsche, Unamuno, and Kafka.

I should like to acknowledge gratefully the bibliographical assistance of Enrique Espinoza, Arnaldo Orfila Reynal, Sheilah R. Wilson, and Carole Goldman. I owe special thanks to Otis H. Green for his careful reading of the text and his suggestions, and to Agustina M. de Martínez Estrada, the writer's widow, for her generosity and cooperative spirit in allowing me to consult a large amount of unpublished and uncollected material. Finally, I wish to thank the American Philosophical Society for a grant that made possible an indispensable research trip to Buenos Aires and Bahía Blanca.

P. G. E.
Drexel Hill, Pennsylvania

PROPHET IN THE WILDERNESS

The Works of Ezequiel Martínez Estrada

Y ahora, al final de tu camino,
buscas a Dios, que sabes que no existe.

—Ezequiel Martínez Estrada

1 · Introduction

The Man

When in 1933 Martínez Estrada published *X-Ray of the Pampa* (x-ray of Argentine culture, history, character, and psychology) a new epoch in Argentine literature was born. Although he was not the first in the twentieth century to attempt a critical analysis of Argentine life and tradition, he was the first to call directly for a change in his countrymen's evaluation of their past and present. Others had approached the matter tangentially: Leopoldo Lugones as an aesthetically oriented poet (in prose as in verse), Ricardo Rojas as a literary historian, and Manuel Gálvez as a novelist.[1] But Martínez Estrada, with greater impact than Gilberto Freyre in Brazil (*The*

[1] Gálvez admired Unamuno and corresponded with him, as did Ricardo Rojas. See Manuel García Blanco, *América y Unamuno*, pp. 31–52, 247–340. From about 1910 (see Manuel Gálvez, *El diario de Gabriel Quiroga*, 1910, and *El*

Masters and the Slaves, 1933) or Samuel Ramos in Mexico (*Profile of Man and Culture in Mexico*, 1934), awoke in his own country a revitalized national consciousness comparable in many ways to that of the Generation of 1898 in Spain.

The Argentine political crisis of 1930—the culmination of serious latent problems and the beginning of others equally serious—took place in psychological circumstances similar to those of 1898 in Spain, and the intellectual reactions were also similar: pessimism, skeptical appraisal of traditional values, renewed interest in the symbols of national life, and enthusiasm for contemporary foreign cultures.

But there were important circumstantial differences between the Spanish and Argentine generations. The Spaniards, as reflected in the sensitive meditations of Unamuno, Baroja, and Azorín, were predominantly "time obsessed," and the substance of their works was the meaning of Spanish tradition, religiosity, individualism, and decadence against the general background of Western history. The Argentines, on the other hand, were "space obsessed." Lacking the rich, chaotic tradition that the Spaniards had always lived and re-lived, they began in their age of intellectual awakening after 1920 the imaginary reconquest of their imaginary pampa. The Spaniard lost himself in his history, the Argentine in his spaces; the former was oriented toward the past, the latter, toward the future. His life, as the reader is constantly reminded by Martínez Estrada, was always a succession of illusions shimmering on the horizon, illusions that included an idealized image of himself as an adventurer certain to achieve great things in the future. But the future, like the horizons

---

solar de la raza, 1908; Ricardo Rojas, *La restauración nacionalista*, 1909; Leopoldo Lugones, *El payador*, 1916), centenary of Argentina's independence, there is a marked trend toward nationalism in literature. Manuel Gálvez, prolific and popular novelist, had great ambitions as interpreter of his country's history and spirit (see Otis H. Green's three articles in *Hispanic Review*: "Manuel Gálvez, *Gabriel Quiroga* and *La maestra normal*," 11 (1943): 221–252; Manuel Gálvez, *Gabriel Quiroga* and *El mal metafísico*," 11 (1943): 314–327; and "Gálvez's *La sombra del convento* and its relation to *El diario de Gabriel Quiroga*," 12 (1944): 196–210). Aspiring to the social and psychological understanding of Pérez Galdós, the spiritual depth of Tolstoy, and the regenerative mission of Unamuno and Ganivet, he matched none of them in achievement. His characters were superficial and his thought platitudinous.

of space, always evades one's grasp, merging the real and the unreal, what is done and what is merely hoped for. Martínez Estrada could not have failed to read two of José Ortega y Gasset's essays written during a 1929 visit to Argentina. In the first of them ("La pampa . . . promesas") is the following:

The Pampa promises, promises, and promises. . . . From the horizon it makes infinite gestures of generosity and concession. Here everything lives on distances, and from the vantage point of distances. Almost no man is where he is, but rather ahead of himself, far out on the horizon of himself; and from *there* he controls and fulfills his life which is *here*: his real, present and effective one. The Argentine's mode of existence is what I would call *the concrete futurism of the individual*. Not the generic futurism of a common ideal or collective utopia, but rather the living of each man in the perspective of his own illusions, as if these were already a reality.[2]

It was within this framework of philosophical solitude that Martínez Estrada developed his writings from 1930 on, having first thoroughly absorbed the pessimism of his favorite European philosophers.

Eduardo Mallea (author of *History of an Argentine Passion* and numerous philosophical novels), Jorge Luis Borges (creator in poetry, stories, and short essays of a new world of the imagination), and Ezequiel Martínez Estrada were the three principal leaders of the Argentine literary renaissance that began in the late 1920's and the early 1930's.

Martínez Estrada began his literary life in 1917, publishing his first essays in *Nosotros* (Buenos Aires), and worked intensively until shortly before his death in 1964. The two dates encompass crises in the Western World of apocalyptic significance, anticipated in the dark prophecies and ultimate madness of Nietzsche and recorded as an awesome existential presence by Kafka, Sartre, and Ortega y Gasset. Beset from within by the continuing struggle between his skepticism and his idealism, he placed the precarious historical period in which he lived in the context of the whole Argentine and Hispanic American past. Though always sensitive to history, he recognized no

[2] José Ortega y Gasset, *Obras completas*, p. 639. The other essay on Argentina is "El hombre a la defensiva."

important evolutionary development. If superficial circumstances differed from age to age, men remained the same and experienced the same basic problems. The sterile existence of colonial society in America was repeating itself, he thought, in the cities and provinces of the twentieth century.

In the period from 1917 to 1964, civilization reached the paradoxical point of tacitly accepting organized destruction as a major and *normal* fact of historical life. Spengler, who considered Western civilization to have reached the end of its cycle, Ortega y Gasset, who saw in the growing power of the "mass-man"[3] a serious formalization of violence and primitivism, and Martínez Estrada, who reached the disconcerting conclusion that civilization and barbarism were integral parts of the same phenomenon, "like centrifugal and centripetal forces in one delicately balanced system," recognized this major and normal fact.

Ironically, the first great political stimulus to bring the diverse national forces of Europe and America into a permanent, multiple relationship was World War I. A destructive rather than constructive event thus inspired what would later be called the virtue of "internationalism." Primitivism and technology, as Ortega y Gasset convincingly points out in *The Revolt of the Masses*, go quite as well together as do technology and civilization. Thus twentieth-century man could understand, said Martínez Estrada, what the great Argentine statesman and educator of the past, Domingo Faustino Sarmiento (1811–1888), could not understand: that civilization and savagery had turned out to be complementary rather than opposing forces. As a poet and entirely "self-made" student of philosophy and sociology (he had little formal schooling and no university training), Martínez Estrada became a stern revisionist of Argentine history and culture, expressing in his perspective of the past the same articulate despair that several Germans (including Schopenhauer, Nietzsche,

---

[3] Ortega presents the mass-man—in *Invertebrate Spain* (1922) and more fully in *The Revolt of the Masses* (1930)—as an inevitable result and the "spoiled child" of modern civilization. The mass-man resents excellence in others, recognizes no authority, and considers himself automatically endowed with the same talents, rights, and privileges as all other men. He is, in effect, an up-to-date (and very influential) barbarian in the civilized world.

and Thomas Mann) had expressed in their perspective of the future. Like Spengler, Martínez Estrada considered civilization as he knew it to be the final stage ("old age" and "death") of culture; and the history of Hispanic America from the time of Columbus' voyages to the twentieth century was a long, almost uninterrupted chronicle of deception, of figuratively blind explorers struggling across an empty and borderless plain. The promised land of the New World was, in more realistic terms, a land of promises.

Like many fine Spanish American prose writers of the twentieth century (Argentina's Jorge Luis Borges, Cuba's Alejo Carpentier, Guatemala's Miguel Angel Asturias, and Mexico's Alfonso Reyes, to mention but a few), Martínez Estrada was also a poet. Although he had an intense interest in history, sociology, and politics, his interpretation of reality was basically lyric and temperamental, and the inevitable conclusion in all his works from 1929 (year of publication of his best book of poetry, *Humoresca*) to his death was one of romantic despair. As early as 1922 his perspective is set: 'Sad but true, the world is our own invention,/ and the sea and the star, a mere emotion,/ and out of this chaos of mysterious things/ comes the woeful truth; we alone are real."[4]

Things, the objective world ("las cosas") vanish before the poet's eyes; ultimately the poet, like the pessimistic philosopher into which Martínez Estrada progressively develops, is left with nothing but himself—a soul in voluntary exile. In a characteristically entitled "Useless Prologue" published the year of his death, Martínez Estrada recalls the era in which he wrote his six books of verse (1918–1929) as his "mental adolescence and phase of life devoted to the games, speculation, and cult of letters."[5] *X-ray of the Pampa* (1933) was the certain sign of his maturity, the "nearly total cancellation" of the relatively playful period of literary experimentation in the 1920's. But this gravity of purpose was by no means sudden. His basic pessi-

---

[4] Da pena, pero es cierto que creamos las cosas
que el mar y que la estrella son sólo una emoción
y que entre este tumulto de cosas misteriosas
somos la triste y única realidad de las cosas.
(From "La nueva razón pura," in *Poesía*, p. 80.)
[5] "Prólogo inútil," in *Antología*, p. 12.

mism had expressed itself fragmentarily and sporadically since his first published essay, "Tesoros Velados" (1917),[6] in which he emphasizes his interest in Schopenhauer and defends the spontaneous spirit—"mysterious little light"—against the dark ravages of reason. Here it appears that Martínez Estrada may have read *The Book of Divine Comfort* by Meister (Johannes) Eckhart (1260?–1328?), who refers to the "divine spark" (*das Funkelein*) that every man should seek within himself. If this was the case, Eckhart was probably instrumental—together with Schopenhauer and Nietzsche—in Don Ezequiel's early separation from Catholicism. By 1928 one can appreciate the maturity of his thought and his clear cognizance of life as a progressive dilemma:

> At 15 we were convinced Catholics, at 20, metaphysicians and utopian socialists (*falansterios*), but at 30 we are a syncretic amorphous whole, because we have sacrificed our most precious natural impulses and acquired mental and physical habits that properly belong to others and other circumstances. "Know thyself" becomes an impossible goal, and a psychoanalytic overflow sweeps us into the labyrinths of the mysterious isle we dream on, which Socrates thought to be no more than a luminous peak.[7]

The typical literary adolescent (a term that, in accordance with Martínez Estrada's self-appraisal, refers to a young writer's initial experimental stage) is intensely concerned with himself and his own subjective point of view. So much so that in his emphatic solitude we find little that reveals a true awareness of the complexities of the world surrounding him. But Martínez Estrada slights himself by calling *X-Ray of the Pampa* the "cancellation" of his immaturity. In the first place, he never entirely abandoned the rather unnatural grimness of his literary adolescence. The childlike enthusiasm that sometimes vitalizes a mature writer's style (Unamuno, Thoreau, García Lorca, Goethe, Wordsworth, Balzac) showed itself only in these ecstatic moments when (for example, on reading the natural descriptions of William Henry Hudson) he was able to escape from the gloomy world that he metaphorically built around himself. Secondly,

[6] *Nosotros* 11 (Oct. 1917): 193–199.
[7] "Reflexiones acerca del error," *Síntesis*, no. 14 (Buenos Aires, July 1928): 187–188.

the preferred philosophical readings of his youth (Nietzsche, Schopenhauer, Spengler) were the basis of his enduring pessimism. Finally, one can trace, from his first published volume of poetry, *Oro y
piedra* (1918), to the last, *Humoresca* (1929), as well as in the essays of the same period, a steadily growing preoccupation with the
world around him and its naturally mortal condition. No abrupt
changes took place; there were no disenchantments (rather he often
had presentiments of future dilemmas); no illusions inspired him ("I
must confess that I can remember no time in my life when I experienced the simple innocence of childhood," he wrote in 1945).[8] Martínez Estrada's intellectual development seemed to fulfill his earliest
premonitions; the darkness he saw in the future reflected the darkness he had seen in the past.

His work is best understood, I think, through an interpretation of
the critical milestones of his life; moments both of psychological and
spiritual significance in his personal existence and of historical and
political significance in the life of Argentina. The close parallel he
believed to exist between his own experience of growing disillusionment and the collective experience of his country is the emotional
basis of his work. Four of his books, *X-ray of the Pampa* (1933),
Sarmiento (1946), *Death and Transfiguration of Martín Fierro*
(1948), and *The Marvelous World of William Henry Hudson* (1951)
emphasize—in their detailed description and prophetic view of
the Argentine tradition—how meaningful to him that parallel was.
The vital link between his country and himself is personified, in three
of these books, in the solitary protagonist, exiled or alienated from
Argentine society. What Martínez Estrada saw in Sarmiento, the in-
domitable political exile and prophet, in Martín Fierro, dolorous
singer of the lost gaucho race, and in William Henry Hudson, nostalgic defender of a pastoral and partly mythical golden-age Argentina
of the 1850's and 1860's, he saw also in himself, the exile in his own
land and the moral and spiritual misfit of his age.

The four greatest Argentine writers of the first half of the twentieth
century—Ricardo Güiraldes (novelist and poet and author of *Don
Segundo Sombra*), Jorge Luis Borges (poet, master of fantasy fiction,

[8] "Carta a Victoria Ocampo," *Sur*, no. 295 (July–August 1965): 4.

and stylistically the most original prose writer in Spanish America to date), Eduardo Mallea (philosophical novelist and literary critic), and Ezequiel Martínez Estrada—are all "nationalists" as far as their permanent interest in Argentine tradition is concerned. Of the four, Martínez Estrada had the least formal education and was the least "literary" in his specific interests. Quite rightly, he thought of his *X-Ray of the Pampa* as a sequel to Sarmiento's *Facundo: Civilization and Barbarism* (1845), for both are very subjective interpretations of the origin and growth of the basic dilemmas of Argentine national life, and both reveal a more sociopolitical than literary purpose. But the fact that these two works are indispensable reading for serious students of Spanish American Literature suggests significant characteristics of that literature: its strikingly heterogeneous quality; its continuing obsession with the problems of a multiple cultural heritage (Spanish, Indian, African, Creole, "Mestizo," European immigrant, and American "coca-colonization"); its frequently unliterary or marginally literary content (such as the greater part of Argentine masterpieces of the nineteenth century, the novel of the Mexican Revolution and the novel of social protest in several countries, and Afro-Cuban poetry directly inspired by music and the dance); its curious oscillation between the most primitive and most refined styles.

Martínez Estrada saw little merit in most of the Argentine works written *en buen estilo literario*. For him, the first two prerequisites of literary consciousness were love and knowledge of one's country. But the latter implied no tin-drum patriotism; what he really meant was that one's country is necessarily the object of criticism and even vituperative ideological attack, but never, ultimately, of shame. For the citizen as well as the moralist and the humanist—in trying to be all three, Martínez Estrada found both inspiration and nervous exhaustion—literature is a mighty weapon and great revealer. "Only literature, and in the secondary sense, music and painting, can reveal the social spirit, the superego. But life demands sincerity, not shame, just as we cannot be ashamed of our souls or our bodies, for God gave them to us. Still less can we be ashamed of our country."[9]

[9] "Cuestionarios e interrogatorios," *Cuadrante del pampero*, p. 177.

Sarmiento, statesman and educator, José Hernández's Martín Fierro, fictional reincarnation of the lost freedoms of the gaucho age, and William Henry Hudson, Argentine by birth and sentiment, had become, several years before the publication of *X-Ray of the Pampa*, Martínez Estrada's "representative men." Sarmiento, the activist and teacher who concerned himself first of all with the children of the nation and strove to convert Argentina into an "immense laboratory for progress"[10] was for Don Ezequiel the man of action who could accept no defeat, notwithstanding the near hopelessness of his task. Martín Fierro, by contrast, was the anachronistic victim of a new society in growing pains. Like his creator, José Hernández (1834–1836), Martín Fierro did not feel the urge for knowledge or self-improvement, nor did he retaliate except in the most futile and symbolic way against the formidable series of obstacles he encountered —from the time of his abandonment of his home and family and flight into the wilderness until his assimilation into society in Part II (*The Return*). But Hudson was especially meaningful to Martínez Estrada and in many ways more congenial to him than Sarmiento or Martín Fierro, for, although he was one of the purest mystics of nature and an inhabitant of the pampa for thirty-three years, the Anglo-Argentine writer also moved within the mainstream of the nineteenth century intellectual world and, like his twentieth century admirer, he discerned dark and fatalistic designs in the history of modern Western civilization. These three solitary figures—their legends and their reality—were permanent models of Martínez Estrada's thought and literary art. They were, like him, exiles in their own land.

In the intellectual world of his time, Martínez Estrada was a "self-made man" who painstakingly elaborated his reputation and influence with only isolated literary contacts: the modernist poet Leopoldo Lugones and the Uruguayan short-story writer Horacio Quiroga, both suicides; the critic, writer, and editor Enrique Espinoza, almost continuously absent from Buenos Aires since the 1930's; and Victoria Ocampo, *grande dame* of Argentine letters ever since she founded *Sur* in 1931. He lived out his solitary career in a world, as he thought, increasingly confused by abstractions. "Civilization," in his

[10] *Sarmiento*, p. 23.

Argentine and Spanish American perspectives, was as much a wilderness in the 1930's and 1940's as it had previously been for Sarmiento, Hudson, and the author of *Martín Fierro*. The Argentina that he knew intimately was a continuous adventure in disillusionment. The specter of colonial life, in which he could see only aimlessness and autocracy, had persisted and even found reincarnation in the political decadence in Argentina from 1930 to the present. To explain that decadence he felt it necessary to probe—as Gilberto Freyre and H. L. Mencken (albeit with widely differing methods, temperaments, and purposes) have done in Brazil and the United States—the Argentine character in its historical context. The reader should bear in mind that Martínez Estrada's literary power did not lead very consistently to objective conclusions; the title of a book by George Jean Nathan (*Autobiography of an Attitude*) could have been as appropriate a subtitle for Martínez Estrada's works as *La Comédie Humaine* was for Balzac's. But attitudes are not only the mirrors of history, they are also its substance, and it may be helpful to describe the cultural climate out of which they grew. Thus the country whose contemporary era one historian has labeled "a haunted house" may be better understood.[11]

His Argentina

Another historian of our times has said that perspective "is not a state of reality; it is a state of mind."[12] This is a calculated exaggeration for reasons of emphasis, but it is undeniable that, although perspective by definition consists of a *relationship* between reality and the mind, it is necessarily the mind that establishes a perspective and determines its nature. Martínez Estrada's essays—his earliest as well as his latest—give us the impression that his rational skepticism and lyric despair would have characterized his work had he been born in virtually any country of the contemporary Western world. The technique and temperament of the poet underlie the

[11] Arthur P. Whitaker, *Argentina*, pp. 151–169.
[12] Arthur M. Schlesinger, Jr., "On the Writing of Contemporary History," *Atlantic Monthly* 219, no. 3 (March 1967): 74.

fundamental historical theme of his entire work, and the poet's perspective colors his whole view of Argentine, Hispanic American, and universal life. In his writings, Argentina—its wide expanses and remote places, its gauchos, its strong and weak men of past and present, its flora and fauna, the melancholy tango and teeming streets of its capital—is transformed from reality into symbol.

The Death and Transfiguration of Martín Fierro, is, indeed, an elaborate symbolic projection of that exemplary victim into Argentine history, which is his "transfiguration." The subway motorman in Buenos Aires is "a circulatory impulse sealed in its own vein,"[13] the life's blood of the city condemned to travel perpetually the same routes. The geological history of Patagonia, the arid wasteland of the south with its desolate canyons, extinct rivers and glacial winds ("the sterile wind is the sea . . . the sea is the wind") is offered as a natural and psychological prelude to today's loneliness, and the traveler in these parts experiences "ancestral chills up and down his spine."[14] "To mythicize Martín Fierro"—symbol and allegory of the last gaucho; in essence, the sum of social wretchedness in nineteenth-century Argentina—"to abstract him from his world, was to forget that world, to close one's eyes to its sad spectacle."[15]

However, it would be a fallacy to suppose, as some of his critics have, that Martínez Estrada was unique in his affective and intuitional interpretations. Sarmiento had projected his temperament and personality into his civic action as well as his thought and descriptive literature. Like the literary historian Ricardo Rojas in *Eurindia* (1924), the essayist had attempted to trace the development in Argentina and Hispanic America (when in fact much of the development took place in his own mind) of a new "aesthetic doctrine" based on a growing national consciousness since the early nineteenth century. For Rojas, the essence of culture is like that of a tree, of the seed that grows in the "jungle" of human civilization. "Like the ignorant Indian, I am convinced that an animating spirit dwells in my

---

[13] "un impulso circulatorio envasado en su vena," *La cabeza de Goliat*, p. 185.
[14] *Radiografía de la pampa*, pp. 124–130.
[15] *Muerte y transfiguración de Martín Fierro*, I, 296.

tree-symbol; I have called that spirit *argentinidad*, deity of our land and our race, totem of their tradition and culture."[16]

Among the purest of idealists, as among demagogues, the rather easy persuasion that the strongest political party of the moment represents the authentic "Argentine" spirit has prevailed throughout most of Argentina's history since her independence in 1816. As a spokesman for the once-powerful Radical party[17] expressed it, "We are not just a political party . . . we are a force of national and continental history which consists in imparting constitutionality to independence . . . in giving to the nation through its people firm bases for its authentic development, which conceived the Republic as a moral idea."[18] There can be little doubt that a strong Messianic feeling—of the individual functioning within the design of a collective, historical destiny—evident not only in Juan Manuel de Rosas and Juan Domingo Perón, but also in Sarmiento and Hipólito Irigoyen—contributed much to the obstinately personal, even anticonstitutional approach of so many leaders to political, economic, and social life.

Progressive, relatively prosperous, and democratic by intention, Argentina has nevertheless frequently demonstrated a typically Hispanic (some call it "Mediterranean") disdain for constitutional politics and systematic government, and Martínez Estrada does not exaggerate very much in stressing the "invariable" aspects of her history and the ineffectiveness of virtually all of her "revolutions" since the first proclamation of independence in 1810. "The reason it is so hard for us to overcome the past is that we *are* the past and want to continue being it."[19] Martínez Estrada then attacks the aristocratic attitude as expressed in Argentine literature; in his view cultural "aristocracy" for most Argentines is not a positive defense of excellence but rather a mere synonym for "contempt." Accordingly, "we

[16] *Eurindia*, in *Obras*, V, 151, Rojas also wrote a book entitled *La argentinidad*.
[17] The Unión Cívica Radical, a coalition of opposition groups officially organized shortly after the abortive yet significant Revolution of 1890. Rojas (just quoted) was a Radical.
[18] K. H. Silvert, "The Costs of Anti-Nationalism: Argentina," in *Expectant Peoples: Nationalism and Development*, ed. K. H. Silvert, p. 356.
[19] *Cuadrante del pampero*, pp. 155–156.

[Argentines] constantly scorn everything, including ourselves. Is there among us adoration or reverence for anything? Are we Christians, or democrats or idealists—of any kind of ideal, even a barbarous one. . . ?"[20]

Essentially, he agrees with Ricardo Rojas, who has interpreted Hispanic-American and Argentine history as a series of "defeats" for each succeeding social group. First, the pre-Columbian Indians were vanquished by the Spanish conquistadors and colonizers, who in turn succumbed to the Argentine gauchos, who reached the height of their power in the eighteenth century. Then, toward the end of the nineteenth century, waves of Spanish and Italian immigrants displaced the gauchos. Finally, by 1920, there was a rebirth of anti-European attitudes that had previously characterized the gaucho literature up to the 1870's.[21] The phonemenon of social change, which in some respects was similar to that of the United States, seemed detrimental to Argentina, or at least it did to Rojas and Martínez Estrada. In their view, the changes did not at any point signify an evolution, but rather a series of frustrations; for in each change the established group failed because of its inadaptability to new conditions.

Unlike the militant Bolivian pessimist Alcides Arguedas,[22] Martínez Estrada does not indulge in fanatical denunciations of the Latin American mestizo as a biologically and morally inferior being. But throughout his work he does imply that there is a *psychological* inferiority in the average inhabitant of Latin America. Martínez Estrada attributes this alleged inferiority to a complex that indeed has lurked in the thoughts of every sensitive Latin American from earliest colonial times to the present: the persistent tendency to reject all three of his basic historical backgrounds—the peninsular Spanish, the indigenous American, and the blending of the two in a kind of synthesis of the worst of both.

Some of the younger Argentines who, in different ways, have been

---

[20] Ibid., p. 156.
[21] *Eurindia*, pp. 19–20.
[22] See *Pueblo enfermo* (1909). In the revised, 3rd edition of this work (1936), Arguedas uses Hitler's *Mein Kampf* as part of the substantiation for his theory of the superiority of unmixed races.

strongly influenced by Martínez Estrada (among them H. A. Murena and Julio Mafud) essentially agree with him. They agree that the overwhelming majority of thoughtful Hispanic Americans are combative and—in the existentialist sense—even feel guilty about their countries' lack of steady and progressive historical evolution since the wars of independence. Only a few, mostly extremists or utopians, have felt proud of any achievement as "Americans." The majority, nurtured in pessimism and feelings of solitude from generation to generation, have denounced the real and withdrawn into splendrous dreams of the possible, that is, of possibilities so remote that they are virtually impossible. As a result, Argentine literature since the publication of Leopoldo Lugones' *La guerra gaucha* (1905)—stories based on the struggles for independence in the northern provinces of the country—became increasingly nationalistic. The best-known examples are Lugones' *El payador* (1916), an interpretation of José Hernández' *Martín Fierro* as epic poetry; Ricardo Güiraldes' *Don Segundo Sombra* (1926), still the best-known Argentine novel of this century; Ezequiel Martínez Estrada's epic odes in *Argentina* (1927) and his nihilistic appraisal of national history and contemporary life, *Radiografía de la pampa* (1933); Eduardo Mallea's *Historia de una pasión argentina* (1936), his interpretation of the continuing struggle between two "Argentinas," the authentic and the superficial; Leopoldo Marechal's Dantesque and Homeric novel *Adam Buenosayres* (1948). These and other works, including the essays of Ricardo Rojas and Carlos Alberto Erro, come to grips with the enigmas of Argentine character and culture. All seem to confirm the following opinion of H. A. Murena: "Our protestations of nationalism have always been genuine [but] just as in many countries nationalism is due to a heavy preponderance of the past, to an effacement and distortion of its origins, in ours it is due to an absence of the past, the historical solitude, to a totally impoverished history."[23]

But Murena (as well as Martínez Estrada and other authors just

[23] "El acoso de la soledad," in *El pecado original de América*, p. 57. Elsewhere Murena quotes José Fernando Abascal (Spanish viceroy of Peru from 1806 to 1816) in a dark prophecy: "[Latin] Americans are men destined by nature to vegetate in obscurity and dejection." (*Homo Atomicus*, p. 219)

mentioned) recognizes the fact that conditions have usually favored the strong individualist, from the reformer (Sarmiento) to the demagogue (Perón).[24] In this country of great spaces, personal initiative and the love of personal freedom have seldom been transformed into social, political, or institutional values. Rather, they have traditionally found *direct* expression in the isolated individual—the dynamic caudillo of the provinces, the anonymous gaucho, the persevering immigrant, even the decidedly vain "Hombre de Corrientes y Esmeralda"[25] portrayed by Raúl Scalabrini Ortiz. Accordingly, the obvious subjectivity of Martínez Estrada's view must not obscure the fact that many other writers (the representative men who in themselves seemed to bear the whole message of his country's history) were equally subjective, equally emphatic in stressing always the *symbols* of their national life over the realities. Even Alberto Palcos, one of Sarmiento's most level-headed and perceptive biographers, wrote that, had the great educator and statesman not been so close (in time and circumstance) to twentieth-century Argentines, "we would be tempted to consider him as a mythological being, symbolic of man's millenial struggle to surpass himself and to eradicate the hidden roots of barbarity incrusted in his nature."[26]

This symbolic inclination has led Martínez Estrada to think of Argentine history as a static rather than an evolutionary phenomenon, in which past and present seemed identical. Two important lectures he gave in August 1947, in Buenos Aires, bore the pointed title, "Historical Invariables in Facundo" ("Los Invariantes historicos en el Facundo"). The mass march of the "shirtless ones" in support of Juan Domingo Perón took place in October 1945, exactly one hundred years after the publication of Domingo F. Sarmiento's *Facundo: Civilization and Barbarism*. Perón, leader of impoverished laborers, and Rosas, Sarmiento's arch enemy and the nation's first large-scale

[24] "Sarmiento, in spite of his democratic intentions, belonged like Juan Manuel Rosas and Juan D. Perón, to the true line of Argentina's 'personalist' presidents." (George Pendle, *Argentina*, p. 53.)

[25] Corrientes and Esmeralda are busy streets in downtown Buenos Aires. "The Man of Corrientes and Esmeralda" is the enigmatic and evasive *porteño* (inhabitant of Buenos Aires), described in Scalabrini's popular essay, *El hombre que está solo y espera*, first published in 1931.

[26] Alberto Palcos, *Sarmiento: La vida, la obra, las ideas, el genio*, p. 13.

organizer of its primitive gauchos, were both masters of demagogy and each solicited public support in the name of fanatical nationalism. Martínez Estrada was aware of these and other parallels between the two most spectacular eras of Argentine history. Rosas and Perón could, each in his own time, truthfully say, "L'Etat c'est moi." Martínez Estrada stated—as discreetly as possible under the political circumstances of Argentina in 1947—that Rosas was still "the spectral ruler of our national life, its organizer and hidden legislator."[27]

But this view of historical parallels was not limited to a comparison of two eras and a few powerful men. The Argentina of Martínez Estrada was a near millenium of changelessness, and the first sections of *X-Ray of the Pampa* show conclusively his conviction that the destiny of Argentina was definitively fixed when the first Spaniards arrived, an arrival that, on the very first page, he equates with their "flight" from the realities of recent Peninsular history. They sought, literally and figuratively, "another world," which, with its uninhabited expanses, its lack of a past, and its latent invitation to adventure, led to a persistent faith in the future. And yet, deep down in his conscience, "The Conquistador, who conquered nothing"—nothing, that is, other than a wilderness— knew that he had been deceiving himself; he knew, in effect, that the only true conquest had been "that of his ignorance by his pride." He had been obsessed with conquest when the need was for massive colonization, with "reaping when he should have been planting," with theological and juridical principles instead of tangible constructiveness.[28]

Unlike Sarmiento, whose writing was but a part of his dynamic political and civic activity, Martínez Estrada sacrificed himself and almost all ordinary commitments to his writing. (It is interesting to speculate on how much his tedious and thankless job at the Buenos Aires post office—which he could never take seriously as a profession although he endured it for thirty years—may have influenced the pessimism that began with adolescent readings of Nietzsche.) In Sarmiento we find the talents of the essayist, the journalist, the poli-

[27] *Los invariantes históricos en el* Facundo: *Conferencias pronunciados en la librería Viau en agosto de 1947*, p. 9.
[28] *Radiografía de la pampa*, pp. 15–16.

tician, and the educator combined; in Martínez Estrada the talent of the essayist overwhelms all other potentialities, and the observation of life becomes a morbid exercise in the negation of accepted values. Sarmiento, although he created few, was a believer in systems; Martínez Estrada was the enemy of systems. Sarmiento, by convention and personal belief, was a positivist; Martínez Estrada was spiritually an anarchist who—like so many other anarchists—consumed himself in rebellious thought and restricted his action to the written and spoken word. If that anarchism prevented his active participation in the agitated politics of his country, his aloofness never signified indifference. His refusal to be quiet became one of his basic stylistic principles, and after 1930 more and more of his writings were done in the tone of protest.

It was precisely his anarchism that contained the seeds of a spiritual bond with Sarmiento, for not only was each of these two vigorous writers the biggest egocentric of his literary era, but each was also an ethical purist. In a letter to an Argentine friend in Mexico in 1956, Don Ezequiel wrote: "Do you realize that I am sixty years old and still (an ideological) virgin? I haven't even dreamed of coveting power, wealth or knowledge. Even when poor and having to work very, very hard for a living, I've never compromised with radicals, conservatives, nationalists or communists (and all have courted me). Rather, I preferred persecution and poverty."[29] Other affinities, like their common disdain of the Spanish heritage, unite Sarmiento and Martínez Estrada; but most of all, an ardent feeling of indignation at all forms of corrupt self-interest—forms so pervasive that together they seemed to constitute the substance of Argentine political and social history—drew them ideologically together. One of the main messages in Martínez Estrada's *Sarmiento* (1946) is the lament for a leader who lived by principles and fought for reforms too far above the moral level of his time. Although Sarmiento damned barbarity for the sake of civilization, and his twentieth-century successor attacked civilization as he knew it as a mere out-

[29] *Cuadrante del pampero*, p. 106. This letter was addressed to Arnaldo Orfila Reynal (not identified in this text), then director of the Fondo de Cultura Económica in Mexico City. It was written shortly after the overthrow of Perón in 1955 and has interesting autobiographical passages.

growth of the barbarity described by Sarmiento, the two had much in common. Martínez Estrada's morbid view of all the symbols of Argentine life was fundamentally, he insisted in his sixtieth year, an optimistic view: "It am convinced that I have been incredibly optimistic and that I have faith in genuinely human values. I refuse to conform with evil because I believe that good is possible. I am a religious man, that's all there is to it. If I were to accept what I have always rejected with great revulsion, I would take pity on myself. Reread St. Matthew, Chapter V, Verse 48."[30]

A writer and teacher by vocation, Martínez Estrada sacrificed action to words. Words as used by some have an effect comparable to that of direct political or social action; Martínez Estrada's words were rather like an invitation to withdrawal into a limbo of despair. To some extent, his meditative inclination was due to a somber view of civilized humanity and an intellectual restlessness that Sarmiento literally never had time to develop. The Argentina of Martínez Estrada was an immense world of specters—not fantasies, but rather artistic magnifications of certain aspects of reality, such as the lonely and derelict gaucho, the agonizingly twisted *ombú* tree, and the head of Goliath as a symbol of Buenos Aires. The spectral Argentina first took form in the delicate abstractions and cosmic imagery of his poetry (1917–1929). But throughout the 1920's the young writer's critical acumen was growing apace, and the reader can easily discern in the essays from about 1927 the process of growing involvement in the ebb and flow of national life.

The series of economic and political calamities in Argentina from 1929 to 1932 coincides exactly with Martínez Estrada's conversion into an apocalyptic writer. Economic depression, an echo of the Wall Street crash of October 1929; what Arthur P. Whitaker has called "anti-democratic contagions from abroad";[31] the total ineptness of the aged though erstwhile distinguished president, Hipólito Irigoyen; and an almost universal discontent from left and right led to the military coup of September 6, 1930. It is no exaggeration to say that

---

[30] Ibid., p. 104. The passage from Matthew 5:48 is "Be ye therefore perfect, even as your Father which is in heaven is perfect."
[31] *Argentina*, p. 80.

Argentina has not recovered politically from the death of the Radical party on that date, nor from the fraudulent and dictatorial methods that have been sporadically repeated ever since. Although Martínez Estrada tended always to accentuate the adversities of life and to invent infinite symbols of gloom, no objective observer can deny that the dark political and social overtones of *X-Ray of the Pampa* (1933), *The Head of Goliath* (1940), and *Sarmiento* (1946) reflect quite truthfully the extensive deterioration of Argentine civic life over the period in which those books were written.

But Martínez Estrada's role was that of the tutor, not the reformer. He could—he felt—go no further than the psychoanalyst in the first stages of treatment of a deeply disturbed patient: he could only begin to dispel delusions and injurious defense mechanisms. This is what he wanted to do for his collective patient—Argentina— by writing *X-Ray of the Pampa*. In later writings his role was substantially the same, that of the revealer, if seldom an objective one; that of the intellectual awakener, if only on an emotional basis. He thought of his average reader, the average Argentinean, the average person, as a good (impassioned) or bad (indifferent) student. The good student, "suffered or matured in a kind of sacred affliction or unfortunate fatality" that involved a permanent dissatisfaction with the limitations of his knowledge and spiritual power.[32] The bad student sought only the rewards implicit in his diploma and accepted all convention as if it were the highest standard of excellence. Martínez Estrada's temperamental tone, his frequent falling back on nihilism, did not contradict his persistent hope for better political and cultural leadership. But that hope consisted entirely of his dogged refusal to accept things as they were before, during and after the Perón era.

As the realities of Argentina appeared more and more ominous to him—with the military revolts (traditionally and euphemistically referred to in Argentina as "revolutions") of the 1940's, the pro-Axis leanings of Argentine diplomatic neutrality until World War II was nearly over, the increasingly anti-intellectual stance of Perón, and the subversive revival after 1955 of some of Perón's methods and

[32] *Exhortaciones*, p. 40.

attitudes—Martínez Estrada withdrew gradually into voluntary exile, from Buenos Aires to Bahía Blanca, from Bahía Blanca to Mexico, and from Mexico to Cuba (from 1960 to 1962). He was even accused (falsely) of becoming a Cuban citizen.[33] Even the final return to his Bahía Blanca home must be interpreted as an extension, not the end, of his exile, for by then Don Ezequiel was more embittered, solitary, and world-weary than ever before.

His enmity with the officialdom of his country during the last eight years of his life found expression in a series of intensely polemical works, such as *What Is This?*, *Exhortations*, *The Quadrant of the Pampa Wind*, *True Story of Uncle Sam*, and, of course, in the Cuban adventure.

His Fate

What was his fate? The writer himself would certainly have answered—and in several ways and on many occasions he did answer—that it was to be misunderstood. Emerson ("to be great is to be misunderstood"), however, could not have consoled him in his unrelenting anxieties, for Martínez Estrada was convinced that his personal life, a progression from artistic humility to ideological defiance, from poet to prophet, was a representative *life*. To date, no one—least of all the man himself—has seen fit to consider Don Ezequiel a representative *man*. Although many have acknowledged his influence and value as a teacher, only two or three have considered themselves his disciples. His position with regard to the world, his country, and his fellow man was hermetic and solitary. His critical method was coldly intellectual at one moment, passionately emotional the next. The tension was great between his exacting moral principles and standards of excellence on the one hand, and the drab realities his mind's eye converted into eerie specters of doom, on the

---

[33] On July 16, 1961, *La Nación* (Buenos Aires) reported that shortly after his arrival in Havana he became a Cuban citizen and "has lived here ever since." The report is refuted by Martínez Estrada himself in an article in the Sunday supplement of *La Nación* (Guayaquil, Ecuador), Oct. 29, 1961, and five years later by Pablo Lejarraga in a letter published in *Confirmado* 2, no. 59 (Buenos Aires, Aug. 4, 1966): 73. Lejarraga's letter was in reply to a published statement by the Argentine novelist Beatriz Guido, who also asserted that Martínez Estrada had renounced his Argentine citizenship.

other. Who, indeed, could join this tormented man on a crusade that, from the beginning, was impossible to organize? In cultral and literary histories of the future I think he will appear in the intellectual family of Friedrich Nietzsche and Miguel de Unamuno, for, like them, he was not "a man of his time" but a man against his time, a utopian at heart, forced to settle for the role of the philosophical agitator and to disguise his ideals in the bitter language of spiritual anarchy.

The position of Martínez Estrada is not unique in Argentine letters. Like his nineteenth-century predecessors José Hernández (*Martín Fierro*), Esteban Echeverría (*The Slaughter House*), Sarmiento (*Facundo*), José Mármol (*Amalia*), Juan Bautista Alberdi (*Daylight's Pilgrimage*), and Lucio Victoria Mansilla (*An Expedition into the Territory of the Ranquel Indians*); and like Eduardo Mallea (*History of an Argentine Passion*), Leopoldo Lugones (*Ballads of Río Seco*), Julio Mafud (*Uprootedness in the Argentine Tradition*), H. A. Murena (*The Original Sin of America*), and Ricardo Güiraldes (*Don Segundo Sombra*) in the twentieth century—writers of widely differing styles and attitudes—Martínez Estrada was bound, like a modern Prometheus, to the traditions, destiny, and life-pulse of Argentina. That in itself could scarcely be called a fate. The relationship of Don Ezequiel to the realities he deals with can best be described as *tropistic* (in Webster's second definition, "any innate tendency to react in a definite manner to stimuli"). In most of Latin American literature, cultural nationalism and collective self-analysis with an increasingly critical spirit have been common since 1900. Yet more than any of his compatriots just mentioned, more even than Sarmiento and Hernández, Martínez Estrada identified himself psychologically with his country; in his work Argentina becomes a complex and enigmatic personality. His obession with certain legendary and fictional personalities—Sarmiento, Martín Fierro, William Henry Hudson, and others—led him to submit them to a kind of "temperamental adjustment," extending the real role of each into a symbolic role. Unamuno had expressed his tropistic relationship with Spain by saying, "Me duele España" ("I am sick at heart over Spain"). It has been suggested that Don Ezequiel could well have said, "Me enferma la Argentina" ("I am ill over Argentina"). Indeed, he took ironic pleasure in reminding his readers and friends that his ugly skin ailment of over five years' duration—which saw him bedridden and totally inactive during most of that period (1950 1956)—coincided with the worst part of the Perón era: "You will recall that my illness and that of my country ended simultaneously, within a few days of each other."[34]

Surely Martínez Estrada's limited international fame can be explained, at least in part, by his seemingly limited subject matter. Not only are his five most important books (*X-Ray of the Pampa, The Head of Goliath, Death and Transfiguration of Martín Fierro, Sarmiento*, and *The Marvelous World of William Henry Hudson*) intimately and obsessively concerned with Argentine life, but so is the major portion of the rest of his work. However, one of the main purposes of this study will be to show that his obsessive nationalism —nationalism in the deepest and widest sense, the will to examine, interpret, and criticize his own culture and civilization—demanded a great deal more than the direct observation of Argentine local color, traditions, and institutions. As an insatiable reader and an ingenious synthesizer of all he read, he sometimes sought in other histories and other cultures substantiation for his interpretation of Argentine life. His own land, especially that part of it he recollected from childhood —its pampas, its wildlife, its lonely villages—was his basic habitat and the symbolic substance of his writing. Europe and the United States, on the other hand, were his school, in which he formed very early the definitive pattern of his thought with extensive readings in the "Biblioteca Blanca" collection of world authors.[35]

A curious fact of the lives of solitary men is their susceptibility to other lives, their innate tendency to become, to some degree, the vicarious agents of the writers they read. The solitary writer in our century is likely to be a derivative writer (for example, Proust, Gide, Unamuno, Thomas Mann, and D. H. Lawrence), who, through

[34] *Cuadrante del pampero*, p. 162. See also Bernardo Canal Feijoo, "Los enfermos de la patria," *Sur*, no. 295 (July–August 1965): 20–25.

[35] "The fragrance of earth infuses my flesh and Nietzsche is my most revered writer." "Carta a Victoria Ocampo," *Sur*, no. 295 (July–August 1965): 7. The statement synthesizes well the natural and intellectual elements of his thoughts.

reading as experience and experience put to the test of reading, is not so much an absorber of other men's attitudes as a participant in previous experiences. Or, stated another way, he is the culminating point of experiences begun long before his own birth to consciousness. There is, then, a solidarity within solitude. With greatest ease the solitary can choose his company, and he can draw it from any time and any place. Martínez Estrada chose exiles, heroes, and a variety of intellectuals as his companions. His contention that they shared with him a largely futile existence, full of noble intentions but doomed to ultimate failure, has been widely disputed regarding Sarmiento and Martín Fierro, unofficial national heroes and symbols, respectively, of progress toward civilization and of the romantic glories of personal freedom.

The distinctive feature both of what Martínez Estrada wrote and most of what has been written about him to date is its polemical tone. The poet-essayist seldom failed to incite discussion, and almost all that discussion led the reader to contemplate not the quality of what was written or the depth of the character and personality of the man who wrote it, but the message and the judgment contained therein, its direct applicability to Argentina at the moment, "the issues." While his combativeness and unconditional commitment were essential parts of Don Ezequiel's vitality, these qualities have not been my main concern in writing this book. Rather, I have chosen to consider the huge breadth and subjectivity of his reading, the anxieties of his personal existence, and the enigmatic symbolism of his works as the decisive factors in the development of a great writer. No single event in his life amounted to personal tragedy, yet it was a somber life marked by many frustrations, each of which he thought confirmed the generally tragic quality of his existence ("Sometimes I doubt that even Dostoyevsky has imagined an existence as tragic and sorrowful as mine.")[36] He shunned as many experiences of the physical world as he could, and his ideological purism and his hypersensitivity added much to his suffering as well as to his creativity. His method, confirmed in the structure and style of each of his works,

[36] Ibid., p. 4.

finds adequate definition in a passage from his mammoth study
(889 pages), *Reality and Fantasy in Balzac*, the last of his books to
be published before his death. "True experience is mental experience;
the rest is simple mechanics, the work of stonecutters. In this sense
no great naturalist—from Pliny to Darwin—has done more than
interpret, decipher, translate reality into a system of symbols."[37]
This "naturalism" was his own persistent philosophy.

Most of the debate that has centered on him can be related to the
question of how faithful a chronicler of Argentine times and traditions he was. Analyzing him on these terms is necessary if we judge
him as a historian, but erroneous when we interpret him as a literary
artist. "More faithfully than any historian," writes Peter Ustinov,
"the artist reflects the atmosphere, the pith, and the prejudices of
his epoch. He is the chronicler of moods, the distiller of style. He
translates life into poetic and organized terms."[38] That is, the artist
or the writer is likely to provide, whether he intends to or not,
whether he is obstinately subjective or coldly analytical, a truthful
glimpse of the world he lives in and which is his heritage. It is the
duty of the literary critic as well as that of the literary scholar to
comprehend not only the writer's style and point of view, but also
—insofar as this is possible—his life, in both its limitations and its
expansiveness.

In Martínez Estrada's case that duty has not yet been fulfilled.
His dialectic, his theses, his public defiance of a variety of traditions
are the trees that have not allowed most to see the deep forest of his
spirit. Juan José Sebreli, author of the only book-length study on
Martínez Estrada to date, concentrated mainly on a polemic, a con-
demnation of Martínez Estrada's alleged disbelief in historical progress (Hegelian-Marxist), his "irrational pessimism," and his critical
perspective, always "from the outside." Sebreli believes that the
nineteenth century did not reach its point of ideological extinction
until 1930—the year of his own birth, the year of world-wide economic awakening to the Wall Street cataclysm of the preceding
October, and the year, as we have already observed, of political chaos

[37] *Realidad y fantasía en Balzac*, p. 226.
[38] "Politics and the Arts," *Atlantic Monthly* 219 (March 1967), No. 3.

in Argentina. To be sure, much of the obstinate fatalism of which Sebreli accuses Martínez Estrada we find concentrated in Sebreli's own phrase: "When I was born (in 1930) everything had ended; it was the morning after the party.[39]

Martínez Estrada himself was convinced that the pattern of his intellectual existence was set very early, that rather than possessing an exceptional intelligence he had experienced "a premature awakening to the meaning of life." Such persons, he adds—and here is his peculiar manifestation of the tragic sense of life—normally die at a very early age, "and it is a misfortune to survive the conditions established by nature," as he had done.[40]

The poet and scholar Rafael Alberto Arrieta recalls his first meeting, in April 1918, with the neophyte author:

I was surprised by the gloomy aspect of his personality, his pale face with its prominent jaw and snub nose of a boxer, and the dull, straight black hair, parted in the middle, which extended aggressively into long sideburns. And the eyes, eyes with long, curved lashes, submerged their darkness in the anguish of sadness that his glance seemed to reveal. His suit and tie, like those of a recent and devout mourner, completed his funereal appearance. But a clear voice pronounced my name with a questioning intonation, and, awaiting no reply, he added: "My name is Ezequiel Martínez Estrada; I'd like to offer you a copy of my first book."[41]

Arrieta's portrait shows a young man of great sensitivity and volatile temperament and also the image of a puritan.[42] The man described is so exacting that in his persistent dissections of Argentine reality he came to equate its weakest aspects with its basic characteristics.[43]

---

[39] "Vida de un pequeño burgués," *Confirmado* 2, no. 59 (Buenos Aires, Aug. 4, 1966): 43. See especially Sebreli's book *Martínez Estrada: Una rebelión inutil*. In fairness to Sebreli, it must be said that his insights and general grasp of Martínez Estrada's view of history are superior to the quite doctrinaire conclusions of his book.

[40] *Sur*, no. 295, p. 4.

[41] Rafael Alberto Arrieta, *Lejano ayer*, p. 156.

[42] See, for example, Ludevic Ivanissevich Machado, "El puritanismo en Martínez Estrada," *Ciudad* 1 (Buenos Aires, 1955): 20–23.

[43] "Martínez Estrada can be legitimately criticized for summoning up elements of Argentine reality and evaluating the worst of them in such a way as to indicate that they contain the whole truth." Dardo Cúneo, "Sobre Ezequiel Martínez Estrada," in *Aventura y letra de América Latina*, p. 135.

Arrieta recalls that in the early 1920's the poet and his recent bride "did ascetic oriental exercises, from sleeping in a sitting position to eating handfuls of raw wheat."[44]

What seems to have given dramatic tension to Martínez Estrada's tragic *sense* of life was that puritanical *ideal* of life, so uncompromising—according to Sebreli—as to be destructive of the last hope of progress. Unlike Jose Martí, the Cuban patriot to whom Martínez Estrada was to devote his last and one of his most voluminous works, his Argentine biographer was never to have the satisfaction of transforming his own puritanical concepts of history, society, and politics into action. A decisive majority of his readers have thought that this failure was all to the good, for Martínez Estrada was just as much of an anarchist as he was a puritan, and on those very few occasions when he actually came forth with a concrete proposal for reform, he did not generate much enthusiasm for its realization. One particularly recalls a series of requests to the president and his minister, in 1955, that Buenos Aires be "dismantled" as capital of the Republic and that the capital be reestablished in Bahía Blanca, Martínez Estrada's place of residence since 1949, some five hundred miles to the south.

The events and style of Martínez Estrada's private life make it easy to see how convinced he was that there was a fatalistic affinity between his personal existence and the infinite and unfathomable forces of the universe. *Motivos del cielo* (1924), his third book of verse, includes, among other somber meditations, "Night," or the final phase of his four-part poem "One Day's Cycle":

> The dark sea runs up only to die on the sand
> and silence is but a shadow reaching out to the abyss
>
> .   .   .   .
>
> And the star that once illuminated my way
> will now show me how to vituperate life.[45]

---

[44] *Lejano ayer*, p. 157.
[45] El mar oscuro viene a morir en la arena
　　 y el silencio es la sombra tendida hacia el abismo.
　　 .   .   .   .
　　 y la estrella que antes me alumbraba el camino

The gist of the book is that individual life, time, and the celestial bodies all move along a predetermined path. Death, deception, and the ephemeral mess of nature are its constant themes. In "Sleep" he imagines a second awakening of Adam in Paradise, and Adam prays "to a God who had tried to reduce all evil to a bad dream." Martínez Estrada himself would later think of *Motivos del cielo* as part of the "playful" and innocent phase of his literary life, but it reveals much of the tragic sentiment that he elaborated in such abundant detail later on.

The bleakness of his life was not purely metaphysical. The post-office job (1916–1946) showed him the dehumanizing effect of a labyrinthine system of bureaucracy, later portrayed in the novelette *Holy Saturday*. Economically, life was very hard for him until after 1927, when he began to win important literary prizes. As a teacher of world literature at the preparatory school of the University of La Plata in the morning, and as an employee in the Central Post Office of Buenos Aires in the afternoon, Martínez Estrada wrote his six books of poetry and a multitude of essays both long and short, including *X-Ray of the Pampa* and *The Head of Goliath*, in his spare time—on the train between Buenos Aires and La Plata and at home at night. Without university training he became a fine university teacher, as several of his students later to achieve success in the academic and literary world would testify.[46] Arrieta, poet, editor, and professor of Spanish literature at La Plata, proposed him for the job, and the two became close personal and professional associates. Undoubtedly the teaching position, which offered the young writer not only additional income and an increased incentive for extensive and varied reading, but also a much-needed sense of filial relationship between himself and his students, contributed a great deal to his emotional stability from the first year (1924) to the year of his retirement (1946). Martínez Estrada's marriage was childless; his

---

me enseñará la forma de maldecir la vida.
Poesía, p. 138.
[46] See Eugeno Pucciarelli, "La imagen de la Argentina en la obra de Ezequiel Martínez Estrada," and Enrique Anderson Imbert, "Martínez Estrada en 1926," both in *Sur*, no. 295 (July–Aug. 1965): 34–48, 49–54. See also, Rafael Alberto Arrieta, *Lejano ayer*.

social life was minimal; his literary relationships few, although very good, including Leopoldo Lugones, Horacio Quiroga, and Enrique Espinoza (pseudonym for Samuel Glusberg). But by 1938 the three friends were to disappear, the first two by suicide, the last by emigration to Chile.

In late 1932 a literary scandal erupted that greatly increased Martínez Estrada's progressive disillusionment with professional literary life. On November 19 the Argentine Academy of Letters awarded him the National Prize in Literature (dating back to 1929, year of the publication of his last and best volume of poetry, *Humoresca*), in the amount of thirty thousand pesos. The second prize of twenty thousand went to the popular and much more widely known novelist, Manuel Gálvez. Although Martínez Estrada had won two previous prizes for his poetry (in 1921 and 1927) he was still, by the end of 1932, a relatively obscure man of letters, modest in all his literary undertakings, unattached to either of the leading literary groups of the 1920's (the avant-grade and elitist *Martín Fierro*; the more sociologically conscious and combative *Boedo*).

But *Humoresca*, his sixth book of poetry, and *Argentina*, for which he had won the Municipal Prize of Buenos Aires in 1927, showed originality and depth of spirit. The panel of judges—composed of the dean of the Faculty of Philosophy and Letters of the University of Buenos Aires, Alfredo Francheschi, and the writers Leopoldo Lugones, Carlos Obligado, Jorge Max Rohde, and Miguel Angel Carcano—voted three-to-two for Martínez Estrada.[47] Manuel Gálvez exploded with indignation when he discovered he had received only second prize. His letters to Rohde and Obligado appeared in several Buenos Aires newspapers on November 24 and 25. To Obligado he wrote:

> Your behavior has been that of a second-rater, an ingrate and a coward. An ingrate because you owe your academic prestige to me; a coward because you gave in to that perverse mulatto [Leopoldo Lugones]. Surely you couldn't believe that a second-rate poet, without personality, significant works or prestige, deserved the prize. Lugones doesn't believe it either, but the wretch has been my enemy for 29 years.

[47] *La Prensa* (Buenos Aires), No. 23, 1932.

P.S. I'll tell you the same I told Rohde; don't bother sending me your seconds. I'm a Catholic and cannot accept a duel.[48]

Only one paper seems to have supported Gálvez—*El Diario* on November 23, 1932—and that was before Gálvez had issued his irate proclamations. Raúl González Tuñon, a poet of the then-disbanded *Martín Fierro* group, deplored the awards to both Martínez Estrada and Gálvez, as well as the third prize to a little-known historian:

A caveman's criterion: Sr. Martínez Estrada is a poet in Lugones' style, but, to be sure, quite inferior to all the rest of the disciples of the author of *Gardens in the Twilight*. Sr. Manuel Gálvez has won scarcely enviable popularity among seamstresses and seminary students, as the result of a few cheap novels without noteworthy characters, atmosphere or descriptions. . . . As for Sr. Enrique de Gandía, an academic-type historian, a scavenger of research done many times before, how did he get into a literary contest?[49]

In the anti-Gálvez periodical *Crítica* the following headline appeared on November 25th: "L. Lugones Spoils Gálvez's Attempt at Literary Bribe." And on November 30: "Sr. Gálvez Reminds Us of Tolstoy. He's So Different!" In *La Fronda* of November 25, Lugones wrote that Gálvez, as a second-rate writer, had clearly deserved a second-rate prize, and he quoted the French critic Daniel Rops (*La Vie Intellectuelle*, October 1932) who in turn, had criticized Gálvez ("mediocre creator of myths and characters, good at descriptions of environments") for seeking in 1932, on his own, the Nobel Prize for Literature. The bad feelings extended, on Gálvez's part, to Martínez Estrada himself, and as late as 1960, when asked to contribute commentary to an issue of the magazine *Atlántida* (Buenos Aires) in which Martínez Estrada's antagonistic position with regard to the Argentine government was discussed by several writers, Gálvez replied simply that his relations with Martínez Estrada were "strained" because they had long been enemies.[50]

The Gálvez affair reveals the quite hostile atmosphere of the lit-

[48] *La Fronda* (Buenos Aires), Nov. 25, 1932.
[49] *La Acción* (Buenos Aires), Nov. 25, 1932.
[50] "Los escritores frente a una actitud: Martínez Estrada y el país," *Atlántida* 43, no. 1123 (Sept. 1960): 22–28.

erary community in Buenos Aires in the 1930's. On more than one
occasion Martínez Estrada suggested that by winning the National
Prize he incurred the enmity of the greater part of that community.
Part of it took form in negative reviews of *X-Ray of the Pampa*, but
most of it was silence, which was what hurt the most. "For many
readers," he said, "the sixth edition (1958) has been the first, for they
read it now as if it had been completely forgotten."[51] In an interview
published three months before his death, all the old bitterness was
reborn: the Gálvez affair, the political turning point of 1930, the virtual abandonment of his writing from 1933 to 1940 (years in which
he devoted himself to the "intensive study" of the violin), the suicides of Quiroga (1937) and Lugones (1938), the sickness from 1950
to 1955 ("with my skin as black as coal and as hard as the bark of a
tree"), and the sojourn in Cuba, for which he was attacked as an
antipatriot and accused of renouncing his Argentine citizenship.[52]

Although Martínez Estrada's life, as I have briefly portrayed it,
was a story of progressive disillusionment and bitterness, in no sense
did he abandon his combative function as a writer. On the contrary,
in his last eight years, following the five-year hiatus in hospital beds,
he produced fifteen books and several articles of widely varied content, including the extensive work on Balzac and the three-volume
biography of Jose Martí. It was in this period (1956–1964) that he
lived and acted out in a symbolic way his complex role as voluntary
exile, prophet ("Ezequiel") and *excitator Argentiniae.*

In this period one notices a growing tendency to self-dramatiza-
tion, to a belief in life as a pilgrimage destined to fail in the ugly
circumstances of twentieth-century history, yet to succeed as inspiration to unknown readers of the future. We have in the angry *Exhortations, Quadrant of the Pampa Wind,* and *What is This?* in 1956
and 1957, and the books written in Mexico and Cuba from 1959 to
1962, a curious mixture of anarchism, revolutionary enthusiasm,

---

[51] "Placa de una *Radiografía,*" *Revista do Livro,* no. 10 (Rio de Janeiro,
June 1958): 202.
[52] "Martínez Estrada, el hombre que soslaya la muerte," *Primera Plana* (Buenos Aires), Aug. 4, 1964, pp. 36–38. See also note 33, above.

utopian and Marxist idealism, anti-Yankee and anticapitalist propaganda, and Cassandra-like pessimism. Yet the personal involvement and, in most of these works, the rising tone of indignation, seem to have weakened the artistic mastery that characterized his books, brief essays, stories, and poems up to and including *The Marvelous World of William Henry Hudson* (1951). Sarmiento, Juan Facundo Quiroga (gaucho leader and, together with the tyrant Juan Manuel Rosas, subject of Sarmiento's most famous book), José Hernández (author of *Martín Fierro*), and the Argentine-born North American William Henry Hudson were his representative men. As a revisionist of history he gleaned many political, social, and spiritual symbols from their lives.

With José Martí he did the same, and more. In his lengthy work the Cuban patriot appears as the last of a race of incorruptible men, the purest of heroes in what seems to have been the last great century for heroes. The final volume of *Martí the Revolutionary*[53] is ideologically similar to his *Sarmiento*, in that each describes a man confronted with political and civic tasks a step beyond the limits of possibility. But there can be little doubt that most of the tragic sentiment and feeling of futility emanated not from them but from himself. While, in a rationalistic sense, he recognized the positive achievements of both the great educator (Sarmiento) and the great liberator (Martí), he could measure their lives only in the light of what he considered to be the objectionable traditions that preceded them and hampered their attempts at reform, and in light of the course of history following their deaths (in 1889 and 1895)—the history not only of Argentina and Cuba, but of the whole Western world.

Martínez Estrada's view of Argentina and the Latin American world, we must not forget, was inseparable from his interpretation of Spengler, Nietzsche, Montaigne, Kafka, and Simone Weil, all of whom accompanied him in his alienation. There is symbolic significance in the fact that on his first visit to Martí's tomb at Santiago de

---

[53] *Martí: El héroe y su acción revolucionaria* is the third and final volume of *Martí, revolucionario* (scheduled for publication in its complete form by Casa de las Américas in Havana), but the first to be published.

Cuba in November 1961, his main impression was one of self-consciousness. The anticipated inner experience did not materialize; the strong emotions had come before.

> Old, feeble and foreign, an expatriate and an unknown person, I had approached his remains in silence, so as to experience in my soul his solitude rather than my own, to offer him my companionship and leave it with him. But before the casket in the mausoleum I confess that I felt no strong emotion, as I had expected I would; and I even felt—as had been the case on other occasions—that my natural inclination to the hero cult might actually have been a self-delusion concealing my congenital coldness and irreverence.[54]

This attempt to preserve an idealistic spirit against a cold, analytical disposition, the ceaseless struggle between his propensity to love humanity in circumstances that should have been and his inability to discover circumstances even remotely satisfactory, was the permanent stimulus for his writing.[55]

In 1959 Martínez Estrada had lost all hope of arousing anyone to promote the Argentine political reforms he had clamored for in early 1956, and his interest turned from Argentina to Latin America as a whole. In 1959, invited by the Fondo de Cultura Económica to take part in the celebration of their twenty-fifth anniversary, he came to Mexico City where the following summer he would give a seminar at the National University on "Latin American Problems." His revision of these lectures became *Differences and Similarities among the Countries of Latin America* (1962). In late February 1960 the Casa de las Américas, the most active publishing firm in Cuba since the Revolution, invited him to Havana to receive a prize for essay writing and to give a series of lectures. From May to September he was again in Mexico City for the university seminar. From September 1960 to November 1962 he remained in Cuba, where he was contracted by the government to write an extensive biography of

---

[54] *Mi experiencia cubana*, p. 209.
[55] Plato's suggestion in the *Symposium* and *Phaedrus*, recalls Norman O. Brown (*Life Against Death: The Psychoanalytical Meaning of History*, p. 7), was that "the fundamental quest of man is to find a satisfactory object for his love."

Martí, which he did with great enthusiasm. He returned to Argentina, via Mexico City, in late November 1962, physically and mentally exhausted, but with still more writing ahead of him.

The feeling of isolation grew until his death. His enthusiasm and admiration for the Cuban Revolution, Fidel Castro (whom he never met), and the late Ernesto ("Che") Guevara was constant and complete. But in a personal sense he suffered some disillusionment, the feeling that in both Mexico and Cuba he did not receive the attention he had expected. At the National University of Mexico his seminar was not well attended; government officialdom in Cuba paid him little heed; and in a late, unpublished letter (September 16, 1964) he complained of the slowness and apparent indifference with which Casa de Las Américas was preparing the publication of the first two volumes of his *Martí the Hero*. Earlier that year,[56] he complained that he had been treated in Cuba as a *desocupado internacional*, that he had not been granted the privilege of meeting Premier Castro, and that the G2 Police had unjustly arrested and imprisoned a person whom he (Martínez Estrada) knew and trusted.

The last published interview with Martínez Estrada,[57] which his widow and friends claim was exaggerated and written in poor taste, leaves little room for doubt, however, of the bitterness and disillusionment he then felt. Like Simón Bolívar, he felt he had "plowed in the sea." Afflicted by abdominal cancer, his frail body steadily weakened and he died in the afternoon of November 3, 1964. Two months before, he had given as his intellectual last will the "Useless Prologue" to his *Anthology*: "I hope that some day my work will be read with impartiality, as the creation of an artist and a thinker."

[56] From a letter from Haydée Santamaría (Havana, May 18, 1964) to Martínez Estrada (unpublished to date).

[57] "Martínez Estrada, el hombre que soslaya la muerte," *Primera Plana* (Buenos Aires), Aug. 4, 1964, pp. 36–38.

2 · Sarmiento

The Historical Background

In all that Martínez Estrada wrote about Sarmiento two purposes
are constantly evident: a liberal and antitraditional revision of Argentine history, and a sustained attack on all the varieties of antidemo-
cratic forces in twentieth-century Hispanic America. Sarmiento's
character, achievements, and failures became the touchstone for
Martínez Estrada's interpretation of the formative years of the
Argentine nation. Accordingly, a brief review of Sarmiento's era
may improve our understanding of Martínez Estrada's historical
ideas.

The seventy-seven years of Domingo Faustino Sarmiento's life
(1811–1888) include a complete cycle of history, from the collapse
of Spanish colonial rule to the thriving economy of the Gilded Age

of Buenos Aires, roughly parallel to and contemporary with the Gilded Age of the United States in the last quarter of the nineteenth century.

In 1811 the pampa was no more than 250,000 square miles of wilderness; its rich, rolling expanses, which many travelers likened to the ocean, were uncultivated. It was the lonely habitat of nomadic men, wild horses, thin muscular cattle, burrowing animals, and pumas. In 1890, two years after Sarmiento's death, there were over 5,800 miles of railroad; cattle and sheep were raised for meat (not just for hides, tallow, and wool, as they formerly had been); and European immigration, predominantly Italian and Spanish, had approached the million mark (in a total population of less than 3,500,000). Refrigerator ships for beef had been in regular service between Buenos Aires and British ports for over a decade; a federal constitution had been ratified (1853) and amended for the whole nation's adoption in 1860; the best public school system in Latin America had been developed; wheat and other agricultural products were fast gaining on the cattle industry. Immigrants' agricultural colonies and huge, quickly prosperous *estancias* (haciendas) replaced the lands of the Pampa Indians, who were displaced, starved, and decimated by a military campaign that surpassed in cruelty the routing of the Indian tribes in the United States. Sarmiento himself, as governor and educational reformer in his native province of San Juan, as ambassador to the United States, and as president (1868–1874) and senator, could take credit for many of the advances that would ultimately make Argentina the most prosperous of the Latin American republics.

The symbols and realities of progress and the general aura of well-being should not, however, obscure the evidence of strong currents of discontent and civil strife that rises persistently to the surface in the essays of Sarmiento's chief ideological opponent Juan Bautista Alberdi (the motivating spirit behind the 1853 Constitution), in Hernández's *Martín Fierro*, and in most of Sarmiento's writings after his return from exile. In 1852 Juan Manuel Rosas was overthrown, but Martínez Estrada was convinced that he left a malignant heritage, and that the forces which had elevated Rosas to power "would continue, institutionalized, in action long afterwards."[1]

Because Sarmiento, in his classic work *Civilization and Barbarism: The Life of Juan Facundo Quiroga,* set up a rigid distinction between the urban liberalism and provincial primitivism that makes up the ideological nucleus of his message, and because many serious readers inside and outside Argentina have accepted Sarmiento's terms of interpretation for their own appraisal of Argentine history, Martínez Estrada felt the need to reexamine the complex relationship between Sarmiento the observer and Sarmiento the doer. In his view, the great leader was not simply the champion of liberalism and progress against the dark forces of reaction, but "the full embodiment of the good and evil aspects of his country,"[2] including much of the "evil" he attributed to the Spanish. Indeed, it does not enhance the prestige of the Spanish colonial system in America very much to consider that the last and least firmly established of its vice-royalties (Río de la Plata, 1776) was to become, from entirely non-Hispanic causes, the most modern and progressive of the Spanish American republics.

In *Facundo,* Sarmiento emphasizes the roughness, the "American" quality (i.e., the characteristics of perpetual civil war in the Argentine backlands and provincial cities) and the *predetermined* ingenuousness of his protagonist, Juan Facundo Quiroga, the wild-tempered gaucho leader, "for in Facundo I don't see simply a caudillo, but a manifestation of Argentine life just as it has resulted from the colonization and the peculiarities of the land."[3] It was not only the late and unsystematic character of the colonization that produced what Sarmiento called *barbarie* in Argentina, but also the lack of an indigenous pre-European culture. Thus, from the first, merely token founding of the city of Buenos Aires in 1536 (the second, definitive one came in 1580) until the struggle for independence[4] beginning in 1810, the wide expanse of territory that included in one colonial

---

[1] *Sarmiento,* p. 57. "Rosas," he adds, "is a chapter of Argentine history adapted to a colonial system without Spain."

[2] Ibid., p. 17.

[3] From Sarmiento's introduction to *Facundo,* ed. Emma Susana Speratti Piñero, p. 34.

[4] Argentines, past and present, prefer the term *emancipación.*

province present-day Argentina, Uruguay, Paraguay, and a part of Bolivia offered little incentive for civilization. Spain neglected it; it had virtually no connection with the Europe of the Renaissance or the Europe of the Enlightenment; it had no indigenous past. The prohibited but nonetheless active book importations from Europe and the open publishing enterprises that, throughout the colonial era, operated in Mexico City and Lima, found no home in Buenos Aires. It was not until 1776 that, "the one printing press in the area was moved from inland Córdoba to the capital, and Buenos Aires became the cultural, economic, and political center of a vast region."[5]

From the two factors just mentioned—late, unsystematic colonization and the lack of an indigenous culture of the past—came a third: the phenomenally rapid development of the independent republic in the nineteenth century—too rapid, in Martínez Estrada's view, for the moral and cultural values of modern civilization to grow apace with material progress. By mid-century so much land was yet to be conquered and cultivated, so much was yet to be accomplished in the way of civic organization that the tasks appeared formidable beyond hope. In an article signed May 25, 1847, commemorating the Proclamation of May 25, 1810, Juan Bautista Alberdi mixes sarcasm, despair, and hope. After characterizing the Rosas regime as "established anarchy, converted into a permanent institution," he wryly concludes: "Whatever the solution, one thing is undeniably true; and that is that the Argentine Republic awaits her finest hour of prosperity and good fortune. The rising sun on her coat of arms is a historic symbol of her destiny: for her everything is the future, ultimate greatness, and fanciful hopes."[6]

For the same reasons that Sarmiento was in an ideal position to set up new institutions and to change the whole course of national history, he was also extremely vulnerable. Gaucho society over many decades, and more than ever during Rosas' rule (1829–1852), had instilled in the region a formidable resistance to all the cohesive ele-

---

[5] Lewis Hanke, *South America*, p. 60.
[6] "La República Argentina, 37 años después de la Revolución de Mayo," *Obras completas*, vol. III, p. 242.

ments of modern social and political organization.[7] Martínez Estrada thought that, as a logical product of the old colonial and undisciplined gaucho atmosphere Rosas and Facundo came to epitomize, Sarmiento was at the same time an idealistic anomaly (an exile who enthusiastically assimilated foreign attitudes and points of view, a utopian who inevitably lost contact with the drab realities of his homeland but who could nevertheless see things, from abroad, in their clear and proper perspective) and a psychological synthesis of the most restrictive aspects of the Hispanic colonial tradition in Argentina. He took an arbitrary, personalist approach to problems, he was egotistical and quite prejudiced against the indigenous American. First, as an exile and militant political moralist, second, after 1852, as a direct participant in his country's development, Sarmiento became the composite image of nineteenth-century Argentina and, by extension, the key to many of the enigmas in Argentina today. So, at least, thought Martínez Estrada.

An Ideological Stimulus

When Juan José Sebreli says that in three successive years (1930–1932) Martínez Estrada "remains silent," reappearing with *X-Ray of the Pampa* (1933) "totally transfigured," and that he has exchanged not only poetry for prose but "optimism for pessimism and harmony for chaos," he greatly oversimplifies the truth.[8] I shall deal later with Martínez Estrada's poetry in some detail. For the present it is enough to say that some of his starkest pessimism appears in his last volume of poetry, *Humoresca* (1929). His serious reading of Nietzsche and Schopenhauer began before 1920, and one of the deepest influences in *X-Ray of the Pampa* was Spengler, whom he began

[7] Without specifying countries, Hans Kohn writes: "By 1823 the Spanish rule was terminated. But the development was different from that in Anglo-America. Spain had offered to its American subjects as little training in self-government and democracy as to its own subjects at home. The Ibero-Americans could as little overcome this political and social backwardness in the nineteenth century as the Spaniards could. Like Spain herself Spanish-America could not apply the principles of democracy and federalism which Anglo-America introduced, both in the United States and Canada. In most Spanish-American republics anarchy and dictatorship alternated" (*Nationalism: Its Meaning and History*, pp. 43–44).
[8] *Martínez Estrada: Una rebelión inútil*, p. 19

reading in the mid-1920's. A series of essays published in literary periodicals of Buenos Aires between 1926 and 1931[9] leave little room for doubt: Martínez Estrada was a pessimist by personal conviction and by logic, as he already had been for some years by lyric inclination. The last of these essays, "Sarmiento: A Hundred Twenty Years Later" is the most important, because it is a fitting prelude not only to a number of other essays on Sarmiento, including the book published in 1946, but also to his masterwork of 1933. The difference between the Sarmiento piece and most of the the essays preceding it is its concrete, historical nature, in contrast to the more abstract and universal pessimism of the others.

The main impulses behind Martínez Estrada's thoughts in this period of his transition from poet to prophet are pessimism and idealistic nationalism, attitudes that go very well together in an imaginative critical mind. The fatalistic emphasis that characterized *X-Ray of the Pampa* and *The Head of Goliath* is anticipated in a short essay written on the occasion of Columbus Day, 1930, scarcely more than a month after the coup d'état that in Argentina was to mark the beginning of a long period of political rigor mortis. The "Revolution" of 1930 marks not only the downfall of the once-dynamic Radical party, but, in George Pendle's words, the restoration of "the monopoly of government to the old landed aristocracy."[10] The popular Hipólito Irigoyen, the first freely elected Argentine president (1916), grew progressively more autocratic. Reelected in 1928, he became a recluse, and his last years of office were totally inactive and his administration corrupt.

It was against this bleak political background that Martínez Estrada turned his attention permanently to Argentine history. One of the first official acts of General Uriburu's military junta—symbolic, in Martínez Estrada's opinion, of neocolonialism—was to change the name of the "Day of America" (October 12) to the Spanish peninsular term used since 1905, "Day of the Race" ("Día de la

[9] See "Reflexiones acerca del error," *Síntesis*, no. 14 (July 1928): 187–192; "Doce de octubre, fiesta," *La Vida Literaria* 3, no. 25 (Nov. 1930); "Drama y comedia de la juventud," *La Vida Literaria* 4, no. 30 (April 1931); and "Sarmiento a los ciento veinte años," *La Vida Literaria* 4, no. 28 (Feb. 1931).
[10] *Argentina*, p. 88.

Raza").[11] "The equivocal Day of the Race," retorted Martínez Estrada, "a degradation of the most vivid symbol of our sovereignty." His conclusion was that "if we Americans are to celebrate something together, it should be what we have become (despite the fateful heritage that weighs on our thought, our sensitivity and our will) and what we are going to be (when we discover—for good or ill— the most adequate means of freeing ourselves from everything European and of embarking on our new destiny). Accordingly, the continental holiday of October 12th must be the day of our reality and our future; it can no longer be a commemoration of the worst features of the past." Columbus Day was still, as far as conscientious Argentines were concerned, the Day of America, as indeed it has always been for North Americans. The old image of a forced unity of all Spanish-speaking peoples by virtue of only one of its racial origins ("la Raza" had a discriminatory connotation) was unacceptable a full century after colonialism had been pronounced officially dead.

The too-great separation of literature and life that Martínez Estrada, Ricardo Rojas (*La literatura argentina*), Juan Agustín García (*Sobre nuestra incultura*), and others saw in Argentine culture of the colonial period ended with the social Romantics, or the "May Association" (Asociación de Mayo) led by Esteban Echeverría (1805–1851). Enrique Anderson-Imbert calls 1830 "the delimiting year," or the break between a very European "Age of Reason" based on largely abstract libertarian principles, and a very American Romantic Age. "Only in Argentina, . . . in the decade of 1830, did a generation of young Romantics, educated by the same books (mostly French), tied together by the same vital attitude toward historical reality, arise."[12] Much of the political anarchy revealed in the works of Echeverría and his slightly younger contemporary, Sarmiento, had actually existed long before. "As early as the year 1580," writes Pendle, "the people of Santa Fe (largely *criollo* in origin) deposed, though only temporarily, all the chief Spanish office-holders in that term."[13]

[11] "Doce de octubre, fiesta." See note 9.
[12] *Spanish American Literature*, trans. John V. Falconieri, p. 164.
[13] *Argentina*, p. 16.

But no reflection of turmoil or, for that matter, of the true substance of life, permeates the dry chronicles of the colonial era. It would be up to an outsider, a traveler from Lima, to introduce in a vital way the gaucho and his customs to the eighteenth-century reader.[14] The first important writers to describe the Argentine condition *from within* were Echeverría, Sarmiento, and José Mármol (1817–1871). Like their spiritual descendant, Martínez Estrada, they felt the intimate relationship between their vocation as writers and their existence as members of a turbulent society. Whereas Echeverría and Mármol concentrated on the more truculent aspects of Rosas' oppression within their personal experience and were (like Sarmiento) forced into exile because of their violent criticisms, Sarmiento attempted to place Rosas, his gaucho underling Facundo, and the whole Argentine people in their proper historical and sociological perspective. He had begun a critical enterprise that the author of *X-Ray of the Pampa* would continue a century later. More than to any other man, Martínez Estrada owed inspiration for the largest and most important part of his work to Sarmiento.

"Sarmiento, A Hundred Twenty Years Later" is an expression of historical disillusionment. Martínez Estrada's ideas about Domingo F. Sarmiento did not change very much between 1930 and 1950, although, as the contemporary political scene changed, he incorporated new analogies. In this dense little essay of 1931 is the nucleus and synthesis of most of what he said about the great man in *Sarmiento* (1946), "The Historical Invariables in *Facundo*," and "Sarmiento, escritor" (1950).[15]

Significantly, Martínez Estrada associates the publication of *Facundo* (1845) with the *third* in a series of "multiple" phases of the "Spanish domination of America." The first was the official colonial period; the second was the period of the wars for independence; the third was the long era of sporadic civil wars in the nineteenth

[14] See Alonso Carrió de la Vandera ("Concolorcorvo"), *A Guide for Inexperienced Travelers between Buenos Aires and Lima.*

[15] Martínez Estrada completed this study of some fifteen thousand words in June 1950. It was not published, however, until 1958. See Rafael Alberto Arrieta, ed., *Historia de la literatura argentina*, II, 369–434.

century, in which colonialism was dead in name but not in administrative and social practice. The use of the word "multiple" is more meaningful than "third," because the essayist is telling us, in effect, that Argentina and America may never find themselves free of the disorderly methods and attitudes of their Hispanic ancestors. Absolute disorder, he is careful to point out, is more fatal than anarchy. Anarchy comprises, negative as it is, a system and philosophy of absolute freedom. Disorder is, at bottom, absolute nullity; chaos is the inevitable result of a situation in which "each individual aspires to become the center of that universe of ruin" that was Argentina of the 1830's and 1840's. Sarmiento and the other distinguished patriots of his time (Mitre, Alberdi, and Vélez Sarsfield, among others) created a new reality, but since it was by "superfetation" (conception during pregnancy) they did not destroy, but only temporarily arrested "the corrosive forces that agitated our history in the period covered by *Facundo*," and when these men passed from the national scene, so did the force behind their ideas and innovations.

Though Sarmiento has been accused of impulsive and arbitrary public behavior, it was obvious to Martínez Estrada that his entire work, in writing and in action, expressed "the beautiful unity of his life" and his singleness of purpose. In later writings Martínez Estrada said a great deal about the inevitable gap between that singleness of purpose and the evil practices against which Sarmiento struggled. In the light of subsequent events and attitudes, he characterized the nineteenth-century leader's struggle for "civilization" as a colossal failure. "If someone had pursued the question, I'm sure he would have concluded that civilization and barbarity are synonyms in our language, with the important differences that civilization is what we are going to be, and barbarity is what we have been."[16] Right here we have the prelude to disillusionment. The civilization "that we are going to be"—Martínez Estrada persistently emphasized—is little more than a horizon and, as everybody knows, horizons always maintain their distance.

[16] This and the preceding quotation are from "Sarmiento a los ciento veinte años," *La Vida Literaria* 4, no. 28 (Feb. 1931).

Sarmiento: The Anti-Spaniard vs. Rosas

In literary style and in life Sarmiento was a romantic who would have liked to make over the nation in his own image. The extent to which he was able to effect changes is still a matter for discussion, but, in the name of "civilization" and in violent opposition to "barbarity," Sarmiento made his position emphatically clear. Rosas was not a monster of nature or any kind of aberration. "On the contrary, he is a social manifestation, the formula of a people's way of being."[17] From François Guizot (*History of Civilization in Europe*) the author of *Facundo* adopted the idea that in the New World there were two parties or sociopolitical forces, the "European" and the "American," and that the latter was the stronger and more primitive of the two.[18] In *Facundo* he set out to explain, through the description and interpretation of Juan Facundo Quiroga's career as a gaucho leader, "the Argentine Revolution," or the intermittent civil war from 1829 to 1852. If Rosas was the formalization of barbarity (Rosas himself was of a Spanish colonial family of some distinction) in the seat of ultimate power, Facundo Quiroga was the natural exponent of barbarity, the true spirit of the backlands, "the most American figure" of the civil-war period. Sarmiento was not the first to express such pro-European (and anti-Spanish) opinions. Indeed, Bernardino Rivadavia, the first president of independent Argentina ("the United Provinces of the Río de la Plata") was himself an image of revolutionary France. J. A. B. Beaumont, one of the first of a long line of English travelers in nineteenth-century Argentina, described Rivadavia as a caricature of Napoleon or as a member of the French Directory: "His coat is green, buttoned *à la Napoléon*; his small trousers, if such they can be called, are fastened at the knee with silver buckles, and the short remainder of his person is clad in silk hose, dress shoes and silver buckles."[19] The truth of the matter is, of course, that there were not two "parties" at all, but rather a tiny intellectual minority, and the great nonpolitical mass of inhabitants

[17] *Facundo*, p. 31.
[18] Ibid., p. 30.
[19] *Travels in Buenos Ayres and the Adjacent Provinces of the Río de la Plata* (1828), quoted by George Pendle in *Argentina*, p. 35.

whom Rosas, with the help of Facundo, Friar Felix Aldao, and others, would eventually round up into the Federalist party.

The small group of founding fathers and theoreticians that organized the independence movement had little influence during the 1820's and early 1830's. Significantly, several provinces refused to ratify the Constitution of 1826. It was designed for strong centralist rule, and the gaucho caudillos were not willing to give up any of their local power. The liberal revival of Rivadavia's centralist concepts did not begin until after 1838, year of the founding of the underground liberal group, the *Asociación de Mayo*. Although Rosas was nominally no more than the governor of the province of Buenos Aires, his rule eventually extended to all the provinces. His rough-style propaganda was based on total intolerance; his supporters were expected to wear red ribbons with the motto "Death to the Savage Unitarists," the small but secretly active party of the May Association. Rosas distrusted and hated foreigners and opposed all liberal ideas of European or North American origin. His solidarity with the Catholic Church, whose ecclesiastical appointments he controlled, was symbolized in the custom of "permitting portraits of Rosas the Restorer to be placed on altars alongside statues of Christ the Redeemer."[20] A fierce parody of his regime is Echeverría's *The Slaughter House*, in which a child, an Englishman, and a defiant young Unitarist leader are the victims of a blood-thirsty, orgiastic horde of Federalists, including their terrorist special police, the Mazorca ("ear of corn"; but also a pun: *más horca*, "more hangings").

By virtue of his despotism, Rosas was, in the period between 1829 and 1852, the strongest unifying force in Argentina. He was nationalistic and xenophobic in an era when memory was still fresh of the abortive English invasions of 1806 (spontaneously disrupted by the populace of Buenos Aires without the help of the Spanish viceroy, the Marques de Sobremonte, who ungraciously fled to the interior). He was a "states-righter" at a time when effective administrative controls over the provinces were unknown. He was a patriot with a prominent role—even as an adolescent—in the defense of Buenos

[20]Arthur P. Whitaker, *Argentina*, p. 29.

Aires against the English. He was a caudillo and horseman of legendary prowess. Basically he was a dynamic and popular leader, but his hunger for power and fanatical belief in "gauchocracy" as the natural form of political life for all Argentina led him ultimately to terrifying excesses. One source estimates that by 1843 he had been responsible, through executions and civil war casualties (not including the badly wounded who would die shortly afterwards, or the deaths inflicted by Rosas' enemies) for over 22,000 deaths.[21]

According to Sarmiento, Rosas embodied the Spanish heritage, which would have to be eliminated if Argentina were ever to enjoy a free and democratic society. Sarmiento's own line of propaganda, as evidenced in a letter from Chile in 1843, reveals some conflict between his wrath and his objectivity:

Rosas is the political inquisition of old Spain personified. . . . In Spain thought has been prohibited for three centuries and there has been a tribunal to persecute and to burn alive those who speak against, write against, or even those who are suspected of disloyalty to the king and to the dominant ideas; Rosas has created that same tribunal in his own person, to drown all murmur of disapproval, to suffocate every seed of liberty. Freedom of the press was unknown to Spain until 1833; Rosas has destroyed the libery that we enjoyed since 1810. Spain has known no constitutional powers during the past centuries; Rosas hates even the word constitution. Despotic, cruel, enemy of all that is national, that is to say, a barbarian, Spanish—he has trampled all under foot, he has destroyed all; and he has finally realized after sacrificing twenty thousand victims the old Spanish government, which is his model, which is his type.[22]

If Rosas was the Spanish heritage, Facundo Quiroga—subservient in his primitivism to the violent will and perverse "Spanish" principles of the former—was the son of the American plains. "Americanism" as Sarmiento and his contemporaries understood it, and Americanism as Spanish Americans of the twentieth century understand it are two quite different things. In 1845 Rosas and his supporters

[21] Rivera Indarte, *Tablas de sangre de la administración de Rozas*, quoted by Lucio V. Mansilla in *Rozas: Ensayo histórico-psicológico*, p. 193. (Originally. Rosas' family spelled their name with a *z*.)

[22] From "Quinta carta a Don Rafael Minvielle," *Gaceta del Comercio*, Oct. 28, 1843; quoted by Allison W. Bunkley in *The Life of Sarmiento*, p. 173.

thought of themselves as defenders of Argentine freedom against a host of enemies from abroad and subversive ideas from within. Their mission was to defend the "Confederation" and the sanctity of personal privilege among the caudillos in power. On the other hand, Facundo was "American" only in the sense that he was wild. Those whom the Argentine liberals of our own time like to think of as true Americans of the 1830's and 1840's (e.g., Sarmiento, Echeverría, Alberdi, Juan María Gutiérrez—Hispanophobes all) were romantic revolutionaries at heart and European libertarians intellectually.

Mariano José de Larra, a rebellious romantic with a keen critical mind, was—significantly—the only Spanish writer of the century appreciated by the Argentine liberals (and also one of the very few in all Spanish literature appreciated by Martínez Estrada). And one need only recall that the theaters of Buenos Aires during the Rosas regime offered but two kinds of works: Spanish plays of the 1830's and 1840's (predominantly the uncontroversial romantics such as García Gutiérrez, Bretón de los Herreros, Zorrilla, and the Argentine-born Ventura de la Vega, who also adapted works of Scribe) and virulent propaganda dramas aimed at the enemies of Rosas. A good example of the latter was *Happy John, or the Fate of All Traitors*, by J. de la Rosa González, performed on July 15, 1851, as an attack on Justo José de Urquiza, a caudillo and former supporter of Rosas who then was beginning the revolt that would result in the latter's overthrow the following year. The protagonist, who closely resembled Urquiza, barely escaped being lynched on stage by the indignant Federalist audience.[23] Since Rosas rigged and regulated it with a heavy hand, local culture deferred to Spanish importations. Melodrama was the order of the day, and the only deviation from this fare was the rapidly increasing number of propaganda pieces after 1840. The subversive culture generated by the May Association and its sympathizers was, by contrast, markedly antitraditional and anti-Spanish.

Civilization and Barbarism: The Life of Juan Facundo Quiroga had a primary and a secondary purpose. Its secondary purpose was the evocation of a man, assassinated ten years before by the very

[23] See Raúl H. Castagnino, *El teatro en Buenos Aires durante la época de Rosas (1830–1852)*, pp. 445–446.

Federalists he had been serving. Facundo symbolized the raw power and naïveté of a typical adventurer of the provinces; he was the "Tiger of the Pampas," and, as such, a good example of Johann Gottfried Herder's theory of the strong influence of a physical environment on the course of history[24] and of Sarmiento's more subjective view of the compatibility between primitivism (as the inevitable outgrowth of New World nature) and Old World colonialism. Sarmiento does not present him as a simple criminal, but as a historical figure of great power. In this unruly leader Sarmiento saw "a man of genius: Caesar, Tamerlane, Mohammed. He was born that way and it was not his fault."[25]

The primary purpose, as everyone who reads *Facundo* through to the end knows, is the overthrow of Rosas. As Raimundo Lida points out, Sarmiento had no scientific interest in the philosophy of history.[26] But he was an enthusiastic reader of Guizot, Herder, and Cousin, for in their writings he found theoretical ammunition with which to attack the tyrant of the Argentine Confederation. In Herder, Sarmiento found that the will to *affective comprehension* surpassed the will to rational knowledge, that there was a thorough exploration of the meaning of national spirit or *Volksgeist* in history.

In place of the Lockian conception of the universal similarity of human nature, [Herder] set up the diametrically-opposed conceptions of national peculiarity and development. . . . Unlike Rousseau, from whom nevertheless he drew much of his inspiration, Herder proclaimed the national group rather than the individual the agent of this development. Here, for the first time, appeared the pregnant idea, not clearly worked out but expressed in emotionally potent iteration, that the nation is a natural organic unit.[27]

Sarmiento thought, and, more important, *felt* that nationality was not simply the coincidence of race, language, and religion, but the whole context of the nation's natural elements. And this context signifies, as Darwin was to demonstrate so convincingly in his theory

[24] See Raimundo Lida, "Sarmiento y Herder," *Memoria del Segundo Congreso Internacional de Literatura Iberoamericana*, pp. 155–171.
[25] *Facundo*, p. 96.
[26] Raimundo Lida, "Sarmiento y Herder," p. 159.
[27] Wallace K. Ferguson, *The Renaissance in Historical Thought*, p. 116.

of evolution, time and history as well as space and environment: in the sense that the fulfillment of individual characteristics necessitates a certain continuum for development. Thus, for example, Facundo Quiroga reveals a synthesis of traits that explain his "natural" history, traits that stem from his forebears as well as from his primitive habitat; from the Spanish sense of personal worth in combination with the Spanish inclination to idleness; and from nomadic and unproductive life in the wilderness, which leads Sarmiento to compare the Bedouin hordes of North Africa with the Argentine *montoneras*, or bands of gaucho horsemen.[28] In Sarmiento's mind, and in Martínez Estrada's, the peculiarities of national spirit *develop* but they do not, to any appreciable extent, *change*. This is one of the reasons why both of them remark so persistently on the inevitable Spanish heritage, as if it were some indestructible weed in the Hispanic American social and political garden. "Rosas invented nothing," said Sarmiento; he had simply coordinated into an intuitive system the instincts and traits that made up his colonial and primitive heritage.

Martínez Estrada: Interpreter of Sarmiento

Martínez Estrada inherited from Sarmiento Herder's organic view of history, which was instrumental in his development of the idea of historical invariables (for example, "The Historical Invariables in Facundo"). His *Sarmiento* (1946) was to become one of his most seriously read works, not only because of its brevity, but because of the critical reassessment of the great writer and leader, and because of the analogies he was able to make between two eras. Or more precisely, and in keeping with Herder and Sarmiento, he interpreted these two eras as successive phases of one, quite homogeneous historical process.

The continuing significance of Domingo F. Sarmiento for Martínez Estrada is best understood through an analysis of *Sarmiento*, which according to his widow, Doña Agustina M. de Martínez Estrada, he composed in three months, dictating the text extemporaneously to a stenographer.[29] However, the book was not of sudden inspiration.

[28] *Facundo*, pp. 77–78.
[29] Interview with the author, July 31, 1960.

As in *X- Ray of the Pampa*, Sarmiento was the representative man who set in motion the thought processes that would result in almost all Martínez Estrada's works after 1930. *Sarmiento* is not a carefully organized and unified treatment, but rather a series of thirteen meditative essays, which, like the essays of *X-Ray of the Pampa* and *The Head of Goliath*, point always toward an interpretation of Argentina's problems, past and present.

Chapter I: Sarmiento was primarily an educator, both in exile and after his return. Since in the mid-nineteenth century the country had no tradition of democratic or representative government, Sarmiento had to do everything himself. He lacked collaborators and created personal enemies. When in high office he saw "his enormous capacity for action," stretched out and diminished by an infinity of petty obstacles and problems. Martínez Estrada believes that Sarmiento's great achievements in public education and government required Sarmiento himself to be a watchdog. In his old age, when he no longer had the energy or the authority to protect them, they were doomed to failure. In this chapter, Martínez Estrada quotes himself several times (pp. 17–18) from *X-Ray of the Pampa*, passages that emphasize the abyss between the hard reality of Argentina as it actually was and 'the other reality" that Sarmiento dreamed of and fought for. However, Sarmiento was not precisely a bastion of order amidst chaos, but rather "the product—by reaction—of barbarism," and the "embodiment of all that was good and bad" in his country.

Chapter II deals with social decadence since Sarmiento's time. The struggle between civilization and barbarity was largely illusory. The ironic effect of Sarmiento's innovations in law, education, and public administration was their ultimate adaption to fraud. These innovations were the "pseudo-structure" that Martínez Estrada first discussed in *X-Ray of the Pampa*; the trappings of order and civilization that conceal the primitive bases of chaos, self-interest, and injustice.

The meaning of Sarmiento's exile is discussed in Chapter III. From the 1820's to the overthrow of Rosas, "the true Argentineans were the exiles." Exiles, in fact, formed Argentine culture, and this explains the "foreign tone" it has had ever since. In this chapter there is a meditation on solitude (also a basic theme in *X-Ray of the Pampa*), which undoubtedly has autobiographical overtones: "The feeling of solitude is characteristic of persons who live for themselves within themselves, and who find only that terrible emptiness which usually leads to the correlative sentiment of death" (p. 43).

There is much in both the poetry and prose of Martínez Estrada that confirms this feeling as his own. Here he has used it for the purpose of contrast; Sarmiento, the constant traveler and man of the world, was not by nature a solitary. "He gives us the impression of a man lacking that dimension which allows him to penetrate his own life" (p. 43). Only in those poetic moments of tenderness incited by recollection of his childhood (*Recuerdos de provincia*) does Sarmiento appear to experience a nostalgia that makes him aware that he has never given much thought to his inner self.

Sarmiento's greatest achievements, thinks Martínez Estrada, were realized abroad; it was in exile that he fulfilled his most vital mission and did his country his finest service: "to accuse, to denounce and to judge" its characteristic evils (p. 47). Here again, of course, an autobiographical element creeps in, for he has always, since 1930, aspired to a similar role, and the essays from 1956 until his death intensify that aspiration. Finally, Sarmiento "had the superiority of his mind working against him. It placed him beyond the reach of his contemporaries; also damaging was the excellence of a literary style that caused him to be admired as a writer but to be underestimated as a thinker and ignored as a prophet" (pp. 49–50).

Chapter IV is a theorization on the ideological civil war that has been waged in Argentina—even in the most peaceful periods—between the forward looking, socially concerned leaders and thinkers who took inspiration from the May Association, and the backward looking, traditionally concerned descendants of "colonialism." Rosas was defeated as a person, but not "as a representative of that colonial status which was theoretically spurious after 1810" (p. 57). Sarmiento was not aware of the fact, says Martínez Estrada, that "civilization and barbarism" (which he thought synonymous with Europe vs. America, and Argentina vs. Spain) were progressively merging since the early nineteenth century, eventually to form a complex, hybrid, and enigmatic "bastard culture."

Chapter V is a further development of the hybrid-culture concept set forth in Chapter IV. Ortega y Gasset and Count Keyserling had noted the impact of industrial and commercial interests on Argentina and other "littoral" cultures, always more susceptible to the circumstances of modern history than the cultures of countries like Mexico, Peru, and Colombia, in which the pre-European past has survived (p. 64). Sarmiento insisted too much on "imported" ideas of progress, mainly from the United States, which was another world with a culture much more closely adapted to its needs than had been the case of Argentina. Sarmiento's main error was oversimplification. In addition to ignoring most of the realities indigenous to the land and its past—minimizing thereby the possibility of radical reforms—he sacrificed a qualitative concept of culture for a "quantitative" one, an idea Martínez Estrada adapts from the anthropologist Ralph Linton. He quotes Linton to the effect that an imported culture is purely quantitative if limited to what the receiving society deems as "the most elevated and desirable" characteristics, and, accordingly, not shared by all members of that society as a *natural* adjunct to their lives.

As a representative of the *realidad artificial*, a "pseudostructure" concealing detrimental personal interests and the "forces of dissociation," Sarmiento was out of touch with *el status social natural* of the everyday citizen. He was an exile (ideologically and psychologically, even after 1852) in opposition to the "acclimated ones" (Rosas, Facundo, and their antiprogressive supporters). Culture in Argentina was, in Martínez Estrada's opinion, imported and theoretical; Sarmiento struggled valiantly for its absorption by the masses, but in vain. The chapter ends on a starkly pessimistic and ironic note. Sarmiento, in many senses, had tried to Europeanize (that is, "civilize") nineteenth-century Argentina, when the gulf was great between the Old and New Worlds. Now, in the twentieth century, the gulf has been dramatically reduced, but only because Europe has been "South Americanized" (that is, barbarized) to a greater extent than Hispanic America has been civilized. Argentina's corruption is only part of a universal corruption in our time, of a "social state structured on immorality, might, injustic, atheism, . . . and the characteristic elements of class institutions, which have converted the world into a brothel, a forced-labor prison, and a diplomatic and political gambling den" (pp. 76–77).

Chapter VI, shortest in the book, condemns the unchanging Spanish bases of Hispanic American unity. Irony once again. The invariable forces, institutionalized in the colonial era, are the military, the clergy, and the bureaucratic system of government peculiar to Spanish tradition; thus what "unites" Hispanic Americans is what Hispanic Americans most want to avoid. Chapter VI contains some of the strongest criticism of Sarmiento, directed mainly at his attitude toward immigration and the indigenous Argentine population. Not only did the famous leader despise the Argentine Indian,[30] but also those of Mexico, Peru, and Bolivia, all of whom he considered a permanent threat to "civilization."[31] The author attacks the "war of extermination" against the Pampa Indians, which took place mainly during Sarmiento's administration (1868–1874). For Don Domingo, the great anticolonialist, the army became a new colonizer.

Sarmiento's ideas on immigration are criticized for quite different reasons. Here we are surprised to learn that Don Ezequiel has been influenced by Hegel, Keyserling, and possibly by his compatriot José

[30] "One day an Indian chief by the name of Calfurcará came to Sarmiento's office in the government house in Buenos Aires. Sarmiento ordered the windows to be opened. The Indian said something to the interpreter, who turned to Don Domingo. 'Mr. President, the chief asks why the windows have been opened.' 'Tell him, [replied Sarmiento] that Indians have a smell of ponies that is unbearable for Christians.' " The Indian chief held his own, replying that it was a good idea to keep the windows open, for "Christians smell like cows." (From Belín Sarmiento, *Sarmiento anecdótico*, quoted by Allison W. Bunkley in *The Life of Sarmiento*, pp. 466–467).

[31] Martínez Estrada quotes (p. 87) from Sarmiento's *La educación popular*. José Ingenieros later adapted Sarmiento's racial point of view to Darwinian principles, claiming superiority for the white man over the "inferior races" destined ultimately to vanish in the universal "struggle for life." As the Argentine son of Italian immigrants, Ingenieros is noticeably more tolerant of the Italians, Spaniards and other recently arrived Europeans than of the lowly autochthonous masses. "Nacionalismo e indianismo," *Revista de America* 2 (May–Aug. 1913): 185–194.

Ingenieros (1877–1925). Hegel and Keyserling, like many French naturalists of the eighteenth century, believed in the inherent inferiority of all nature in the New World—the Hispanic American part of it in particular.[32] Martínez Estrada not only accepts their premise but also extends it to include nineteenth-century European immigration: "Here the immigrant obliterates his good qualities and develops bad ones, lowering himself by adjustment more than by his open resistance to our social status, and that's why I say he takes the place vacated by the Indian" (p. 99).

To help prove his point of the need for a selective immigration, Martínez Estrada compares the relatively simple problem of assimilation of the immigrant in the United States (precisely because the immigrant of the nineteenth century entered a new world with new customs, language, and culture) and the Spanish immigrant in Hispanic America, who, despite the homogeneity of customs, language, and culture, altogether lacked the will to be "assimilated." He was still, in many senses, at home; he injected nothing new into the bloodstream of his new society and preferred to live in the past. Sarmiento failed to see, as Alberdi had seen, the need for a *varied* immigration as well as a *qualified* immigration. For Martínez Estrada the superior nineteenth-century immigrants in Argentina were English, a theory that would be quite difficult to substantiate statistically; he refers not to the English entrepreneur, but to the intellectual traveler (Head, Hudson, Cunninghame-Graham, and but a few others) who could scarcely be construed as constituting a significant class of immigrants. Although Sarmiento as president followed a policy of steadily increasing immigration, he developed no plan for accommodating, educating, or employing the new citizens. The last words of the chapter are, "Without a plan for social justice, progress is damnation."

In Chapter VIII the author returns to his topic of the three colonial ogres: the military, the clergy, and the bureaucracy, all of which Sarmiento failed to check. Martínez Estrada detects an ambivalence in his subject's character. Intellectually he was liberal and

[32] For a complete and exhaustive discussion of this and analogous theories, see Antonello Gerbi, *La disputa del Nuovo Mondo*.

progressive; temperamentally he tended always to accede to vested conservative interests. One of the least fortunate legacies of the Rosas regime, he thinks, is the Argentine wedding of politics and religion. "Our patriotism is the Catholic kind and consists in disbelieving yet affirming." Actually, he adds, the close affinity between religion and politics began with the work of "fraudulent emissaries" in the sixteenth century, who made religion "an adjunct of political power." It was continued by Juan Manuel de Rosas and Doña Encarnación, his red-robed spouse, both of whose portraits adorned Argentine altars on either side of the Redeemer. "All usurpers find consolation and profit on an altar" (p. 113).

With Chapter IX begins a series of four essays concentrating on Sarmiento as a writer. Chapter IX reiterates a favorite thesis of Martínez Estrada's, the defective reading of nineteenth-century texts in the twentieth century. Argentineans of the present, he feels, have no right to read such committed and combative works as *Facundo*, *Martín Fierro*, Echeverría's *La cautiva*, and Mármol's *Amalia* as descriptions of a remote age of atrocities or as a source of entertaining anecdotes. The villains of yesteryear are alive. *Facundo*—"panorama of a fraudulent regime"—is ostensibly about barbarism, but basically it is a rewriting of the eighth-circle section of Dante's *Inferno*. "For what is barbarism, if not a copy, in the rough, of civilization?" (p. 124). Chapter XI, a more appropriate sequel to Chapter IX than Chapter X, is an essay on the twentieth-century meaning of *Facundo*, neither formal literature nor history, but "living history." This means, of course, that Martínez Estrada goes considerably beyond the text and its immediate implications. While in one sense *Facundo* was, in Unamuno's words, "a caricatural portrait," in another sense it was the product of a crucial combination of historical forces visible in both the author and the subject of the work. Like Herder, the philosopher of history, and Freud, the psychologist, Martínez Estrada searches for fixed laws and permanent causes, but in dynamic, organic relationships, to explain the riddles of Argentine life: "Works like *Facundo* are not conceived in the imagination or by analytical reasons, but in the 'id,' the impersonal 'I' of historical experience and reason-free intuition. *Facundo* is an autobiography and a sociology, a literary work and a fragment of history, an accusation by a defender of the poor and the banished, and a chapter in American anthropology" (p. 140).

Sarmiento's own rhetorical question about Rosas ("Why persist in fighting him, then, if he is a fatal, inevitable, logical and natural phenomenon?") is clearly within the Herderian scope of thought. Martínez Estrada reads into *Facundo* and all subsequent Argentine history "the tragic recurrence" of certain genes of "hybridization"—by which he refers to the merging of the least desirable elements of Spanish and native American traditions. Unlike Sarmiento, Martínez Estrada sympathizes with the gaucho, but he nevertheless interprets the gaucho as the result of essentially destructive forces, as the symbol of all that is static, 'invariable," and incurable in Argentine life.

One of the most surprising outgrowths of Spanish colonialism in Latin America, according to the author of *Sarmiento*, is "Anglo-Saxon Imperialism"; that is, Spain prepared the way for the great powers of 1945 through an ambivalent policy of neglect and exploitation until the time of independence. Thus in the nineteenth and twentieth centuries Great Britain and the United States took over the functions of Spain, developing imperialism out of colonialism.

Sarmiento, like the rest of Martínez Estrada's work, is, of course, intended to be part of an extensive critical analysis of Argentine history and life. In this sense the essayist feels that all resistance to Sarmiento and his message, both in his own time and later, can be explained by the fact that Sarmiento struck too deep into the sensibilities of those "who do not want the truth." That conclusion leads logically to another, says Martínez Estrada: it explains the abundance of great literary raw material in Argentina (including a number of valuable but misunderstood books like *Facundo* and *Martín Fierro*) together with a lack of great literature, of "a truthful literature" of deep revelations, such as the Russian (p. 144).

Chapter X is an interpretation of the biographical method of Sarmiento. History and geography, as for Carlyle and Taine, have "biographical projections." For Sarmiento, men are always archetypes predestined to certain kinds of existences. Martínez Estrada compares Don Domingo's method—thinking, no doubt, of his descriptions of caudillos, pathfinders, guides, and outlaw-gauchos—with Spengler's theory of civilizations and cultures, predestined like individual men to youth, maturity, and old age, or, like the year, to seasons of growth and deterioration (p. 129). He believes that Sarmiento was fortunate to have lived in a world "which revealed itself to him flowering on the surface," and one can only wonder if Martínez Estrada's nineteenth-century predecessor did not influence him strongly in his artistic (and moral and psychological) obsession for converting all the surface objects of life into symbols of the hidden trends of fate and of individual and collective souls. Sarmiento, he concludes, was "a novelist who wrote other things," for his literary genius was not analytic, but "temperamental and glandular."

Chapter XII is the best-conceived essay in the book, the most meaningful commentary on Sarmiento's thought and style, and perhaps the clearest mirror of the author's own spirit and character. The reader of this chapter has the impression of an idealistic pragmatist being judged by an idealistic theorist, and one feels that the utopia of the latter was appreciably more remote than the utopia of the former. Sarmiento, in Martínez Estrada's view, was both a materialist and a dreamer, but a dreamer of specific things. He was an idealist in the making, particularly in his writings done in exile, when he set forth the plans and reforms for the republic of the future; yet he never lost sight of basic realities, such as the constant propensity in his time to political authoritarianism and social disorder, which he identified by the term "barbarism."

As should be evident by now, Sarmiento's professional life is divisible into two distinct phases: (1) that of exile, the romantic period in which the writer and thinker predominate, and (2) that of political and administrative action (after 1852), the pragmatic period in which the activist and compromiser predominate. Martínez Estrada makes quite clear his refusal to forgive Sarmiento for this second phase. Sarmiento should have remained in exile permanently, so as to be judged exclusively on the noble indignation of his literary attacks on injustice, on his dreams of progress, and on his prophetic intuitions. His return to the native soil, thinks his sympathetic yet critical biographer, was also his fall from the pedestal of the uncorrupted.

He returned to the game as a direct participant, and it is Martínez Estrada's thesis that he was not equal to the task—no single man could have been—of eradicating the surviving elements of colonial life. Rather, he would have to use some of them to his own advantage, such as the restrictive use of army, caudillo or personalist politics, and a strong belief in a caste system, from the "civilized" level down to the "barbaric."

Martínez Estrada presents Sarmiento as a "mystic of action" but without a "social credo" (p. 158). As a *tactician* he fought valiantly against all that was negative: caudillos, Indian marauding, illiteracy, and separatism. As a *theorist* in the positive sense, he had little to offer. He did not enjoy thinking for the satisfaction of thinking, and the thought that we do find is extremely eclectic—"mutilated fragments" like ornaments knocked off "an architecturally complete building" (pp. 161–163).

He had no system of his own, though he unreservedly admired parts of the systems of others. His thinking was never inner-directed, for he did not consider men individually and personally in a cosmic relationship with their God (or their missing God), or with their universal problems. All relationships were social, and the historical environment in which he moved was strictly local and "American." He was always "vital, robust, pugilistic"; his thought was like "the gestures and mannerisms of a man who says everything out loud" (p. 165). This aspect of Sarmiento's thought is a good key to his style, which is the main subject of discussion in the rest of Chapter XII.

Sarmiento, like Echeverría, rejected all that appeared to be part of Spanish literary tradition, but, as Martínez Estrada points out, he was also a member of that psychologically Spanish family including Mariano José de Larra, Joaquín Costa, Angel Ganivet, and the Cuban José Martí, who were sternly critical of the oppressive aspects of the Hispanic tradition.[33] Like these, he included always the power of his own personality in everything he wrote, "the spoken tone," the sermon, the exhortation. "According to Nietzsche's precept he has the ideal style, that of transmitting to the reader his ideas in the form

[33] "Sarmiento learned from Larra, and Larra was a Spaniard liberated from the Spanish tradition" *Sarmiento*, p. 187.

of convictions" (p. 179). It is also significant that Unamuno, the Spaniard who would accept uncritically no Spanish convention, is quoted several times in this essay as one of the most sensitive interpreters of Sarmiento. Whereas the author is frequently critical of Sarmiento's role as a political leader, he has only praise for his talent as a writer. As a romantic, Don Domingo expressed with great power his nostalgia and his social idealism. He had also the spontaneous gift of characterization and vital description, a biographical talent that Martínez Estrada likens to Shakespeare's and Montaigne's skill "in the reconstruction of a life through a single trait" (p. 181).

The final chapter is a final evaluation, and it is important to point out that here Martínez Estrada amends with consideration and tolerance the critical judgment of Sarmiento's political role after 1852 that he expounded in the previous chapters. Sarmiento's strength is found in his role of the opposition and in the "dramatic tension" (not the originality) of his thought (p. 191). His criticism was basically negative, but, Martínez Estrada now adds, it was necessarily so: "No fundamentally honorable and religious man, of a predominantly ethical spirit—from the Prophets to the 'dissidents' of our time, has lowered himself to flattery, or condoned injustice, indignity or fraud. It was the same with Dante, Leonardo, Spinoza, Rousseau and Nietzsche" (p. 192). Furthermore, he admits that "the magnitude and character of our evils," and Sarmiento's desperate attempts to correct them, show that he was destined to failure anyway.

In this and other equally harsh judgments it is clear that Martínez Estrada did not want to limit his criticism to Sarmiento or to other men of Sarmiento's time. The purpose of this book (1946), like that of his first published essay on Sarmiento (1931) and of "Historical Invariables in *Facundo*" (1947), is clearly a skeptical diagnosis of Argentine problems from colonial times to the present. Germán García is quite right in calling *Sarmiento* "the offspring of *X-Ray of the Pampa*" and in saying that it could even have been included in the latter, "for it is the continuation of the same monologue."[34] The skeptical line of his previous writings does not enter into "Sarmiento,

[34] "El *Sarmiento* de Martínez Estrada," *Cursos y Conferencias* 17, nos. 199–200 (Buenos Aires, Oct.–Dec., 1948): 40.

escritor," written in 1949 and 1950 at the request of Rafael Alberto
Arrieta for a six-volume *History of Argentine Literature*, which
would include the work of diverse contributors. The volume, including Martínez Estrada's essay, was not published until 1958.[35] "Sarmiento, escritor" is an objective account of his subject's life and
work. While there are no second thoughts over what he had previously written, this essay emphasizes the more personal writings—
*Recollections of Provincial Life, European Travels, Africa and
America*, and *The Life of Dominguito* (Sarmiento's elder son, killed
in the Paraguayan War)—to which he had given relatively little attention before. The basic thesis is still present: "the writer is a richer
and even more forceful personality than the man of action."[36] However, Martínez Estrada here is not at his best. He is writing literary
history, which is not his forte, for, among other reasons, the force of
his personality is missing.

"Historical Invariables in *Facundo*" is a reiteration of many of
the viewpoints expressed in *Sarmiento*, but with still greater attention to what the author considers contemporary analogies. Spain and
its American colonies are still presented as the basis for Argentina's
and Spanish America's nineteenth- and twentieth-century misfortunes. The "army, Church and public administration" are still desig-
nated as the principal determinants of Argentine social and political
life; Rosas continues to be "the spectral master of our national life,
the organizer and the hidden legislator."[37] The basic "invariable" is
barbarism, not, however, as Sarmiento conceived it, but as Martínez
Estrada conceives it in its present and past psychological effects. The
"psychosis of terror" fomented by the Rosas regime has not only per-
petuated itself but is more complex and, therefore, more destructive
in our age of technology. Of the "fixers" of historical invariables in
Argentina, some are institutional (the army, the Church, public administration), some are natural (cattle, horses, sheep), some are
psychological (the inferiority complex generated by *mestizaje*, or
the marriage of European men and native American women; the fear

[35] *Historia de la literatura argentina*, II, 371–434.
[36] Ibid., p. 383.
[37] "Los invariantes históricos en el *Facundo*," p. 9.

and panic generated by the violent rule of the caudillos). All are negative and detrimental.

Of these three classes of unchanging forces, Sarmiento himself had a lot to say in *Facundo*. In *Sarmiento*, Martínez Estrada wrote a great deal about the institutional ones as they were known in the 1830's and as they continued to be known in the 1940's; they were the irrevocable legacy of "Spanish colonization." In "Historical Invariables in *Facundo*" he is primarily interested in the natural and the psychological.

It seems certain from the names mentioned in this essay (Alfred Weber, Franz Boas, Malinowsky, Lévy-Bruhl, and others) that in 1946 and 1947 he was reading a lot about primitive societies and cultures and the origins of modern civilization. Weber's *History of Culture* appears to have been of particular interest to him, insofar as fixed and basically unchanging "ethnospiritual" phenomena are concerned. Keeping in mind Argentina's basically rural tradition, he quotes Weber on the remarkable "internal cohesion" of cultures based on horse and cattle raising (India, Egypt, Babylon, and China) and Boas on the unchanging qualities of cultural activity over thousands of years. Sarmiento himself had referred to Rosas' Argentina as the *Era del cuero* ("The Leather Age"). Martínez Estrada recognizes an "internal cohesion" revealed in customs, habits, and character, at the same time pointing out the essential instability of social life in rural Argentina; its "static equilibrium," its variety of "taboos," the association by unstable and unrefined groups, such as gaucho guerrillas, the Mazorca, *montoneras*, which were drawn together more by collective instinct than by civic purpose.

Spain, the "invariante España," is the structure and the "organism" that explains for Martínez Estrada Argentina's accumulated ills. By "Spain" he means, of course, "Spain in America" and all the effects of her colonial institutions. "Barbarity, *campo*, and colony are synonyms," Sarmiento said, just as "civilization, city, and republic" are synonyms. Martínez Estrada adds ("Historical Invariables," p. 14) that the first are the stationary and the permanent, while the second group constitute "the dynamic" and the changeable. In 1947, under the lingering shadow of World War II and the anti-intellectual atmosphere of the Perón Era, the author had little doubt that "permanent" evils would triumph over "dynamic" virtues. The totalitarianism of the 1930's and 1940's is a rebirth of barbarism, with the aid of technical advances, and totalitarianism is the twentieth-century force that rekindles the third, and for Martínez Estrada, the most important of the three invariable forces: the psychological. In the psychological ambiance of the Rosas era the most significant force was fear. Fear, he states, had a "double origin": religious custom and gaucho life. Written on the banners of Facundo Quiroga's followers (which also bore the skull and crossbones) was the motto "Religion or Death," key words in "Rosas' psychosis of terror," which survives long afterward. The same "psychosis" is to be found in 1947 "throughout Hispanic America, Spain and Portugal, . . . disciplining the spirits of these peoples so that they will accept any outrage backed up by force" (p. 11).

In the second of the two lectures that make up this essay, Martínez Estrada lists six dates between 1852 and 1943 that to him signify not only political crises but successive steps in a steady process of political and moral decadence, and of the "formation of a totalitarian state" (p. 29).

Each of the most important works (*X-Ray of the Pampa, The Head of Goliath, Sarmiento,* and the *Death and Transfiguration of Martín Fierro*) is, in part, a moral and intellectual response by the author to Argentina and the world of the moment. Thus, his purpose, as well as his frame of mind, leads him to draw patterns that unite or relate the most ominous events and the most depressing social situations.

Most objective readers sense that his presentation of Argentina, Spain, and Hispanic America is founded on an anti-Spanish bias, and that to blame all modern problems on the deficiencies of the colonial structure (or the failure of progress, democracy, and "civilization" on the evils of reaction, authoritarianism, and "barbarity") is a misrepresentation of the historical truth. However, in Martínez Estrada as in Sarmiento before him (and in both the Spanish historian and philologist Ramón Menéndez Pidal and the Spanish essayist Miguel de Unamuno) there is an important basic agreement: the concept of Spain—and, by extension, the Hispanic World—as two antithetical forces in continuous conflict. The concept is well developed in Unamuno's essay *On the Meaning of Traditionalism* (*En torno al casticismo*) and in Menéndez Pidal's *The Spaniards in Their History*, the fifth chapter of which is entitled "The Two Spains." Menéndez Pidal traces the sporadic struggle, from the Middle Ages to the end of the Spanish Civil War (1936–1939) between the forces of tradition and progress, between "the two sons of Oedipus, who would not consent to reign together and mortally wounded each other."[38]

It is true that Martínez Estrada has not seen this struggle between tradition and progressivism in the same proportion of power or within the same territorial limits. But, like Unamuno and Menéndez Pidal, he is dealing with essentially the same problem. What might be called "the temperamental approach" is the distinctive quality of Martínez Estrada's view.

Unlike *X-Ray of the Pampa*, *Sarmiento* had quick critical repercussions in Argentina. Two of the leading critics, Germán García and Carlos Alberto Erro (the latter's essay has the meaningful title, "Un Sarmiento ahistorico") basically disagree with Martínez Estrada's interpretation, removing much of the "blame" for twentieth-century failures that Don Ezequiel attributes to Sarmiento.[39] Two others, José Luis Romero and Dardo Cúneo, are more inclined to share his pessimism and are quick to praise his insights.[40] But all

---

[38] *The Spaniards in Their History*, trans. by Walter Starkie, p. 141.

[39] Germán García, "El *Sarmiento* de Martínez Estrada"; Carlos Alberto Erro, "Un Sarmiento ahistórico," *Realidad* 1, no. 2 (Buenos Aires, March–April 1947): 267–275. Erro considered most of the doubts raised by Martínez Estrada as constituting an unfair distortion of Sarmiento's character and purpose.

[40] José Luis Romero, "Martínez Estrada: Un renovador de la exégesis sarmientina," *Caudernos Americanos* 6, no. 3 (Mexico City, May–June 1947); reproduced in *Argentina: imagenes y perspectivas*, pp. 99–107. Dardo Cúneo, "Sarmiento" (section of the chapter "Sobre Ezequiel Martínez Estrada"), in *Aventura y letra de América Latina*, pp. 125–132.

agree that Martínez Estrada awakened new thought, not only about the historical role of Sarmiento, but about the historical reality of Argentina.[41]

[41] In addition to the writings already mentioned, Martínez Estrada published three essays in *Cuadernos Americanos*: "La inmortalidad de *Facundo*," 4, no. 5 (Sept.–Oct. 1945): 207–220; "Sarmiento y Martí," 5, no. 4 (July–Aug. 1946): 197–214; "Sarmiento y los Estados Unidos," 11, no. 3 (May–June 1952): 186–204.

3 · Trapalanda

The New World That Was an Old World

The same thesis that inspired Martínez Estrada's writings on Sarmiento led also to *X-Ray of the Pampa*. As a continuation of medieval Spain, colonial Spanish America was from the first moment in full decadence, and independent Spanish America—save a few constitutional formalities—was the continuation of colonial Spanish America. *X-Ray of the Pampa*, which its author claims "was born of necessities of the moment [ca. 1930] and conceived without sin,"[1] nevertheless bristles with ancestral resentment against Argentina's past in general and its Hispanic heritage in particular. Furthermore, it would be no exaggeration to say that Don Ezequiel's essays after 1933 were in

---

[1] "Placa de una *Radiografía*," *Revista do Livro*, no. 10 (Rio de Janeiro, June 1958): 201.

many cases extensive supplements and appendices to the complaints
first registered in *X-Ray of the Pampa*.

Martínez Estrada, of course, is hardly alone in recognizing survival
of the Old World in the New. A Mexican historian has maintained
that the Middle Ages lived on in Hispanic America considerably
longer than in Europe because "an appropriate setting for the development of medieval ideals existed for an extended period in the
Spanish New World while, contemporarily in Europe, the Religious
Reformation and the so-called Italian Renaissance were causing the
abandonment of the essentials that sustained medieval Christen-
dom."[2] Under the eye-opening title "The Legacy of the Middle Ages
in the American Wild West,"[3] Lynn White, Jr., shows in an informa-
tive article that many of the instruments and practices of the pioneers
were known in different parts of Europe several centuries before (for
example, the covered wagon, spurs, the log cabin, the stagecoach,
distilled liquor, and execution by hanging), and that beyond the
typically romantic interpretation of the Middle Ages by researchers
into "feudalism and the hierarchical church, scholastic debates and
the aubades of troubadours" were the unenlightened and forgotten
but nevertheless very real and vital masses of common people. The
patterns of life of these people lingered long after them, in the earliest
colonists of New England and in the latest pioneers of the nineteenth
century. Moreover, the explorers of the Far West were not victims
but beneficiaries of medieval tradition, retaining from it certain
mystic and ascetic tendencies of simple believers within a relatively
rigid socioreligious structure. Accordingly, they were able to consider the wilderness "not merely a dread place of struggle and suffering but also an arena in which spiritual perfection may be won—a
land where 'men are men' "[4] with the continuing possibility of self-
realization.

[2] Luis Weckmann, "The Middle Ages in the Conquest of America," *Speculum*
26 (1951): 130. The Spanish historian Claudio Sánchez Albornoz has called
colonial Hispanic America "the posthumous daughter of the Hispanic Middle
Ages." See his chapter "La edad media y la empresa de América," in *España y
el Islam*, pp. 181–199.
[3] Lynn White, Jr., "The Legacy of the Middle Ages in the American Wild
West," *Speculum* 40, no. 2 (April 1965): 191–202.
[4] Ibid., p. 193.

But whereas westward expansion in the United States took place in the great dawn of the railroad era and in a period of many technological advances in agriculture and gold and silver discoveries, the Spanish exploration and colonization of a much vaster territory (including what was later to become our own Southwest) was virtually completed a little over a half-century after the first voyage of Christopher Columbus. The medieval tradition brought to America by the Spaniards had little in common with the "medieval legacy" described by White; the former was contemporaneous and took the form of a specific mission, the latter was a collective reminiscence and, as such, mainly subconscious. Much has been said about the personal pride, the love of adventure, and the rugged individualism of the sixteenth-century Spaniards in America, and most of it is basically true. What is often forgotten, however, is the prestige and power of the Spanish monarchs from Isabella the Catholic to Philip II, leaders not only of imperial Spain but of the Catholic world, and their strong material and psychological impact on Spanish Americans up to the end of the colonial period. (Sarmiento and Martínez Estrada would say their impact went *beyond* the colonial period.)

The Spaniards did not come to America with the conviction that they were building a new world. Rather, their temporal and religious mission was to expand the world that was inherently and unchangeably theirs, that of Spain dominated by Castile. This was their historical role and purpose—combined, of course, with the universal human desire of all times to satisfy their natural curiosity about the unknown.

The circumstances were these: (1) The Spaniards carried out their conquest of America in a time of deep ideological ferment, only a few decades after what Huizinga calls "the waning of the Middle Ages," directly after the reconquest of the Peninsula from its Moorish inhabitants, and directly after the expulsion from the Peninsula of unconverted Jews. Renaissance concepts of the dignity and power of individual man were in open conflict with the medieval emphasis on man defined according to his specific social and religious functions. (2) The conquest, exploration, and settlement of isolated places was the work of men either intensely loyal to Spanish royal power or intensely eager to reap the benefits resulting from its favor. (3) Imperial Spain, like other European powers of the 1500's, was not "progressive" but rather a nation involved in the consolidation and militant defense of its dominions.

While there was ample opportunity for personal initiative and ambition, the Spaniard in America was relatively unconcerned with the future. In Martínez Estrada's dialectic "possession" (land, dignity, status) was his incentive, and disillusionment (*desengaño*) with what he found was the climax. The Argentine historian José Luis Romero imagines what must have been the frame of mind of the Spaniard en route to the New World: "On shipboard no one wasted time examining maps, obscure memoirs or old manuscripts that might reveal secrets of the recently discovered world, because none of that seemed worthwhile. The conquistador's greatest asset was his irrevocable decision to arrive at some unknown place where he might find something that had not previously occurred to his imagination. That was all there was to it."[5]

Most historians have given insufficient attention in their accounts of the sixteenth century in the New World to the abstract character of the Spanish conquest and early colonization. By "abstract" I mean that the enterprise itself—the founding of cities and towns, the establishment of boundaries, the collective baptisms of sometimes thousands of Indians into the Christian faith, the organization of Indian groups into *encomiendas*,[6] and the teaching of the faith by "peaceful and reasonable" methods—amounted in practice to a great deal less than it did in theory. The abstract impression that one gets when studying the history of the period is increased by the fact that there

[5] *Argentina: Imágenes y perspectivas*, p. 56.
[6] See Lewis Hanke, *The Spanish Struggle for Justice in the Conquest of America*. The encomienda system was first formally established on the island of Hispaniola in 1502 and later spread to many other regions. Hanke writes, "Inevitably questions arose among ecclesiastics concerning the justice of the system, and by a royal letter of August 14, 1509, it was determined that Indians were to serve for a period of one or two years only, and not for life. This order was not strictly enforced, and pressure was exerted to allow encomiendas to be passed on to encomenderos' descendants as inheritances. Thereafter the question was continuously under discussion in Spain and America. The fact remains, however, that the first two decades of Spanish rule was a period of almost unchecked exploitations of the Indians" (p. 20).

is not very much history to study. Even Lewis Hanke in his accurate and abundantly documented *The Spanish Struggle for Justice in the Conquest of America* complains of the lack of reliable material:

> One would like to know . . . what sort of life the encomendero led in that "solid mansion of stone or other durable material" which he was supposed to build in the town nearest his encomienda. No diaries kept by encomenderos have come down to us, whether because time has destroyed them or because they were never written. Spaniards have always shown a marked reluctance to reveal themselves in autobiographical works. . . . Most disturbing of all, no comprehensive Indian records are available to tell how the Indians felt about the encomienda. Indian declarations against the system, of course, exist, and we may safely suppose that it was a horror to some of them, but the documents available do not provide a complete story. And the Indians put under the crown, instead of being commended, still await their historian.[7]

The Río de la Plata region is even more a blank page than the rest of the Empire. No Indian society was assimilated by the Spaniards (as in Mexico and Peru). The origins of the Argentine nationality include no indigenous heritage. No significant cultural center graced the region. In his *Philosophy in Argentina*, Juan Carlos Torchia Estrada sums up the academic activities at the University of Córdoba: "The Jesuits were in charge of instruction from the foundation of the University (1622) until the expulsion of the Society (1767). But the only data on their activities in the 17th century are the names of the professors, for 'neither their writings nor their students' notebooks,' says Father [Guillermo] Furlong (S.J.), 'have come down to us, nor have we found in the archives a single program of theses or abstracts before the 18th century.'"

There was no university in Buenos Aires, and the first printing press in that city (which was only the second in the whole Río de la Plata region) was moved there from Córdoba in 1780.[9] To make matters worse, Río de la Plata was dominated economically by Peru

    [7] Ibid., pp. 84, 85.
    [8] *La filosofía en la Argentina*, p. 33. The text by the Rev. Guillermo Furlong, S.J., from which Torchia Estrada quotes is *Nacimiento y desarrollo de la filosofía en el Río de la Plata (1536–1810)*, Buenos Aires, 1952, p. 100.
    [9] Ibid., p. 19.

until 1777, when the Port of Buenos Aires was opened for the first time to legal trade with the other Spanish possessions. Before then, not even Spain shipped goods directly to Buenos Aires, but rather by a circuitous route that went from Porto Bello (near the present Canal Zone) over the Isthmus of Panama by land, by sea again to Callao (next to Lima) on the Pacific coast, and finally by muletrain or covered wagon some two thousand miles to Buenos Aires.[10] Therefore, it was no surprise that Buenos Aires became one of the biggest contraband centers in the New World. In short, the colonial Argentine territory, backyard of the Viceroyalty of Peru and the neglected hinterland of an Empire, had existed in theory more than in reality, and it is to independent Argentina's great credit that she has progressed culturally and economically as far as she has in little over a century.

The dynamic Spaniards and their immediate *criollo* descendants, excellent spectators of their own image, dreamers always of a fuller and finer life, soon discovered themselves to be—in Martínez Estrada's apt phrase—"señores de la nada." According to the distinguished Russo-German essayist and traveler, Count Hermann Keyserling, the student of Spanish and Spanish American culture must see things "from the point of view of Earth"—in contrast to the point of view of "Spirit," presumably characteristic of non-Hispanic Europeans, Chinese, and Hindu Indians.[11] Keyserling detects a "cold-blooded" relationship between the Latin American and his natural habitat. That is, the Latin American,[12] is uniquely sensitive, like the most refined artist or poet, to the presence, emotions, and sentiments of his fellow man. This is what Keyserling means by "the cold-blooded modality of life," of which the writings of Martínez Estrada happen to be a convincing example.

Solitude

"The Pampa has made modern Argentina; it has given the country

10 George Pendle, *Argentina,* pp. 14–15.
11 *South American Meditations,* trans. Theresa Duerr, pp. 32–33.
12 I have used the term "Latin American" here, which is what Keyserling means by "South American" (i.e., an inhabitant of Mexico, Central America, or South America).

its wealth, industries and character, and it has shaped the habits and outlook of the people."[13] Few geographers or historians would dispute this view; but the pampa is an enigma, and the wondrous fertility of its soil and the history of its progress from wilderness to civilized productivity is counterbalanced by images of emptiness and solitude and a long tradition of violence in some ways similar to that of our Wild West. Martínez Estrada was drawn to the enigma both by his psychological predisposition to skepticism and by the social and political climate of his time.

X-Ray of the Pampa has often been interpreted as the impressionistic view of a poet—which to a large degree it was—but the author reminds us that, of the three years he spent writing it, a year and a half was devoted to the reading or checking of "about four hundred books."[14] In order to write it, he absorbed the widest possible variety of material on Argentina and the contemporary Western world. Those who accuse him of intellectual violence toward his country and its historical reputation should remember that several of his distinguished contemporaries share in varying degree his skepticism and his misgivings (Spengler, *Decline of the West*; Ortega y Gasset, *Invertebrate Spain* and *Revolt of the Masses*; H. L. Mencken, *Prejudices*; Toynbee, *A Study of History*; and Huizinga, *Shades of Tomorrow*).

The Chilean writer Antonio Undurraga stresses in his commentary on Argentine literature the importance of the "sorrowful or metaphysical recollection," expressed, for example, in *The Poem of Martín Fierro*, and a marked inclination of the writer to entertain himself contemplating the impossibilities of life, both those of the past and those of the creative imagination. Here we are reminded of the themes of Borges, who gives artistic form to entire metaphysical universes and who regenerates figures, legends, and events of the past in circumstances that might have been. Undurraga wonders whether "the immense plain has given the Argentine soul a perma-

13 *The Columbia Encyclopedia*, 3rd ed., 1963, p. 1591.
14 "Placa de una *Radiografía*," p. 202.

nent sadness similar to that of the Russian soul."[15] H. A. Murena identifies "historical solitude" and an acute consciousness of a lack of a past as the distinguishing features of Argentine nationalism, clearly disclosing the impact on his sensibility of this and other passages from the second part ("Solitude") of *X-Ray of the Pampa*.

> The solitude which forces its way into the soul like a mysterious anguish and which removes human interest from panoramic beauty is the absence of history. Nothing of deep significance to man has happened in those regions; thus he does not feel, as Spengler thinks, swept forward by destiny. There a man is as isolated as in the visual field of a microscope or telescope. . . . Crossing our plains and passing by our villages with their inexpressive names, one feels like a transient being without a past, and is repelled by the ostentatiousness of the high-sounding but meaningless labels.[16]

This sadness permeates the whole book and determines its unity of vision. Everywhere we are struck by a close affinity between the writer's emotional state and his surroundings (cf. Keyserling's theory of the "cold-blooded modality of life").

Martínez Estrada was not a devotee of Jung,[17] yet in many works, most prominently in *X-Ray of the Pampa*, he practices to a surprising degree what the psychiatrist preaches. For Jung there are two "modes" of artistic creation. One is drawn "from the realm of human consciousness," or from the experiences, problems, and crises of life as they are consciously experienced; this is the "psychological" mode, by which Jung means the conceptual approach to reality. The second mode, more significant from the standpoint of psychoanalysis and literary criticism, is "visionary." The visionary mode "is a strange something that derives its existence from the hinterland of man's mind." It is "primordial vision," impossible to explain because it constitutes a direct apprehension of reality, preceding both language and concept. One finds it in Wagner's *Nibelungenlied*, in William

---

[15] "Encuesta sobre la literatura hispanoamericana, argentina y chilena," *Ciudad*, nos. 2–3 (Buenos Aires, 1955): 69–70.

[16] *Radiografía de la pampa*, p. 121.

[17] In his *Panorama de las literaturas* (p. 359) he accuses Jung of not having understood a single word "of the 754 pages" of Joyce's *Ulysses*.

Blake's poetry, and, fused with historical situation, in Dante's *Divine Comedy.* "The value and force of the experience are given by its enormity. It arises from timeless depths; it is foreign and cold, many-sided, demonic and grotesque. . . . The disturbing vision of monstrous and meaningless happenings that in every way exceed the grasp of human feeling and comprehension makes quite other demands upon the artist than do the experiences of the foreground of life.[18]

Martínez Estrada has understood and repeatedly confirmed the theory, developed in part from his readings of Count Keyserling and Georg Simmel, that "the foreground of life" is nothing in itself. It is meaningful only as a reference point for the illumination of the inner self: "Contemplating the map of the world is like watching in the depths of oneself the outline of the history of man."[19] In the Argentine wilderness one feels "ancestral chills up and down one's spine."[20] The pampa is "the land in which man is alone, like some abstract being about to begin again in the history of its species—or to conclude it."[21] One of the many annotated passages in a Spanish translation in his personal library of Simmel's *Schopenhauer and Nietzsche* reads, "Every philosophy is based on the premise that things are more than they appear to be; multiplicity is also unity; the simple, compounded; the earthly, divine; the material, spiritual; the spiritual, material; the stationary, moveable, and the moveable, stationary."[22] And on the first page of a French translation of Keyserling's *South American Meditations* he underlines the following: "For 'facts' do not exist in their own right; they are artificial creations of arbitrary abstraction."[23] Keyserling, Simmel, and Martínez Estrada continually emphasize the ambiguous and abstract character of the most common reference points of human existence—or what are commonly referred to as facts, events, and natural phenomena.

[18] Carl Gustav Jung, "Psychology and Literature," in Brewster Ghiselin, ed., *The Creative Process*, pp. 211, 212.
[19] *Radiografía de la pampa*, p. 124.
[20] Ibid., p. 125.
[21] Ibid., p. 12.
[22] Georg Simmel, *Schopenhauer y Nietzsche*, trans. Francisco Ayala, p. 34.
[23] Hermann de Keyserling, *Meditations Sud-Américaines*, trans. Albert Beguin, p. 9.

Reality, they say, is not to be found in these things but only in their impact upon our inner selves.

Elsewhere I have observed that the literature of solitude is rich in Argentina long before Martínez Estrada's time.[24] Sarmiento wrote that there was "a source of poetry" in the pampa, for poetry, "like religious sentiment, . . . needs a spectacle of the beautiful, the immensity of space, of formidable power, of the vague and incomprehensible."[25] William Henry Hudson, the great Anglo-Argentine who esteemed wild nature more than civilized man, is without doubt the writer who felt most strongly attracted to the lonely expanses of the land of his birth. José Hernández's poem, *Martín Fierro*, is the story of a perpetually displaced person, projected at last into society only when Argentine history has begun a new cycle.

The romantic and Parisian educated Esteban Echeverría published in 1837 the first significant work on life on the pampa. *The Captive* is a verse romance of melodramatic adventure and death, which includes panoramic descriptions of great beauty and which apprehends the persistent loneliness of its two errant protagonists. As Rafael Alberto Arrieta points out,[26] Echeverría is not simply a poet but a man obsessed with the political and social problems of his time, to the extent that he was the guiding spirit of the liberal May Association secretly organized against the regime of Juan Manuel de Rosas. But in none of these nineteenth-century masters nor, for that matter, in Martínez Estrada, have these preoccupations weakened the lyric spirit. From the Romantic to the Existentialist age, the spectacle of wilderness has made Argentine literature unique in Hispanic America. In Martínez Estrada the literature of solitude reaches its culmination, for it is in his works that the sentiment of desolate loneliness and a sensitivity to nature and the landscape are skillfully combined in a unique form of geographic fatalism.

The pampa is in the "empty" category of landscape, as opposed to the "full" category of the tropical, mountain, and urban areas. On the

[24] "Espacio y soledad en la literatura argentina," *Sur*, no. 279 (Buenos Aires, 1962): 30–40.
[25] *Facundo*, p. 55.
[26] "Esteban Echeverría y el romanticismo en el Plata," in Arrieta, ed., *Historia de la literatura argentina*, II, 109.

one hand its spaciousness, uniformity, and atmosphere of isolation overwhelm the literary observer. On the other hand, the observer fills that emptiness—*tabula rasa* for the creative mind—with his most intimate impressions and anxieties. The literary treatment of the emptiness has had a historical as well as spatial dimension. In *X-Ray of the Pampa* Martínez Estrada takes up where Hernández, in *The Poem of Martín Fierro,* left off, deploring in philosophical and intricately metaphorical terms what Hernández's protagonist had deplored in the direct terms of his personal experience: tradition vitiated by self-interest and progress for the few at the expense of the many.

The message did not end with *X-Ray of the Pampa,* nor with the *Death and Transfiguration of Martín Fierro.* A younger generation developed the same theme in the context of intellectual and political problems of the 1950's. H. A. Murena, in *The Original Sin of America* (1954), and Julio Mafud, in *Argentine Uprootedness,* (1959), show clearly the impact of Martínez Estrada's stark historical pessimism. The first six chapters of Mafud's work deal with six varieties of "uprootedness" (*desarraigo,* cf. Simone Weil's concepts of *enracinement* and *déracinement*), including those of the nomadic Indian, the restless gaucho, the perplexed immigrant, and the average citizen of the Perón era. In Chapter V he points to the best-known works of the nineteenth and twentieth centuries in Argentina and severely criticizes two idiosyncrasies: (1) the introspective, abstract, and narcissistic nature of their characters, and (2) their authors' inability to "capture reality."[27] Like Martínez Estrada before him, Mafud denounces the excessively homocentric nature, moody and introspective, of the reality described. One is indeed struck by the self-obsessed protagonists who are islands unto themselves and to whose sensibility the world and all other beings are merely subjoined.

The feeling of geographical isolation is strong in Argentine literature, but, as in the Hispanic tradition in general, there is little feeling

---

[27] *El desarraigo argentino* p. 105.

for nature.[28] Ortega y Gasset is probably right in questioning the conventionally accepted cause-and-effect relationship between environment and man in most realistic literature. Insisting that environment "is not the cause of our acts but only a provocation" and that "our acts are not an effect of the environment but a free response, an autonomous action," Ortega concludes that "each race bears in its primordial soul an ideal of landscape which it strives to realize within the limits of its own geography. Castile is so terribly arid because Castilians are arid."[29] Man by psychological make-up and ideological intention seeks out the surroundings most appropriate to his character. "The world is my idea," the phrase with which Schopenhauer began his great essay, is every man's truth, every man's point of departure, and every man's fate. It has led man to all the varieties of solitude, Utopia, and deception, including those of the Spanish conquistadores who, in the open space of South America, turned out to be "señores de la nada."

Probably Martínez Estrada read the essay by Ortega y Gasset just quoted ("Historia y geografía") before finishing X-Ray of the Pampa, for there is a strong suggestion in the skeptical Argentine's work of the same kind of fatalism found in Ortega's meditations: a fatalism of character rather than one of physical circumstances. Ortega goes so far as to say that geography is significant only in the sense that in history it becomes the "symptom and symbol" of the national character of the people who inhabit it.[30] In like manner, Martínez Estrada diminished the importance of geography as a historical determinant. He could never have shared Sarmiento's dream of the development of river transport from Buenos Aires to the interior, and in his view the true function of the railroads in his country had been merely that of a "colonial" supply route to Buenos Aires and Europe. In Argentina men had not lived as the product of their environment. Rather, they had fulfilled a destiny of unknown be-

---

[28] On Hispanic indifference to nature, see Marston Bates, "Man and the Balance of Nature," in Crane Brinton, ed., *The Fate of Man*, pp. 487–488.
[29] José Ortega y Gasset, "Historia y geografía," *Obras completas*, II, 371–373.
[30] Ibid., p. 373.

ginings, and the lonely existence of life on the pampa was the ultimate expression of that destiny.

Similarly, environment is not the cause but the instrument of poetic expression. Martínez Estrada had prepared for his vocation of solitude before the pampa became the central image and theme of his works. Goethe, Kant, Spengler, Schopenhauer, Nietzsche, and Baudelaire guided him in the initial phase of his pessimistic thought. *Argentina* (1927), his fourth book of poetry, was the turning point from the abstract to the historical. From that point forward, his country became "the symptom and symbol" of his thoughts.

"X-Ray of the Pampa": Philosophy of a Title

From youth to old age Martínez Estrada remained an outsider. Unlike the nostalgic Ricardo Güiraldes who in *Don Segundo Sombra* found ecstasy in solitude ("impressions are swift on the pampa, spasmodic and vanishing traceless into the enormous present"),[31] he was the gloomy foe of exuberance, peering out at the world from his permanent vantage point of spiritual exile. Others have been positive by contrast. His predecessor Sarmiento had thrived on all experience, no matter how adverse, as his incentive to write and struggle for a better day. His contemporary Jorge Luis Borges discovered the magic with which to sublimate ordinary experience, converting the prosaic problems of existence into a fanciful world of his own invention. All were perfectly "serious." Martínez Estrada, however, took direct inspiration from absences, obstacles, and everything that was negative: man's lack of progress, the pernicious effects of colonial tradition, the incommunicability of all persons, political, social, and ecclesiastical corruption, and geographical nature as a fateful projection of human nature.

Spiritual nationalism had already found expression in other Argentine writings, as, for example, in the poems and legends of Leopoldo Lugones and in the essays and criticism of Ricardo Rojas. But *X-Ray of the Pampa* was still a first cry in the wilderness, the first total confrontation in this century by an Argentine with the "real-

---

[31] *Don Segundo Sombra,* trans. Harriet de Onís, p. 48.

ities" of past and present. It was the first interpretation of Argentina in which the interpreter tried to bring a synthesis of social psychology, spiritual pessimism, and raw indignation to bear upon the accumulation of errors that, he was convinced, underlay the history and customs of his land.

Martínez Estrada has alluded to the copious documentation of his great essay. His mention of the documentation was intended as a corrective, because twenty-five years after the publication of X-Ray of the Pampa he wanted to remind his readers, both those of the past and those of the present, of its prophetic value. Although few Argentines accepted the work consciously in its total message, many found themselves affected by it and have shared its pessimism. Luis Emilio Soto, in one of the first critical commentaries, wrote that Martínez Estrada presents a "vision" and not a "conception" of Argentina.[32] To be sure, an x-ray is just that: reality as it is seen, not as it is thought to be. But while the x-ray reveals objects beneath the surface, as the psychoanalyst penetrates beneath external human behavior, it can give us no more than a silhouette or shadow-picture of those objects. Thus, what is offered as a suggestion of impersonal analysis in the title—not a judgment or impression, but an x-ray—amounts actually to artistic license for an entirely free, subjective interpretation. The author himself has denied poetic method in his famous work,[33] but the truth is that he bases almost every observation on a metaphor and presents every historical, social, and political concept in the form of a symbol.

The key to the general meaning of X-Ray of the Pampa appears in a brief but important essay, "Reflexiones acerca del error" (1928),[34] in which we read that "sooner or later one realizes that the process of life is an error that compounds itself." This fatalism was, in a nutshell, the thesis of the book published in 1933. Argentina and all Latin America "had been born by mistake."[35] and their subsequent history aggravated and multiplied that mistake. But Martínez Es-

---

[32] "Análisis espectral de la pampa" (1934), in Crítica y estimación, p. 115.
[33] "Placa de una Radiografía," p. 201.
[34] "Reflexiones acerca del error," Síntesis, no. 14 (July 1928): 192.
[35] Radiografía de la pampa, p. 9.

trada was not content to limit his tragic view to history. He sought to make it absolute, one in which every immediate reality symbolized some feature of the universal march toward catastrophe. Geography, climate, even geology were fused together with human character, traditions, and customs. In *X-Ray of the Pampa* we have a kind of positivism *a posteriori* based on wholly nonscientific motivations. Only after the feeling has been experienced and expressed does the essayist seek a naturalistic explanation of what was originally no more than a fleeting, intuitive notion. Otherwise, how could he assume, for example, that there was a meaningful relationship between the South America of the Tertiary geological age ("that deformed and titanic existence")[36] and the disorderly life of the pampas and cities of the modern era? The geological-social relationship described by Martínez Estrada seems to have been drawn from the first chapter of *South American Meditations* ("The Continent on the Third Day of Creation"), in which Keyserling states that "wherever new life comes into existence on that soil, it at once acquires the character of a primordial beginning. This is true of Argentina. To its original landscape correspond only the extinct prehistoric animals . . . and the few ancient forms of life still extant there impress one as being antediluvian."[37]

Everything had symbolic significance in this period of the anxious life of Martínez Estrada. The landscape was full of signs and portents; the suicides of the great writers Horacio Quiroga and Leopoldo Lugones seemed to him a partial surrender of humanity to the anonymous forces that afflicted the universe. The world-wide decay of democratic processes and the rebirth of racism were a prelude to a new age of violence. The contamination of Argentine politics since 1930 became his permanent obsession.[38] Nothing was right with the world.

[36] Ibid., p. 74.

[37] *South American Meditations,* p. 26.

[38] Martínez Estrada sums up, in an address to the Argentine Writers Association in 1942, the motives for his continuing pessimism since 1933: "I fail to see any improvement in the gloomy climate in which the intelligentsia debate their tremulous orphanhood. Since those days, so remote now, there has been no favorable change that could lead me to a more indulgent interpretation of

But there was, he felt, a personal inner core to the outer sphere of general dissatisfaction. By 1930 the young writer had already steeped his mind in the most fatalistic aspects of Schopenhauer's idealism, in Spengler's vision of the Apocalypse, and in the anguish of the individual as described by Nietzsche. Argentina itself had not been of vital concern, and in 1930 he reminded his readers with some remorse "that on a certain occasion I wrote a book about an Argentina I had not seen."[39] But from the moment of writing that book, just as the persevering scientist slowly and painstakingly approaches a crucial discovery, Martínez Estrada moved toward the vital image, the permanent metaphor, of his tragic sentiment—Argentina.

Luis Emilio Soto's observation that *X-Ray of the Pampa* is a vision rather than a conception of Argentina is food for further thought, for that vision was also a stimulus for the reconstruction of reality. In his extensive *Reality and Fantasy in Balzac* (1964), Don Ezequiel reiterates his own ontology, which is flexible in the extreme:

The world of Balzac is not one of appearances, but *world* (Welt) as conceived by the German transcendentalist philosophers influenced by Plato: a world susceptible to every aspect and content imaginable, to being thought, and hence created, in different ways. Every "Weltanschauung" re-creates the whole world; and, in the words of Eddington, he who discovers something (e.g., as Kirschoff did with the atom) creates it. . . .[40]

With Balzac everything acquires the animation of life and expression; inanimate things that come into contact and coexist with men reveal not only a physiognomy, but a "pathos" and a destiny, a history, a temperament; and this does not derive from literature, which in his case is sometimes of mediocre quality, but from a profound and exact vision of forms and meanings.[41]

---

our reality. Furthermore, I have seen our best men become victims, assassinated by their own hand [the suicides of Quiroga and Lugones], with the acquittal that silence gives crimes when guilt itself—and not any individual person—is to blame" (*Cuadrante del pampero*, p. 76).

[39] "Leer y escribir," *La Vida Literaria* 3, no. 23 (Aug. 1930). The reference is to *Argentina,* a book of poems, many of which are patriotic and idyllic, about the Argentine countryside.

[40] *Realidad y fantasía en Balzac*, p. 308.

[41] Ibid., p. 472.

These two passages reveal much about Martínez Estrada's own perspective. Although he was not a professional novelist, he used his open world of the pampa, its real and symbolic emptiness, in basically the same way that Balzac used his closed world of bric-a-brac, boudoirs, and houses. Each in his own way transformed the phantasmal atmosphere of appearances into a psychic existence of great vitality.

"X-Ray of the Pampa": Structure and Content

"Each of the six parts of *X-Ray of the Pampa,*" we are told twenty-five years after the publication of the first edition, "incorporates a basic technique of social psychoanalysis." The author claims that intuitively he had anticipated by some twenty years the scientific application of those techniques, mentioning as an example Erich Fromm's *Ethics and Psychoanalysis.*[42] On the other hand, he does recognize the precedence and strong influence of Spengler and Freud. By 1930 both had given him new perspectives in which to see society and history. Spengler had taught him to think of history as "the cultural biography of peoples," and "a morphology or anatomy of facts." Freud had convinced him—particularly in *Totem and Taboo*—that what was psychologically true ("vertically") of the individual was also sociologically true ("horizontally") of cultures and civilizations. This led, by Freudian theory, to the collective neurosis of mankind.

Martínez Estrada admits that, ideologically, he has little claim to originality. Anyone, he wrote in 1958, "could have seen that the sociological disposition of *X-Ray of the Pampa* derives from Spengler, with his symbolic interpretation of fact; from Freud, with his examination of disorders in the social psyche; and from Simmel, with his configurative method . . . of themes and their variations, for example, on secrets, sects, the poor, social circles, etc."[43] But his synthesis for the Argentine and Hispanic-American situations was important and unique; in his perspective, and in the graceful expres-

---

[42] "Sobre *Radiografía de la pampa* (Preguntas y respuestas)," in *Leer y escribir,* p. 134.
[43] Ibid.

sion of his exacerbated sensibility, he produced a work of great power. Spengler, Freud, Simmel, and others, including the most representative writers of the Argentine past, had given him theoretical and historical guidelines; Martínez Estrada himself then easily assumed the role of poet and prophet.

The 350-page work is divided into six parts, each with three chapters. The chapters, in turn, have brief subdivisions, many of which have the character of individual essays. If the formal organization of the work is fragmentary, the ideological whole is unified. What appear to be 104 heterogeneous essays in series are actually closely related variations on the theme of Argentine life. The first of the six parts is entitled "Trapalanda."[44] According to Enrique Espinoza, the first idea for a title was "Routes to Trapalanda" ("Las rutas de Trapalanda").[45] In sixteenth-century Indian legend Trapalanda was a kind of Promised Land in the hereafter. By extension, it became in *X-Ray of the Pampa* an "illusory country" for all Argentines from the moment of the Conquest to the present and, generally, a symbol of the impossible. In an unpublished literary interview with himself ("Preguntas y respuestas") written in 1958,[46] Martínez Estrada sums up the purpose of each part of his famous work. Of Part I he says:

Trapalanda. The illusory country, the empire of Jauja, which attracted the conquistador and colonist with its promise of gold and spices which he could carry back to his native land. He did not think, of course, of the pirates who would board his ship. Disillusionment: instead of Trapalanda he found a wilderness which he would have to seed, cultivate, and irrigate with his sweat and blood. [Thus] the disappointed intruder dreamed up

[44] "Trapalanda is called El Dorado in more recent terminology." "Discurso de Ezequiel Martínez Estrada en la Sociedad Argentina de Escritores," published in *La Gaceta* 5, no. 53 (Mexico City, Jan. 1959). Martínez Estrada delivered the address in Buenos Aires on Dec. 3, 1958. It has also been published in his posthumous work, *Para una revisión de las letras argentinas*, ed. Enrique Espinoza, pp. 161–167, under the title "A los 25 años de *Radiografía de la Pampa*."

[45] Interview with the author in Santiago, Chile, in August 1966.

[46] Here and in *Cuadrante del Pampero* (pp. 155–180), Martínez Estrada convincingly demonstrates the superiority of the "self-interview" over the conventional interview, which, since the advent of electronic communication and systematically developed publicity techniques, has slowly but steadily usurped the function of the critical essay.

a pseudo-Trapalanda which despite his frustrations left him oblivious to his failure. He wanted what he did not have, and he wanted it as something he had been denied.[47]

Part I, then, deals with the "structure" of history and culture inherited by the New World from the Old. The colonist had settled in a land which, the more he saw of it, revealed itself to be a fateful abstraction; that is, a steady dissipation of his dreams, a disappointment which—though nearly total—could not destroy his psychological quest, his "will to believe" in the existence of some form of earthly paradise. The very emptiness of the New World incited the newcomer's imagination, for indeed there was nothing in those surroundings to conflict with his preconceptions. The world was his idea. Accordingly, Martínez Estrada tells us that when the coveted Trapalanda proved to be nonexistent, a psychological substitute was necessary. Trapalanda was replaced in the colonist's mind (and in that of his descendants for many generations) by a "pseudo-Trapalanda."

Martínez Estrada thinks that a basic cause of this continuing frame of mind was the Spanish honor cult, which in the New World had just as serious consequences—in a sense, more serious—as in Spain itself. Antiprogressivism was one of them. With regard to the honor cult he makes three points: (1) The Spaniard had not come to settle or develop land but to "possess" it; "the property deed is synonymous with the flair for command." (2) "The present-day dreams of one's own home without the natural feeling of living in it constitute a degenerate and bourgeois form of those impulses of the 'grand seigneur.'" (3) "The third angle of the triangle is the grave," and "the three positions add up to one and the same rejection of life."[48] Of course, this critical view is not intended to define the honor cult itself but merely to suggest the persistent self-centeredness underlying it. Not consciously but psychologically, the inhabitant of the pampa moved steadily toward the fulfillment of his death. His history was "an advance backwards." The self-aggrandizement that

---

[47] *Tesoros velados.*
[48] *Radiografía de la pampa*, pp. 16–17. Subsequent reference in the text to this work will be in parentheses, by page number only.

was inseparable from honor could lead in only one direction—self-destruction.

The writer's vision is not simply tragic but nihilistic to the point of intellectual caricature. Nevertheless, Martínez Estrada does not, in his essays, distort reality (the grotesque is something reserved for his fiction); more precisely he exaggerates and magnifies it, striving always to preserve its original proportions. As readers we are affected more by the tone and the imagery than by the argumentation. Consider the imagery: On the pampa man finds himself transformed into "an abstract being" (p. 12); the pampa is "an emptiness without expression" (p. 13); its expanses do not amount to geographical grandeur but only to "the *idea* of grandeur"; the pampa does not offer wealth but merely "the possibility of mortgage credit"—"it is nothing" (p. 16). The inhabitants of the pampa are "sons of concubinage" (p. 32). Everything toward which the political and military leaders of the independence movement strived could be reduced to "abstract aspirations" (p. 42). In summary, the *homo pampensis* was a pallid and inferior derivative of the feudal lord of Europe, without tradition and without a home; "eternal brother of the stallion"; a Don Quixote "returning in defeat, the last dregs of a ridiculous dream" (pp. 44–45).

Part I is an informal historical introduction extending from the Spanish conquest to the advent of the railroads. The first of its three chapters ("Directions of the Compass") discusses the problems of the first explorers and settlers and sets the desolate tone for the rest of the book. In this first chapter the wilderness is established as the first and last truth and, as such, a synonym of death (p. 16). One truth (death) and one heritage (deception). The longest and most substantial chapter of Part I is the second ("The Rawhide Era"), a description of the gaucho, symbolic bastard son of the Spanish and indigenous races. As the accidental offspring of a Spanish minor nobility (*hidalgo: hijo de algo*, "son of something") and the anonymous and primitive caste of American Indian women, the gaucho was a nobody (*hijo de nadie* [p. 34], "son of no one"). Always a step below his "mestizo" counterpart of the other Spanish colonies, the Argentine gaucho was born into no preestablished tradition or culture. By circumstance, custom, and necessity, he was a loner. The gauchos "were sons rebelling against their fathers; the children of solitude, of the wilderness, of debauchery, of rape—like the fragments of nightmares of feverish drunkards taking form in the far reaches of the plains and then galloping into town" (p. 35).

Although the wars of independence beginning in 1810 did not benefit the mestizo of Mexico, Central America, or Peru, the plainsman of Venezuela or the gaucho of Argentina, it was they who, because of their inherent and tenacious anarchism, made independence politically possible. That was so because in many senses those sectors of the population were already socially independent. By his anarchic and independent nature the gaucho was especially amenable to the caudillo type of loose confederation that began to prevail in Argentina immediately after independence. However, his divisive nature maintained the body politic in such a constant state of weakness that Juan Manuel de Rosas could easily control the country, for he was the only one with a "system."[49]

Unlike Sarmiento, Martínez Estrada does not recognize that chaos to be a historical accident of "barbarism" or a mere result of geographic circumstance. Apart from the wilderness there was a "constitutive and organized social state" (p. 44) that had roots in the Hispanic psyche (in the "dreamers of grandeur") and in the despotic inclination of the Spanish conquerors of the sixteenth century. The gaucho himself, a second-class creature whom the Spanish landowner considered to be on a par with wild horses and Indians, "was a product of that prolonged dream of grandeur; its living ghost, a product of mirages on the plains" (p. 45). The knife, with which the gaucho defended himself, slaughtered cattle, and prepared his meals, clothing, and equipment was more than a simple instrument; it was a dynamic extension of himself. The shortness of the knife led the man wielding it to attribute extra strength and skill to himself. "The winner feels that his victory is due more to the handle than to the blade" (p. 49). Compared to the gun or the sword, it was the weapon *par excellence* of the solitary man, though never of the suicide. The

---

[49] In this regard, Rosas was similar to other caudillos in Spain and Spanish America.

knife is "the weapon of the extrovert" and, in contrast to the fencing foil, individualistic. Not only is it the weapon of forward, chivalric thrusts, its wielder has the option of using the length of the blade in a disdainful chopping motion, or even—for complete ridicule— of slapping at his opponent with the broad side of the blade (p. 52).

Part I ends with the chapter entitled "Routes," referring to itineraries and roads that lead nowhere. The special character of these routes was due in part, writes Martínez Estrada, to the wide-open spaces between Buenos Aires and the isolated points of the interior that they covered. But it was due still more to the personal nature and mental disposition of their travelers. "A people of the plains (the Spaniards, particularly those of Castile, Extremadura, and upper Andalusia) settled on our land: wanderers, knights, pilgrims, beggars. They came alone and as transients. Nowhere did they leave evidence of a will to remain" (p. 60). There had not been, in the sixteenth century, a conquest, but rather the unique historical experience of being "scattered into the unknown" (p. 59). The routes were not laid out in conformity with plans for economic development, but with regard for combat with the Indians and for mere survival. These were not the paths of settlers, but, psychologically at least, of exiles from the Old World; and all distances were simply abstract measurements from outpost to outpost. In connection with his notion of "people of the plains" the author recalls Sarmiento's comparison in *Facundo* of rural Argentines and "Tartars and Arabs."

From 1857 on, the steam locomotive began to follow the same routes, with the same "indecisiveness" and the same lack of purpose, as the first explorers (pp. 62–63). Sarmiento, he might have also recalled, had been enthused to the point of obsession with the possibilities of river travel and had not considered railroads important for Argentina's future. Martínez Estrada did recognize their importance but held that they had not been planned to meet the economic needs of the nation. This "spider web" system was of no local benefit. It was merely an extension of the Atlantic routes from England and France, countries which, "in their ruinous competition with North America," carried off Argentina's natural riches. According to the logic of this chapter, the railroads (like the knife, the horse, the indigenous woman, and the feverish dreams of El Dorado and Trapalanda) have been only one more extension of man (cf. Marshall McLuhan on expression and communication in the "electronic age"), one more vain manifestation of the unextinguishable Hispanic will.

Part II: Solitude. The settler is alone in a lonely world. The mother of his children is of another race. The ocean has reduced his continent to an island. He must struggle to survive. However, his attitude is not Robinson [Crusoe's] but rather that of a great lord reduced to poverty. What he is building is no country; nor is it a home, as was the case with the English in North America. He continues to long for his native land, the mother country which he shows to his children as the Jerusalem of their exile. He himself is but the founder of a colonial business company.[50]

Part II is an essay on solitude, organized under three topics: isolation, distances, and solitude as both a personal and cosmic force ("Soledad del mundo y del hombre"). Isolation was at first general, a pattern of social isolation was set. It was due in part to the spiritual need to defend the Spanish conquest of the New World as an enterprise of great promise for the future. In part it was due to the terrain: the wide expanses that at first were deemed unworthy of agriculture, and the Indian marauders. Here Martínez Estrada expounds a theory of importance for the student of Hispanic American culture, saying that the ethnic and psychological similarity of the Spanish American colonies and, later, countries, has led to mutual *understanding* but not mutual *knowledge*. They were born in isolation and in isolation they grew. "The aggregate history of the countries of South America reveals the same character of an archipelago of mainlands that the map reveals: disunity" (p. 90). Under the heading "Incommunicacion" are listed six conditions contributing to Argentina's isolation: (1) the range of the Andes and the Chilean deserts; (2) the complete separation within Argentina herself of the forest, plains, and mountain regions; (3) the arid, volcanic terrain separating the more fertile pampa areas from the mountains along the Chilean border; (4) Chile's economic collapse of the 1920's, which had continental repercussions and marked a serious decline in commercial relations with

---

[50] *Tesoros velados,* pp. 111–112.

Argentina; (5) the rivers, both those bordering Argentina and those of the interior, which signified less a means of transportation than "ranges of water, deserts of water, abysses of water"; and (6) land-locked Bolivia and the promontory of Uruguay, which are spiritually isolated from Argentina; the former characterized by its "suicidal drive to the sea, the latter by a spirit of independence so strong that she has little in common with the other South American countries.

The second chapter stresses the strange abstractive effect that space and the *idea* of space allegedly had on the Argentine psyche. The league, kilometer, hours of travel, and other terms of distance measurement constantly remind the rural inhabitant of his isolation. The twisted and spongy *ombú* tree (good only for giving shade) has slowly crept ("migrated") south from the jungles of the Paraguayan and Brazilian border country. Similarly, the provincial villages seem to have been created elsewhere: "These villages are like aeroliths, like pieces of inhabited stars fallen on the plains" (p. 101). And the villages are somber, like the cemeteries outside them ("the house of the dead is very similar to the tomb of the living"). Martínez Estrada believes that people of the plains are more self-centered and rebellious than inhabitants of the hills, who demonstrate in their daily lives a deeper love for their land and their traditions (p. 107). On the pampa "solitude transmutes the individual into the center of that infinite circle which is the plain and the keystone of that absurd vault which is the sky" (p. 108).

The striking feature of the rest of this chapter is a description of the *guapo* (roughly, a braggart and troublemaker), a small-town character whose aggressiveness, selfishness, and continual emphasis on masculinity and sexual prowess give him a personality similar to that of the Mexican *pelado* depicted by Samuel Ramos,[51] and the youthful ruffians in black leather jackets in our own society. The *guapo* is a logical offspring of the *gaucho malo* of the past century. He is the contemporary embodiment of the barbarian spirit in conflict with all that is civilized; his profession is vice. The counterpart of the

[51] Samuel Ramos, *Profile of Man and Culture in Mexico*, trans. Peter G. Earle. See especially Chap. III, "Psychoanalysis of the Mexican," pp. 54–72.

guapo in Buenos Aires is the *compadre*, or low-class dandy.[52] In Martínez Estrada's view, everyone among the poor or dispossessed bears the same mark of spiritual sterility as the *guapo*. "Among us, the poor man is a deserter, a fugitive without the right to anything, and we are ashamed of him" (p. 117). As time goes on, the circumstantial differences between cities and the rural areas diminish. The provinces of the 1930's abound in vagabonds in search of work and shelter; with their increase in number, their physical isolation has decreased. But their desperation and loneliness are more acute than ever. Their local world has merged with the "immense world"; they have dragged all the miseries of the provinces into the city (p. 118) and have donated their own solitude to the solitude of the world.

The final chapter of Part II ("Solitude of the World and of Man") is among the most poetic in the book. Geographic and geological terminology are incorporated in powerful images that accentuate the barrenness of the land, on which the inhabitants seem to have been dropped like some accidental astral body. The disappearance, over the centuries, of all evidence of animal and human life—save the fossils of the most remote eras—attests to a lack of history. Even recent events are quickly lost to memory, and the names of numerous villages and railroad stations honoring personages of some prominence two or three generations back are meaningless to the present observer. Why is this so? Among the possible causes are the varied "forces of solitude," the polar winds from the south, the great distances, alcoholism, free love, and the sterile specter of the *ombú* tree. These things have kept the Argentine in his desolation and made him an outcast to his fellow man. The "new pampa" of the twentieth century belongs not to its own people but to Buenos Aires and Europe; its fertility is a transitory benefit denied to the majority of the unhappy descendants of the gaucho.

Part III: Primitive forces. The elementary secret forces of the earth, with the aid of water, wind and sand, begin their task of disintegrating the precarious structures of adobe and animal hides that have cropped up like

---

[52] An essay in Part III (pp. 166–170) is devoted specifically to the *compadre*.

gypsy camps. The earth labors with greater dignity than man, and corrects his blunders.[53]

These "primitive forces" afflict the individual from the outside, but also from the hidden depths of his subconscious. The book, of course, is fatalistic throughout, but it is in this part where the futility of personal hope and endeavor is most strongly emphasized, where, for example, the power of love, faith, and language is described as having been drastically weakened (pp. 175–191).

There are three kinds of primitive forces: "telluric," "mechanical," and "psychic." The chapter dealing with telluric forces is concerned mainly with the geographical and historical background of Argentina in the nineteenth century, with a view to showing that slow disintegration ("erosión y oxidación"), and not progressive evolution, was the sequel to the Rosas dictatorship. That same disintegration, the author declares, has continued down to the present. The first sentence sets the tone: "The more the man of the pampa aspired to, the more of a slave he became, enclosed in his barbed-wire circle" (p. 133). The allusion is to the transformation from the open ranges of the early nineteenth century to the *estancias*—carefully laid out and fenced—since the 1870's. The simple image of the man imprisoned by barbed wire extends to the nation at large, and what survived was more important than what evolved: the "totemism and fetishism" of the gaucho; politics of the clan; the tradition of the manhunt, artfully developed in Rosas' time; and fear of one's neighbor and the unknown.[54] In different ways, and in many more ways, Argentina of the twentieth century is as much an unknown entity as was Argentina of the nineteenth century.

The nineteenth century was a time of preparation for the more complex realities of the twentieth century. However, that preparation was based not on an anticipation of the future but on the nature of the present; more precisely, on what seemed to be *permanent* in

[53] *Tesoros velados*, p. 112.

[54] Here Martínez Estrada seems to have been impressed by Freud's ideas on collective psychology as set forth in *Totem and Taboo*, particularly by those referring to the parallel between the "animistic" (and narcissistic) childhood phase of individual lives and primitive phase of whole societies.

personal experience and culture, independent of civilized history. In Spain, Unamuno called an analogous phenomenon *presente eterno*, which was the basis of his formulation of *intrahistoria*, history within history, the essence of human life. Martínez Estrada, however, gives greater emphasis to primitive elements and archetypes. He tells us that the representative figures of the century were the *baquiano* (guide) and the *rastreador* (pathfinder), the "intuitive" and "analytic" members, respectively, of Argentine rural society. The *baquiano* could orient himself by tasting grass; Rosas himself reputedly could distinguish among the grass flavors of forty *estancias* in the province of Buenos Aires (p. 139). The *rastreador*, "endowed with an acute and cerebral eye," operated by logic, organizing evidence like a detective. His skill was the reconstruction of reality. The *baquiano* was a human barometer in close harmony with "the *modus operandi* of nature." The qualities of each have survived in the hypnotic "leaders of multitudes" (the *baquiano*), and in the "improvisers of knowledge" (the *rastreador*) of the present (p. 138).

Archetypes, of course, are more symptomatic than causal. Something less tangible than the personal dynamism of these figures underlies the Argentine problem. The main flaw is a continuing lack of direction and purpose. There cannot be real progress in a country "with three-quarters of her territory still unpopulated" (in 1933) and the old sentiment of anarchy still alive. The individual citizen is the automatic victim of "deforming and erosive forces" (p. 144). He experiences a loss of will, which Martínez Estrada might have compared with the *abulia* attributed by Azorín at the turn of the century to his own generation in Spain. But this Argentine loss of will is quite different from anything European. In *X-Ray of the Pampa*, as in *The Head of Goliath*, life and intellectual activity in Buenos Aires are interpreted as having been deformed by the "telluric forces" of the pampa. "The loss of will can be considered as the first symptom by the spirit of the plains" (p. 146). The note first sounded by Lucio V. López's book on Buenos Aires, *The Great Village* (1884), is repeated by Martínez Estrada.

"The mechanical forces" were (and are) the government, its bureaucracy and its laws: the awesome leviathan with "107 joints" (the

107 articles of the Constitution of 1853) and "three gullets" (the executive, legislative, and judicial branches). This chapter stresses the dehumanizing effect of the political and economic processes on the population. The influence of Ortega y Gasset, who had published *The Revolt of the Masses* just when Martínez Estrada was starting to write *X-Ray of the Pampa*, is particularly evident (pp. 161–167) in the references to the "intrusive State," the "capricious and antisocial function of the multitude," and especially in the following passages:

The rush to power is the rush to impunity, toward the expansion of personal power residing in the individual with the aid of society; and since [the government official], as always, can count on the obedience of his subordinates, he expresses in himself a little of the collective ego (p. 165). The "compadre" was typically poor; but some time ago the wealthy joined that immense family of plebians in a spurious relationship of characters; so now the word (*compadre*) describes a group of individuals that is majestically plebian (p. 167).

Max Scheler, who seems to have been equally influential on both Ortega and Martínez Estrada, is then quoted (p. 168) on the psychological phenomenon of "great pride combined with an inferior position"—a phenomenon Estrada consistently applies to the Spanish and Spanish-American character. This could only result, says Scheler, in a universal "sentiment of vengeance."

"Psychic Forces" (pp. 171–191) could have been entitled "Sublimation in Argentine History." This chapter is the voice of the puritan who is also the reader of Freud. The values and style of life are the same in 1930 as in 1830, for each of these historical moments is a moment of "dissolution." The "monstrous growth" of Buenos Aires, a topic the author discusses in detail in Part IV of this book and seven years later in *The Head of Goliath*, is interpreted as the reincarnation of the barbarism prevalent a century before. "Buenos Aires has grown without change. 'The great village' of Lucio V. López is the 'overseas business establishment' [*factoria*] of Ortega y Gasset."[55]

---

[55] The Argentine novelist and story writer Lucio V. López (1848–1894) wrote *The Big Village* (1884), a loosely constructed but perceptive work on the customs of Buenos Aires. Ortega, on the other hand, refers to Argentina as a whole in using the term *factoria* (overseas or colonial business establish-

The image of a society in the process of steady degeneration is then completed with a discussion of the functions of religion, language, and love; *love* between arrogant and selfish men and the subservient women of the cruel Hispano-Catholic tradition;[56] *religion* as the perennially bitter fruit of the Spanish conquest ("To convert Christ himself into a Crusade was the ingenious idea, so that the love of Him might be transformed into a struggle, and that prayer and mystic ecstacy might be channeled into the hypnotic discipline of military headquarters"); *language,* the language that the Spaniards brought to America, turned out to be an inadequate system of expression for the chaotic realities of the New World. The "secret resentment" of which Scheler has written in tracing from its origin the civilizing process of primitive societies, reveals itself in language as well as in other forms of life. For example, in the "incorrect" but vibrant style of Horacio Quiroga, in the counterfeit words of the uneducated, in the "parricidal" inclination of resentful men like Juan Manuel de Rosas, who changed the *z* in his surname to *s.*

Part IV: Buenos Aires. Appearing in the middle, it is the keystone of the book. Buenos Aires today is Spain, the Mother Country. Our enemy at home. It absorbs, devours, dilapidates, corrupts. It is a source of infection. The interior, the territory, the nation and the people are dominated by it. It exploits and deceives them. The country as a whole is its colony, which it must subjugate and brutalize so as to prevent another onslaught by rural caudillos on horseback.[57]

This brief diatribe serves as an accurate introduction to the chapter on Buenos Aires, a longer but equally intense diatribe. Martínez Estrada had a phobia against Buenos Aires, an intricate aversion he nurtured emotionally and artistically from 1930 to the year of his death. Sociologists have not taken him seriously, but his insights into

---

ment): "The immoderate appetite for wealth, the audacity, incompetence, incompatibility or indifference *vis-à-vis* one's position or occupation are well-known endemic traits of all *factorias*. It is precisely this which distinguishes a native and organic society from the abstract and alluvial society called *factoria*" ("El hombre a la defensiva," *Obras completas,* II, 655).

[56] Martínez Estrada's view of men and women in their erotic relationships is remarkably similar to Octavio Paz's more recent interpretation of Mexican traditions and symbols in *Labyrinth of Solitude,* trans. Lysander Kemp.

[57] *Tesoros velados,* p. 112.

the life, movement, and atmosphere of the metropolis contain some profound truths. His attitude, as a native of the interior, is also a true reflection of the antagonism traditionally felt between *porteños* (inhabitants of Buenos Aires) and citizens of the provinces. I shall discuss the theme of Buenos Aires in Chapter V.

Part V: Fear, an inhibitive trauma in our national life. The whole thesis is Sarmiento's but I develop it. The topics are Struggle, Defense, and Flight. Fear and its irrational reactions. This part of the work has absolute and unquestionable relevance today.[58]

"Struggle," "Defense," and "Flight" are also the titles of the three chapters of Part V. As in the beginning of the book, the emphasis is again historical, but historical—as Luis Emilio Soto has indicated—in the Spenglerian sense that history is inevitably "poeticized."[59] In writing about "the historical imagination," R. G. Collingwood agrees.[60] The historian cannot avoid imagining the past, for the present is part of his relentless perspective. Try as he may, he cannot do away with it. When, furthermore, the historian not only adheres to a philosophy of history—such as Martínez Estrada's concept of the collective biography of national culture—but is also an impassioned social critic and a poet by vocation and technique, then the imagination becomes the mirror of unpremeditated utopias and infernal regions, as well as of "reality." The important question is not so much whether the historian is *himself* too subjective or too noncommittal but whether, with all his personal idiosyncrasies, his sporadic amateur-

[58] Ibid.

[59] Luis Emilio Soto, "Arbitraje espiritual," in *Crítica y estimación*, pp. 128–129. One of Soto's motives for writing this essay on *X-Ray of the Pampa* in 1937 was Bernardo Canal Feijoo's negative criticism "Radiografías fatídicas" in the literary review *Sur*, no. 37 (Oct. 1937): 63–77. In 1937 Martínez Estrada won (four years late) the National Prize in Literature for *X-Ray*. Also reproduced in Soto's *Crítica y estimación* is "Análisis espectral" (pp. 109–123), first published in 1934 and one of the first critical articles on *X-Ray*. Martínez Estrada was disappointed and disturbed by the silence which greeted his book in the three or four year period following its publication.

[60] See Collingwood's illuminating chapter "The Historical Imagination," in Hans Meyerhoff, ed., *The Philosophy of History in Our Time*, pp. 66–84. Spengler's and Collingwood's emphasis on the creative factor in writing history has a precedent in Voltaire who, as early as 1738, had said, "one must write history as a philosopher" (letter to Nicolas Claude Thieriot, quoted by Will and Ariel Durant in *The Age of Voltaire*, p. 484).

ism, his nervous state, and his poetic deviations, he has still been able to "place himself in the situation" of the people and the time he is discussing. Martínez Estrada—essayist, poet, and prophet—lacked the historian's necessary discipline, yet he wrote *history*, and between what he has intended to say and what he has involuntarily revealed, meaningful conclusions can be drawn.

"Struggle," "Defense," and "Flight" are chapters presenting three basic characteristics of Argentine life. The explorers and early settlers suffered real adversities as well as chronic hallucinations in the face of the unknown. Fear was their guide, and fear bred a peculiar sort of aggressiveness that would reach its first significant culmination in the civil wars of the nineteenth century. "Crime, thievery, and vice, and the frustrated ambition that slowly changed into a longing for vengeance shaped the men of the colonial and independent eras" (p. 254). Basically the struggle was a continuing attempt to acquire "civilization"—a futile struggle in the author's opinion—because in conformity with the Hispano-Argentine tradition, possession, self gratification, or simple greed were too often the motives behind the civilizing enterprise (pp. 264–266).

Twentieth-century Argentina has had the illusion of living and working in an orderly world. But in opposition to the indefatigable Sarmiento, whose rather simplistic contrast between the forces of civilization and those of barbarism probably contributed to that illusion, Martínez Estrada sees nothing but chaos and frustration behind the decorous formalities of life in his own time. In the final analysis all struggles are self-interested struggles, for they are part of the larger and deeper subconscious fight for survival: "Life is a pilgrimage over a quagmire. . . . The man who struggles here to achieve order—whether a pioneer or a late comer—lives unwittingly in the midst of a disorder more powerful than he. If he performs successfully in this chaotic and shapeless world, it is only because he acts as an unconscious instrument of disorder. The upstart, the man without preparation, faith or culture knows the techniques of such a world better than anyone" (p. 260).

"La defensa" is also based on this notion of disorder. "Man is a wolf to his fellow man" (p. 269). But here the focus is on the groups and institutions—mostly under the direct or indirect control of the federal bureaucracy—which organize like medieval "forts" against everything and everyone not involved in the national conspiracy of self-help through intrigue. In Argentina in the 1930's "the two most significant thirds (*sic*) of the population and the national wealth depend on the State" (p. 272). The "aggressive forces" embodied in the weakest individuals seek an adequate structure for their mutual protection. Government, bureaucracy, and material success are equated with the ability of the weak but cunning to command the still weaker and to accumulate money and prestige by spurious means. Behind such people's limitless talent for one-upmanship is the inferior man's innate resentment of his own weakness, and Martínez Estrada appears to have taken Ortega's *The Revolt of the Masses* very seriously when he identifies their motivation as "a hidden scorn of the superior man's excellence" (p. 268).

The most effective "organization of defense" against the world of the disinterested and the *naturally* ambitious is the army. In the armed forces resides "power in the womb of weakness." Their organized energies constitute "armed fear." The author finds a psychological transference of fear more efficiently expressed in the military than in any other institution. Armies need war in order to maintain their self-esteem, and very often when the purpose for which a large contingent of men is mobilized has been fulfilled, their continuing mobilization creates problems.

First organized on a nationwide scale by Bartolomé Mitre (president from 1862 to 1868), the Argentine army was used in the bloody war against Paraguay by Argentina, Brazil, and Uruguay (1865–1870). Soon afterward, it was used to subdue the Indian marauders in Patagonia and other outlying regions. By 1880 the frontiers of battle had disappeared and, as in almost all other Hispanic American countries, the military, in the face of potential and imaginary enemies inside the nation, could maintain its status only on the basis of fear. "Of course this is the nature of the professional military everywhere in the world. But the special function, the civil function *ad honoram* and with a good salary to boot, is a native institution of South American latitudes" (p. 275). Clearly, Martínez Estrada is saying that the

military organizations of Argentina and the rest of Hispanic America
are not simply a social, political, and economic cross for everyone
to bear. Beyond that, they are the dramatic articulation of all the
subliminal fears and aggressions of the insecure, and of the Freudian
"dream censorship," which is distortion by the insecure[61] of everything that, because of its uncommitted or disinterested nature (art,
justice, true personal achievement), becomes suspect and "dangerous."

The causes of figurative "Flight," title of the third chapter of Part
V, are "fear of ridicule," "sentiments of inferiority," and "fear of the
truth" (p. 279). The flight seeks refuge in appearances, in a personality that deceives itself as well as others. When Keyserling states
that the "original sadness" of the Argentines is so overwhelming that
it leaves them passive and devoid of imagination,[62] he does not take
into account the psychological complexities that Martínez Estrada
has clearly seen and which Eduardo Mallea exposes in great detail
in one of his most memorable characters: the self-obsessed yet self-
disdaining Mario Guillén in *The Enemies of the Soul* (1950). I refer,
of course, to a paradox of narcissism by which the subject becomes
engrossed in himself much as a spectator is swept into a new reality
by a skillful actor. That is, his absorption in himself on the conscious
level does not cancel out the still-stronger fear of discovering himself
on the subconscious level. Psychologically, every man tends to see
himself as someone else, and when this desire is exacerbated by such
circumstances as the traditions and social norms enumerated in this
part of *X-Ray of the Pampa*, the result—thinks Martínez Estrada,
reader of Keyserling and Freud—is inevitably depression and the
subconscious search for defense mechanisms. The search manifests
itself in strange and novelistic ways, one of which is the ambiguous
status of the Argentine woman, who by 1930 had begun to emerge

---

[61] Martínez Estrada does not refer in the fifth part of his book ("Fear") directly to Freud. But glimpses of the latter's terminology are frequently found;
e.g., "defenses" (pp. 267–277), "fear" (*passim*), "censorship" (pp. 273, 277,
279). He also read with attention Ortega's "El hombre a la defensiva," and
commented on it in "El guaranguismo de Ortega y Gasset" (*Tesoros velados*,
III).
[62] *South American Meditations*, p. 303.

from the rigid confines of the home, but not from her fundamentally sad fate: "Laws are ratified to protect her, but she has no protection. Tomorrow she will have the opportunity to divorce and remarry; she'll have the right to vote, but she will not be free. A hundred thousand eyes watch her as she leaves her house, when she sits down next to the machines at her place of work or bends over her books, and when she returns home. Neither at home nor in society is she more than she was yesterday, even though now she comes home with wages in her pocketbook" (p. 283).

These observations (and others to follow in Part VI) on the character and psychological traits of the Argentine individual in society reveal the writer's talent for the novel, a genre he developed only in the short form (*Holy Saturday, Juan Florido and Son, Marta Riquelme*). Notwithstanding his obsession, the essayist understood his countrymen in both their historical and personal dimensions. In the novelist Ernesto Sábato's opinion, Martínez Estrada should have been a novelist.[63] There are indeed numerous passages in the more creative essays like *The Head of Goliath* and *Death and Transfiguration of Martín Fierro* that show a great facility for fiction in both the tragic and comic manner. By comparison, many of the passages of *X-Ray of the Pampa* seem ponderous and abstract.

The rest of Part V is less coherent than the portions discussed up to this point. Under the oxymoron and subtitle "Euphoric Fears" the author concludes with a rambling commentary on the "defensive spirit" fused and confused with "the delirium tremens of ambition" and the alcohol of confidence. Here he tries to relate culture to economic history, without, I would judge, much success.

Part VI: Pseudostructures. What we have created without the benefit of a solid foundation, to support a structure that is a labyrinth of ambiguities. The search for a firm base in which agonizing task we still find ourselves [in 1958].[64]

The final message is direct and forceful, one in which the author coordinates his overall vision of an Argentina in a self-defeating struggle, in continuous tension between a reality that only a few percep-

---

[63] Interview with the author in Buenos Aires, July 1966.
[64] *Tesoros velados*, IV.

tive minds have seen, and the fictitious image of itself, which is the creation of tradition and the collective will. Here again, Martínez Estrada's novelistic insight, his sensitivity for concealed but deep motivation of the soul, gives him clarity and power.

The fictitious image is made up of "pseudo-structures" ("Forms," "Functions," and "Values" are the three chapter titles). They characterize what the author considers to have been a counterfeit civilization. Starting with Sarmiento, an impassioned and sincere reformer, the nation multiplied the fantasies of its civilization within certain representative and traditional (but abstract) institutions. The instituitions themselves were mere "forms," superficial and false: (1) religion, (2) law, (3) La Plata (the artificial city), and (4) the cult of the future. This is the way Don Ezequiel interprets them:

(1) Being a "formula" that has simply been taken for granted, religion in Argentina lacks "faith." Thus it is divorced from inner life. Martínez Estrada thinks there is an impenetrable barrier between ritual formality and "the religious subconscious" (p. 299). The spirited cry from Rosas' time (¡Viva la religión!) meant relatively little as religion and a great deal as social psychology. In the pattern of ultraconservative groups throughout the Hispanic world (for example, the Carlists in Spain and the Sinarquistas in Mexico), that battle cry is essentially a political slogan. Like other "superstructures," it had results incompatible with its stated purpose and actually was a pretext for violence.

(2) Just as religion *as a form* covers a multitude of irreligious motives, the law works against the principles of justice; it is merely part of "a new world of written difficulties." The best lawyer is not the man "who makes justice triumph, but the one who has learned to use law as a means of abusing it (i.e., justice)" (p. 302). The law is an open invitation to deceit. When the moral conscience finds itself in conflict with a convention of legal precepts devised by a parasitic society and deformed by "that primary source of discontent," the spirit of the masses, justice is doomed to defeat.

The law is conceived and executed not for the citizen as a free individual but "as a receptacle of the collective subconscious" (p.

302). In the universal fight for individual survival that characterizes society, the individual is an inevitable victim. The "vital force" of which Martínez Estrada speaks is an anonymous, collective, mass force. In these circumstances it is quite logical that "the art of abusing law" should become more complex than law itself (p. 303). However, one should remember that in placing his finger on the festering wound of judicial corruption—as Sarmiento and José Hernández, with differing motives, had done before—Martínez Estrada was condemning something that was not simply Argentine but universal. Given the complexities of the motives behind its interpretation, law everywhere is a venerable "pseudostructure" built upon the swampland of self-interest. The interesting point is the variance of customs and institutions between one national culture and another, and the pseudostructures lead the sensitive observer to a novelistic view of history.

(3) La Plata (under the suggestive title "Hollywood") is described as a commuter's city, and an artificial satellite of the great metropolis, Buenos Aires. The author's autobiographical impressions of La Plata are based on his regular afternoon trips to the university there, where for twenty years he taught world literature. La Plata is not typical of other Argentine cities, but the author has considered the phenomenon of its creation to be typical of the Argentine way of life: rootless, provisional, illusory. "Invented" rather than developed, La Plata seemed to him like a temporary daylight place, a mirage to those *porteños* who work there, returning, as it were, to the reality of their homes in Buenos Aires every evening.

(4) The concluding section discusses a purely philosophical "form." As in every previous era, the Argentine concept of the future in the 1930's is baseless, for it is no more than "a flight from the past" (p. 306). The average Argentine is an abnormal dreamer of great fantasies to come, but they will never come. Mental experience is divisible into two parts: a worthless and obscure past, and a "hypnotic" future. A love of gambling and the predominance of intuition over reason, among other symptoms of an illusory life, help explain the endless dilemma.

We are living on the eve of great events to come, on the threshold of tomorrow; and that tomorrow is pure chance, the chaos of a dream after a long day's struggle in the desert. The dreamer is abnormal; he was created neither as a man nor as a fantasy; he is the offspring of centaurs. The dream that he lives is senseless; the things he does have a phantom-like inconsistency; the ideas he conceives have the peculiar asymmetry of the awakening mind which confuses fragments of its dreams with pieces of its surroundings (p. 307).

When chance takes on the appearance of solid reality, what understanding of life can there possibly be? The only discovery open to successive Argentine generations is the periodic realization that each belongs to a "distinct world" (p. 308) without continuity or compatibility with the others.

Chapter Two of the Part VI lists "functions," which, like the "forms" just discussed, are exercises in futility. Martínez Estrada deplores the conversion of man into a mere adjunct of the machinery and the commercial and political systems designed to serve him as instruments. Instead, man discovers himself to be an instrument of the instruments. The functions, in order discussed, are as follows:

Machines (the tractor, automobile, airplane, and industrial machinery). All are called useless to the country as a whole; only Buenos Aires benefits from them. The peon, the itinerant seasonal worker, and the isolated inhabitant of the remote provinces are not prepared to utilize them.

The *professions* and *politics,* and the *universities* as agents in the development of both. Like the machines, Argentina's fledgling doctors, lawyers, and engineers are more numerous than the places available to them. Together they constitute a one-sided bridge, from which to take a figurative leap into nowhere (p. 314). The universities will be unable to achieve their cultural mission so long as society thinks of culture as mere "levers and hoisting machines" to success (p. 321), rather than as a context of intrinsic values.

Values is the third category of collective illusion, and the title of the last chapter of the last part of *X-Ray of the Pampa.* Like the forms (religion, law, artificial communities, and an illusory future) and the functions (modern machinery, the professions, and univer-

sity education), the values constitute a "mythology." Like the forms
and functions, they exist in the realm of fancy; they are "the image of
what is lacking" (p. 326). The values have been "deities," appropriate for Greeks and Trojans—*living* through fallible Gods with whom
men of those times could at least communicate—but only "sterile
and mummified" figures for the Argentines. The development, or,
more exactly, the fabrication, of these values began with Sarmiento's
celebrated dichotomy: civilization and barbarism (p. 327). Since
that time all that did not exist but ought to have existed was grouped
under the heading *civilization*; all that did exist but ought not to
have existed was called *barbarism*. Ritual honor was done to the
"new deities" (education, commerce, industry, literature); but with
the years, the years between Sarmiento's time and Martínez Estrada's, the new deities were steadily corroded and deformed, while
the Argentine people began their silent return to "the ancestral
forms" of primitivism.

Seeking a historical analogy, Martínez Estrada refers to Gregor
Johann Mendel's research on hybrid forms and their hereditary character. According to Mendel, the two hereditary units or genes found
in the body of an offspring (one from each parent) tend to represent
contrasting factors, and over several generations one of the two factors ("dominant" and "recessive") comes to prevail consistently over
the other. It is clearly Martínez Estrada's contention that, in Argentine life of the nineteenth and twentieth centuries, civilization is "recessive" and barbarism is "dominant."[65] His tragic sentiment seems
to have told him that the intelligence, its flexibility notwithstanding,
cannot in the long run withstand the fixity of instinct.

Persistent recourse to artificial values, to extend a bit further the
Mendelian formula, leads to what Martínez Estrada identifies as a
dichotomy of subconscious "defenses": an inordinate fear of ridicule
and heroism, the two poles of the histrionic mentality (p. 328). The
modern Argentine is described as an actor unsure of himself and his
talent. His "maximum defense" is *la broma*, or the derision of his
fellow man, and it is usually combined with an imposing "mask of
dignity" for himself. The implication I gather from this hybridization

[65] See Mendel's *Experiments in Plant Hybridization* (Eng. tr., 1926).

of "defenses" is the progressive victory of the "dominant" ridicule over the "recessive" heroic factor, because the latter, in Don Ezequiel's terms, usually degenerates into caricature. It is Don Quixote "to the road again," but, so to speak, with all the circumstances reversed. The arts of ridicule and caricature, though superficial, are complex. As Ortega had suggested only a few years before,[66] the agility of the Argentine mind is defensively oriented. Martínez Estrada observes in his compatriots "a feline mental and verbal flexibility" (p. 334), a cleverness that limits and concentrates the intelligence "within the circle of personal defense." Theirs is a way "of living on the alert, converting themselves into sentinels."[67] This is the psychological legacy of "the man of the knife," of Martín Fierro striking terror in the hearts of his would-be captors. Life is the full armor plating of personality, quickness, and improvisation; "but improvisation is death, in the beautiful manner, if you wish" (p. 335).

Improvisation, moreover, is the essence of three archetypes of Argentine history (pp. 337–340): the caudillo (the "anti-engineer"), the *baquiano* (the gaucho guide), and the *payador* (the gaucho folk singer), intuitive types who not only rejected the development of a European kind of civilization in their land but painstakingly developed the arts of improvisation and mental self-defense.[68] This intense individualism, in truth an integral part of Spanish heritage, was the basis of the gaucho tradition. Now, in the twentieth century, a new candor and a realistic appraisal of national character were necessary. Martínez Estrada has taken his x-ray and wishes to offer his diagnosis. To arrive at the nation's fundamental truths, Argentines must expose the dogged specter of barbarism (primitivism, historical resentment caused by the ever-elusive Trapalanda, solitude, aggressive individualism, man on the defensive) that continues to lurk behind the thin façades and "pseudostructures" of civilization.[69]

[66] "El hombre a la defensiva," *Obras completas*, II, 643–666.
[67] Cf. Ortega y Gasset: "Where audacity is an accepted form of social behavior, one must live continuously on the alert" ("El hombre a la defensiva," p. 653).
[68] See, for example, *Martín Fierro*, II, Cantos xxix–xxxiii.
[69] Twenty-five years later (Dec. 3, 1958) the author reaffirmed these ideas: "The fox has the glossy coat of the marten and civic virtue changes into hypocrisy. This is the process I described with the indignant metaphor 'the posthumous

The underlying truth cannot be ignored; "we must accept it coura-
geously, so that it may no longer disconcert us; force it up to the level
of consciousness, so that it will vanish and we can live in a state of
well-being" (p. 346). The abrupt transition from the stark pessimism of all the rest of the book to this faint glimmer of hope in the
final paragraph must have appeared unrealistic to a number of readers, but it is not without justification. The book was written primarily
as an analysis, not a cure; moreover, this final paragraph makes it
quite clear that the only possible remedy lies in the sane experience
of the analysis itself, in the dispelling of the whole apparatus of illusions, great and small, that has deceived the nation.

But by testimony of the author himself, the cure was not forthcoming. His lecture commemorating the twenty-fifth anniversary of
the publication of *X-Ray of the Pampa* amends nothing previously
written. The message of 1958, though dignified, is clearly "I told you
so" and is a strong reiteration of the original thesis. He had advised
his country to "abandon the photographer and consult the radi-
ologist" because it was "suffering from its glands, not just its skin."
At the time of the first edition few were disposed to listen, but more
had begun to listen by 1958, and many are listening today.

---

victory of the vanquished savage'" ("A los 25 años de *Radiografía de la Pampa*").

4 · Homo Pampensis

Nietzsche

Martínez Estrada shared most of Nietzsche's passionate rejection of Christianity and Western civilization. Nietzsche was the voice of frustration and heresy, of the individual will denied, of a human dignity impossible to attain but worth struggling for nonetheless.[1] Like Nietzsche, the Argentine prophet sought a humanistic faith that might bring about the realization of man's best potentialities, despite the fact that his written work is an eloquent testimony of the failure of that search. Like Nietzsche and Nietzsche's Zarathustra,

[1] See "Nietzsche, filósofo dionisíaco in *Heraldos de la verdad*, pp. 157–265. This and the two other essays in the volume confirm Martínez Estrada's preference for champions of the individual will, intuition, and moralistic philosophy: "Montaigne, filósofo impremeditado y fortuito" (pp. 5–96), and "Balzac, filósofo y metafísico" (pp. 97–156).

he would like to have acquired "an apostolic faith in man very similar to the Christian faith."[2] As outspoken descendants of a distinguished brotherhood of dissenters (Erasmus, Luther, Giordano Bruno, Milton, and Pascal)—though far more nihilistic than they—Nietzsche and his Argentine admirer believed that truth was to be found neither in nature nor recorded knowledge, but in the private revelations of "the conscience."[3] Their attitude was much more religious than scientific; not really an atheistic position, but rather the reverse of the Christian coin, an impassioned humanism sustained by a militant, individualistic religiosity. Each would like to have founded his own utopia.

Unlike Nietzsche, Martínez Estrada did not interpret the Christian ethic as the upshot of "an ecumenical synagogue" or "new Judaized Rome" subversively imposed by the indefatigable Jews ("that priestly nation of resentment *par excellence*") on mighty Rome.[4] We do find, however, one aspect of Nietzschean thought that obviously penetrated the ideology of *Death and Transfiguration of Martín Fierro*: the theory of collective resentment. There is a parallel to Nietzsche's notion of defensiveness in the Jews in Martínez Estrada's notion of defensiveness in the Argentines. Martínez Estrada accordingly was convinced that José Hernández's Martín Fierro, a fictional representative man of nineteenth-century Argentina, gave simple and forceful expression to the resentment of a disillusioned people. Hernández and the protagonist with whom he identified himself so closely are portrayed in *Death and Transfiguration* as the pariahs, the victims, but also the spiritual parricides of an illusory tradition, and at the same time the spiritual progenitors of an illusory civilization.

A second basic aspect of Nietzschean thought that strongly influenced Martínez Estrada was the tragic recognition that in human

---

[2] *Heraldos de la verdad*, p. 164. The words are Martínez Estrada's and sum up his interpretation of Zarathustra.

[3] Ibid.

[4] "A stronger and more aristocratic nation has never existed in the world." Friedrich Nietzsche, *The Genealogy of Morals*, trans. Horace B. Samuel, pp. 35–38. The Jews also had, thought Nietzsche, "a unique genius for popular morals." In this sense he considered them analogous to the Chinese and the Germans (p. 36).

existence the concepts of good and evil mean little compared to the will to power. Of course one must make the necessary distinction between Nietzsche's outright advocacy of personal power (never hero worship) as man's only legitimate claim to significance and Martínez Estrada's fatalism. In the latter there is no room for a development of the Superman, either figurative or actual. Skepticism and psychological acumen are what the more existentialist Martínez Estrada assimilates from the more romantic Nietzsche: the perception of real weakness under the mask of seeming strength, immorality disguised as morality, systematic and traditional mores precariously balanced on the brink of subconscious fears and obsessions.

The third influential aspect of Nietzsche is his criticism and prophecy of a growing "fear of the individual by society." Nietzsche lamented the fate of the individual in a society more and more devoted to the principle of systematic, collective progress. Consistently the redoubtable liberal from his earliest writings to the last, Martínez Estrada was ideologically unprepared to accept the social and cultural consequences of progress. He was too much the ascetic to "live dangerously" himself, but his appreciation of the heroic anarchy of others was absolutely sincere. Furthermore, he realized that meaningful—if often futile—self-sacrifice for the sake of individuality could manifest itself in many ways in the labyrinthine world of the twentieth century.

The intellectual apostasy that began with *X-Ray of the Pampa* was not to subside; it reached a new peak of intensity with the *Death and Transfiguration of Martín Fierro* (1948). "Apostasy," because Martínez Estrada singled out a national archetype who, within the formal epic structure of a nationally revered work of literature (published in two parts in 1872 and 1879), reflected the cultural indifference, the social disillusionment, and the ideological confusion he believed to be endemic and permanent in his country. Whereas Don Quixote and Faust had given forceful expression—albeit through a series of spectacular failures and ironies—to the fundamental aspirations of modern man, Martín Fierro was the tremulous innocent, a vague synthesis of the everyday cares of an embryonic society. He was a symbol of the ordinary, moving fitfully within an epic structure. It is true that he was created by an author, but Hernández and his gaucho speak virtually as one. Cervantes identified himself as Don Quixote's "stepfather." Hernández, by contrast, could be called Martín Fierro's twin brother; but even together they lack a specific identity. "Martín Fierro is like an anonymous poem, because its author speaks as an entire people."[5]

Nietzsche, of course, was an intensely personal philosopher, the first great thinker of modern times to bring speculative thought into close alignment with morals and psychology. In this sense he is the midway point between Schopenhauer (d. 1860) and existentialism. I have begun by outlining three aspects of his thought (collective resentment, the will to power, and society's fear of the individual) because they were instrumental in shaping Martínez Estrada's attitude toward Argentine life. He had begun reading Nietzsche at the age of fifteen, and the first impression endured. Combined with a radical skepticism, gleaned eclectically from Montaigne, Spengler, Ortega, Keyserling, and Schopenhauer, and already formulated in *X-Ray of the Pampa*, a Nietzchean despair more intense than that of Nietzsche himself underlies the seven-year preparation of his most serious and extensive work, *Death and Transfiguration of Martín Fierro*, the subtitle of which is *Essay of Interpretation of Argentine Life*.[6] Gaucho, Indian fighter, draftee, deserter, fugitive killer, and singer of his woes, Martín Fierro is the archetype and symbol for that interpretation. Although it was published two years earlier, the hastily composed essay on Sarmiento (1946), discussed in Chapter 2 of this study, actually grew out of *Death and Transfiguration* while the latter was being written. Sarmiento and Martín Fierro appear in these works as the positive and negative poles of nineteenth-century Argentine life: the active agent and passive conveyor of the grand

---

[5] *Muerte y transfiguración de Martín Fierro*, I, 324. José Hernández himself confirms this view in a passage from the prologue, quoted on p. 337.

[6] At the urging of his friend Enrique Espinoza (who had also introduced him personally to Horacio Quiroga and acquainted him with the work of William Henry Hudson), Martínez Estrada "set to work and labored for seven years in composing *Death and Transfiguration of Martín Fierro*" ("Literatura y vida," in *Para una revisión de las letras argentinas*, pp. 149–150). Martínez Estrada was "over forty" at that time, which means he probably began writing *Death and Transfiguration* in 1941.

illusion that Martínez Estrada considers to be the historical legacy of the twentieth century. The illusion was double, of course. Sarmiento was the progressive and the "civilizer" who had struggled in vain; Martín Fierro was the quavering voice of a tradition that existed more in the imagination than in reality. So that Martínez Estrada's interpretation of this figure may be more comprehensible, a brief analysis of Hernández's poem and the guachesque tradition that it crowned is now appropriate.

The Poem of Martín Fierro

Costumbrismo, or the description of local life and traditions, was universally popular in Hispanic literatures of the early and mid-nineteenth century. It aspired to authenticity, but "types" turned out to be of greater concern than persons, the way of life more important than the way of being. The universals of poetry were too often lost in the peculiarities of history. In Argentina, gaucho poetry was the predominant form of costumbrismo, mixed at first with the folklore emanating from the war against Spain, and from the anarchic struggles among provincial caudillos until the late 1820's. The gaucho was the central figure of these themes and, accordingly, the genre of gaucho poetry was doomed from the start to a certain degree of degradation, for the gaucho was considered generally as an undesirable. The gauderio, as he was commonly called in the eighteenth century, was characterized as an outright barbarian, and the first use of the word gaucho connoted always an uncouth being who earned his livelihood as a knife-brandishing outlaw. As Enrique Anderson-Imbert remarks, the word assumed a more favorable meaning during the patriotic years of the fight against Spain,[7] but the gaucho soon afterward reassumed his traditionally negative image, doomed to the role of the disinherited and the delinquent.

The initiator of the poetic and costumbrista genre, later to be known as gauchesque literature, was the Uruguayan Bartolomé Hidalgo (1788–1822). Hidalgo found in the popular gaucho songs an effective form of anti-Spanish propaganda, and propaganda was the

---

[7] Spanish-American Literature: A History, trans. John V. Falconieri, p. 144.

extra-literary subterfuge by which the crude cowhand of the pampa infiltrated Argentine letters. Once independence was won, however, the anti-Spanish image was transformed by the violent circumstances of some thirty years of civil war between the minority of liberal, Europeanized reformers, and the majority of conservative supporters of tradition and local autonomy. The ignorant and apolitical gauchos, backbone of what Sarmiento called barbarism, found themselves in the second of these categories. But the sophisticated as well as the uncultured found inspiration in the idiosyncracies and rustic charm of the Argentine plainsman, who was, after all, the only truly traditional figure in his national history. "Even the most cultured writers, who were moved by a moral passion amidst the civil wars, attracted by the crude spectacle of the plains and, above all, convinced by the Romantic ideals of a literature founded on local color and popular expression, began to mythicize the gaucho."[8]

To be sure, none of the gauchesque poets most remembered today was himself a gaucho. Hilario Ascasubi (1807–1875) was city-raised and a partisan of the centralists (*unitarios*) against the confederate followers of Rosas (*federales*). He did not complete his *Santos Vega*—until 1872—after twenty years' work. The protagonist of this work is the wayward member of a set of twins (*los mellizos de la Flor*) who becomes a rural bandit, repents, and dies a devout Catholic.

Estanislao del Campo (1834–1880) wrote his *Fausto* in five days, a tour de force inspired by a performance of Gounod's opera in the Teatro Colón in Buenos Aires in 1866. Del Campo retells the plot of *Faust* from the standpoint of an ingenuous gaucho ("Anastasio the Chicken") who he imagines has attended the performance. Like Ascasubi, Del Campo was a city man and utilized the gaucho theme primarily for its picturesque value.

It was up to their contemporary José Hernández (1834–1886) to place the gaucho in his proper historical perspective and, most important, to speak in his behalf rather than poke fun at him. Born on a ranch in the southern part of Buenos Aires province, Hernández

[8] Ibid., p. 196.

was an obscure poet, journalist and politician who would have had no claim to fame had he not written *The Poem of Martín Fierro*. As Unamuno described Don Quixote in relation to Cervantes, the fictitious Martín Fierro seems to have been Hernández's *raison d'être*, with more "existence" and a greater immortality in the hearts of his countrymen than his real creator.[9] Hernández devoted much of his life to political journalism and guerrilla war activities in support of the caudillo generals Urquiza, Peñaloza ("El Chacho"), and López Jordán, confederates and enemies of the constitutional governments of Mitre and Sarmiento. In the same year that Senator Nicasio Oroño made an impassioned speech against the draft law enacted to bring the war against the Pampa Indians to a successful conclusion (1869), Hernández began writing *Martín Fierro*. Oroño compared the treatment of the gauchos, who constituted the entire army of conscripts, to that of the Indians during the Spanish conquest.[10] But since the mid-1850's Hernández had already been expressing in pamphlets and newspaper columns his indignation at the injustices perpetrated by the federal government on the rural inhabitants. This indignation was the main stimulus for his *Poem of Martín Fierro*. He wanted "to present a type personifying the character of our gauchos, concentrating on their particular way of feeling, thinking, and expressing themselves," and to inform the general public about "their work, their misfortunes, and their hazards of life."[11]

The non-Argentine reader must bear in mind that *The Poem of Martín Fierro* has three significant aspects: it is a strong social and political protest; it is the last, and by far the most authentic, work in the genre of gauchesque poetry; and it is a vivid, though often subconscious, revelation by the author not only of himself and his composite, allegorical, and symbolic protagonist, but also of perman-

[9] Of historical interest are two other works by Hernández: *Life of the Chacho* (published as a brief pamphlet in 1863, revised and expanded in 1875), and *The Ranch Owner's Manual* (1881).
[10] "José Hernández" (biographical introduction by Guillermo Eliseo Sciarra) in *Martín Fierro* (Buenos Aires: Ediciones Albatros, 1965), p. 31.
[11] "Carta del Autor a don José Zoilo Miguena," which served as a prologue to the first edition (1872), reproduced in *Martín Fierro*, ed. Eleuterio F. Tiscornia, pp. 19–20. Subsequent references to this edition are by title and page number only.

ent aspects and problems of Argentine life. As the subtitle of *Death and Transfiguration* suggests (*Essay of Interpretation of Argentine Life*), the third aspect was of greatest concern to Martínez Estrada.

Like many other great works of literature conceived within the general framework of the quest legend, *The Poem of Martín Fierro* transcends its expository purpose. Just as Goethe's *Faust*, by the richness of an expansive and poetic imagination, carries us beyond the portrayal of intellectual ambition, just as *Don Quixote* is more than the theoretical pilgrimage of a hallucinating, anachronistic knight, or just as *Moby Dick* transcends the pursuit of a symbol by a monomaniacal seaman, *Martín Fierro* has more to offer than the story of the disappearance of the gaucho way of life. In all these works the seeds of ultimate failure form complex roots, and the protagonists' struggle against that failure means more to us than their ideal dream, always so hopelessly far beyond the horizon of concrete experience. The struggle is what gives their lives significance.[12] Behind the ideal dream is the nightmare of dissolution. In all these works the intellectual creator operates in the context of his particular *Volksgeist* (a term suggestive of greater depth of meaning than "nationality"). Against the background, both intimate and panoramic, of that *Volksgeist* he measures the crisis of the values of his time. In all these works the implicit aspiration to a higher national culture is eroded by ironic circumstances and the progressive disillusionment of the main characters.

José Hernández, of course, is not of a literary stature comparable to that of Goethe, Cervantes, or Melville. But he was born at the right time, in the right place, and in the right circumstances to express the spirit and dilemma of a vanishing race. This he did with great sensitivity.

The Poem of Martín Fierro is often referred to as an epic poem. The narration in the form of song, the sustained suffering of the protagonist in Part I, the variety of his experiences, some of which are

---

[12] In *Faust* and *Don Quixote* there is literal salvation (Part II of each work), but the succession—sometimes comic, sometimes grim, sometimes grotesque—of adversities and lost values (e.g., the drowning of Faust's and Gretchen's child) is what has most impressed the modern reader's sensibility.

heroic, and his partial redemption as a member of civilized society in Part II give the work an epic flavor. But, as Anderson-Imbert says, "*Martín Fierro* is not an epic poem. It is a popular poem in which the poet, with all deliberation, puts his song at the service of an oral tradition. The impulse is individual; the source is popular."[13] Arturo Torres Ríoseco also denies any epic spirit in the work, mainly because "it does not denote a philosophy of heroic existence." Torres Ríoseco denies, furthermore, that Fierro represents anything—not a race, "nor even a people in a critical moment of its evolution." He thinks it "absurd" to imagine that such a menial social type as the gaucho could symbolize "the genesis of the Argentine nation," for this would be to deny Buenos Aires its historic role as "heart and head of that country."[14]

In contrast to this negative view, the great Argentine modernist poet Leopoldo Lugones (1874–1938), who together with the Spaniard Miguel de Unamuno,[15] is chiefly responsible for awakening *literary* interest in Hernández's work, gave a lecture in Buenos Aires in 1913 in which he extolled the poem's epic virtues. In 1916 he published *The Balladeer*, in which he expanded the same thesis. "The object of this book, then, is to define epic poetry in the light of this principle (i.e., the popular plant gives the epic flower); to demonstrate that our *Martín Fierro* belongs to the genre; to study it in that sense; to determine, at the same time, through its characteristic elements, the formation of the race; and finally, to discover in that way the secret of its destiny."[16] Unamuno finds a fusion of "epic and lyric elements" in Martín Fierro; "the vigorous gaucho soul is like an emergence of the soul of the pampa, immense, free, sun-drenched

---

[13] *Spanish American Literature*, p. 198. There is, of course, no reason to distinguish between "popular" and epic, for the most epic poems are directly or indirectly of popular inspiration (patriotic, tribal, or nationalistic), e.g., *The Iliad* and *The Cid*. But Anderson-Imbert goes on to note, as Martínez Estrada had done before him (*Death and Transfiguration*, I, 336–337), that "Martín Fierro seems to derive from an anonymous people" and that "ordinary inhabitants of the pampas" doing ordinary things are the nucleus of the work.

[14] Arturo Torres-Ríoseco, *New World Literature*.

[15] *Obras completas*, VIII, 47–63.

[16] Prologue to *El Payador*, in *Obras en prosa*, ed. Leopoldo Lugones, Jr., p. 1082.

beneath an infinite sky, exposed to the open air of God.["17] In Fierro himself he senses a continuation of the combative Castilian spirit, and the gaucho in general was "the hero of the war for American independence that separated us, only to bring us together in a higher and deeper union, in a kind of unity of the differentiated, as a certain evolutionist would say."[18]

Agreeing with neither Unamuno nor Lugones (he had high intellectual esteem for both), Martínez Estrada denies the epic and lyric values of Hernández's work. If he agrees with Lugones that Martín Fierro is a genuine embodiment of the Argentine spirit and with Unamuno that the defiantly independent gaucho of the 1860's and 1870's was a last defense against the growing ravages of urbanization, he finds nothing but futility in the plainsman's existence, nothing but the foreshadowing of a hopeless Argentine future in the steady extinction of the plainsman's function and spirit.

In many respects Part I (1872) and Part II (1879) of *Martín Fierro* are two independent works. Part I is built around the unified action and sentiment of the protagonist. When the disenchanted gaucho smashes his guitar on the ground in the thirteenth and final canto, the reader has already had his fill of woe; the "great web of misfortunes" has finally been woven; society has reserved no place for a fugitive whose antisocial philosophy is absolute. Part II is a longer and quite different story. In the first cantos of the second part, the singer explains his return to song, his final, decisive adventure in the wilderness (the defeat of the wild Indian brave and the rescue of the captive woman), and his return to civilization. From Canto XII until Canto XXX, near the end, Fierro remains in the background, while his two sons and Picardía, the son of his late companion Cruz, carry the story by telling their past experiences. Only in the last four cantos does he return to an active role: the *payada*, or spontaneous dialogue in song with the Negro gaucho whose brother Fierro has killed in a fight several years before; and the fatherly advice he gives his two sons and Picardía on the values of prudence, diligence, and brotherhood.

[17] Unamuno, *Obras completas*, VIII, 53.
[18] Ibid., p. 57.

As Hernández reminds us in the prologue to the 1872 edition, Martín Fierro is a victim representing "that disinherited class of our country." Part I is his flight from one intolerable situation to another, candidly told in the spirit of self-indulgence and bitter humor. The relationship of the successive events, like the whole structure of Fierro's life, is vague and in itself suggestive of a rather purposeless and passive character. No achievement is mentioned, and the protagonist's pride is purely defensive. Narrating in retrospect, he gives a double image of himself: the spontaneous actor and the emotional, reminiscent observer. As a historian Martín Fierro is entirely intuitive; the life he reproduces *al compás de la vigüela* (to the rhythm of the guitar) has the haziness and disjointed quality of a dream. No specific geography is mentioned throughout, nor is there, in this first part, any descriptive physical detail of the characters. Part I is a chronicle of unhappy events blurred by time, of vague intentions and strong desires.

Beyond the self-indulgent, pathetic tone of Fierro's song, we can perceive in the casual yet complete synthesis of his life a representative, historical pattern. Forcibly uprooted from his passive existence of life on a ranch, he is drafted into the army and sent to a lonely outpost in Indian country. Virtually imprisoned, he is forced to stay there for three years and is never paid.[19] Fierro finally deserts and, returning home, finds his house and ranch destroyed and no trace of his wife or children. The local authorities, moreover, have confiscated his right to the property. In his "sad circumstance" he becomes a confirmed *gaucho malo*. "If a man takes it on the chin he's a stupid gaucho; if he resists, he's a bad gaucho." The military and political authorities have dispossessed him of everything—even his family. At a country dance where the gin flows free he is involved in a knife fight with a Negro, whom he kills (Canto VII). The next episode (Canto VIII) is a fight with a gaucho bandit, one who has insulted

---

[19] A military man of Hernández's time writes: "The soldier in the field is allotted for his vices or entertainment 25 pesos or one 'hard' peso a month. The pay is delayed at least six months and, at the most, three years. This, added to the various kinds of harsh treatment they receive, induces the best of them to desert" (Colonel Alvaro Barros, *Fronteras de las pampas del sud*, quoted in a note by Tiscornia in *Martín Fierro*, pp. 235–236).

him in a tavern-general store (*boliche*). Fierro is thus forced to fight
in defense of his honor and quickly kills his opponent. Again he must
flee, and he is soon tracked down by the rural police, who surround
him and order him to give up. Instead he fights them off with incredible fury. So impressive is his courage and strength that one of
the police spontaneously decides to take his side and proceeds to
help him rout his ex-comrades. Sergeant Cruz has also been a gaucho
and understands Fierro's predicament. Together they philosophize
on the gaucho's hopeless fate and resolve to abandon for good the
civilized world, seeking refuge among the Indians. Martín Fierro has
broken his guitar and the poet loses track of the pair as they disappear beyond the last frontier with a string of wild horses. In 1872
Hernández had no intention of continuing the poem.

But in 1879 Martín Fierro expresses his author's second thoughts.
Enough time has passed to convince the hero that "the country is for
the ignorant; the city for the educated." In spite of all the persecu-
tions of the past, he must return ungrudgingly to civilization. After
some two hundred lines of melancholy reflection, of thanks to God
and the Virgin, and a reaffirmation of the pleasure of song, the story
takes up where it left off at the end of Part I. Fierro and Cruz wander
across the pampa until they encounter an Indian tribe. The Indians
decide to make them hostages, keeping them separated for two years.
The two experience constant hunger and hardship; the Indians are
portrayed as cruel and insensitive creatures—"no compassion beats
in the heart of the infidel"—who live exclusively by plunder. Cruz is
stricken by an epidemic of smallpox and, asking Martín Fierro to
look after his son, dies (Canto VI). Soon afterward, Fierro rescues a
white woman, captive for two years of an Indian brave who tortures
her, murders her child, and ties her hands together with the child's
entrails. Fierro arrives on the scene directly after this atrocity (Canto
X) and kills the Indian in a fierce struggle reminiscent of some of the
combat scenes in Homer's *Iliad*. With extreme hardship the gaucho
and the woman slowly get back to the white man's territory and then
go their separate ways.

Up to this point Part II is stylistically and thematically united to
Part I, and the hero proclaims, "I've reached the end of my story/

and cannot add any more" (Canto X). Like Ulysses, Martín Fierro
has undergone ten years of adventure and adversity: "three years on
the frontier/ two as an outlaw gaucho/ and five out among the Indians." All is changed; through an old friend he learns that the judge
who had victimized him has died, and that the government no longer
persecutes the defenseless. He also learns that his wife has died in
a hospital.

Most of the remainder of Part II is taken up with the first-person
accounts of Martín Fierro's two sons and of Picardía, Cruz's son.
Each tells the story of his own part of the ten years of wandering,
indecisive existence that all have shared up to then. Martín Fierro
looks old and feels old as he is hastily recast in the role of a father,
and the novelistic perspective replaces the lyric perspective. Martínez Estrada believes that the poem as a whole shows more concern
with time than with space (I, 167). This is certainly true of Part II,
in which the evolution of individual lives and the suggestion of a
more historical atmosphere are undeniably time-centered. But as far
as Part I is concerned, one is inclined to disagree with Martínez Estrada, for here the sentimentalizing absorbs the entire past into the
lyric present, and the reader is more impressed by the constant reference to vague distances, infinite spaces, and the harrowing experience of separation (from family, home, and civilization) so
repeatedly complained about by Fierro. Part I is not time-centered
but space-centered.

"Viene uno como dormido/ cuando vuelve del desierto" ("One returns from the wilderness/ as if in a dream") are among the first lines
of Part II. It is as if the protagonist had moved from the static, solitary world of his personal experience into the mainstream of society
and history. With the appearance of the characters who dominate
Part II, all suggestion of an "epic" poem is lost, for the potential
here, the returned warrior from the Indian frontier, fades into the
background in deference to the younger generation (the two sons
and Picardía). Political change between 1872 and 1879, moralization
through the negative examples of indolent, picaresque lives, and
Martín Fierro's new sense of social brotherhood set fundamentally

different tones in Part II. Anderson-Imbert sums up the situation this way:

In the "Return" Fierro reappears, but with a European and progressivist vision of work: "for the land gives no fruit/ if not watered by sweat." "Vandalism is ended." Now he avoids fights and explains why earlier he had killed (this he does mainly in the *payada* [Canto XXX] with the brother of his Negro victim and in the fatherly advice of Canto XXXII); they are legal justifications which show that Hernández, down deep, was a conservative who respected the law, the reason being that by 1879— Avellaneda is the new president, Sarmiento no longer holding the reins —Hernández recognizes "society" as legitimate, which earlier he had condemned in the "Departure." There are two moralities in the "Return"; the one that Hernández proposes and the one that the cynicism of the old man Vizcacha documents as a reality. The first morality having ideal goals and the second, opportunistic ones. Hernández's idealism and Vizcacha's realism. An Argentina with a program and an Argentina without principles. Lights and shadows. Civilization versus Barbarism: here is where Hernández, the enemy of Sarmiento, in the end agrees with him.[20]

Correct insofar as the change of direction between Parts I and II is concerned, this interpretation could be misleading; for Hernández offers no "program," but only the vaguest moral advice; no "light," but only the most dubious conclusion—as Martín Fierro, his two sons, and Picardía lead us to believe in the final canto. Each goes off in his own direction, first making a secret promise, which the author refuses to reveal, to the others. Each, furthermore, agrees to change his name, not as a simple gesture of beginning life anew, but with the author's quite sinister suggestion that "he who changes his name/ has some guilt to hide." The anti-idealist Vizcacha's perverse scorn of his fellow man, though in no way accepted by Hernández, assumes monumental proportions. It is no mere coincidence that the only *complete* character in the work, described, quoted, and caricatured in intimate detail, is colossally evil. Little does it matter that Vizcacha dies, thereby freeing Fierro's younger son from his (Vizcacha's) tutelage. For Vizcacha's scorn and cynicism, if not his evil, are con-

[20] *Spanish American Literature*, pp. 199–200.

tagious, and they pervade the attitudes of his pupil as well as those of all who hear about him. Martínez Estrada is quite right in observing that "the scornful tone" is "an organic element" of the work, that the characters tend to compare themselves with animals, and to assume that degradation and poverty, "created, administered, organized," are their natural condition.[21] The attitude of all the characters is essentially picaresque, about the future as well as about the present. The end is not a conclusion, but a drifting away; and we assume, as did Francisco de Quevedo, creator of Pablos the Sharper, that life is not going to be much different simply because its individual participants move from one place to another.

Death and Transfiguration

Martínez Estrada would have us believe that there has been more transfiguration than death in José Hernández's unforgettable gaucho. But, to be sure, that transfiguration amounts to little more than Martín Fierro's defeat, his abortive quest of true freedom, projected into future history. The final image of Martín Fierro and the three younger gauchos setting out on their separate ways ("a los cuatro vientos") is for Martínez Estrada the indelible message. It is the certain sign of spiritual failure for the Argentine people, whose psychological destiny—literarily reflected by Mafud's unrootedness, Güiraldes' and Manuel Gálvez's solitude, Mallea's quiet desperation —is aimlessness and perpetual isolation among men. In the important chapter on the "philosophy" of Martín Fierro, Martínez Estrada reflects on the intuitive attributes of the plainsmen. Just as the *Divine Comedy* is a compendium of culture of the thirteenth century, *Martín Fierro* is a "cryptogram" of nineteenth-century Argentina and the "empirical wisdom" of the uneducated inhabitants of the pampa (I, 401). It is here that Martínez Estrada condemns the erroneous adaptation of foreign values and institutions to Argentine life; the main culprit, by implication, is Sarmiento. Against Sarmiento's progressivist utilitarianism, Martínez Estrada upholds his own concept of natural values and "the moral superiority and superior character of the man of the country over the man of the city." It has been

[21] *Muerte y transfiguración de Martín Fierro*, I, 395–396. Subsequent references in the text to this edition are by volume and page number only.

wrong for Argentina to interpret civilization and culture according to Sarmiento's simplistic formula, by which the urban mentality instructs the rural. Indeed, "the opposite view is equally valid" (I,400). Further on he quotes Max Scheler, the phenomenological philosopher (*Knowledge and Culture*), accepting Scheler's principle of a "personal structure" as the foundation of true culture. The pedantic and the arrogant measure "culture" by the many-faceted reality they are able to perceive or by the universal laws they are able to establish. They see the world as a quantitative or synthetic entity. The phenomenologist, on the other hand, measures culture by his own particular existence and perspective.

In Martínez Estrada's interpretation, Martín Fierro was a primitive phenomenologist, extracting knowledge from the life-pulse of experience, from the "intuition . . . of the universe in man, from the absurdity and incoherence that constitute the laws of gravity and thermodynamics of the history which is not written, which is impossible to record: the true history of living man" (I, 404).[22] It is quite clear that, had he not been influenced by Scheler, Martínez Estrada would have found little of positive value in the character of Martín Fierro. Whereas the Hernández of *The Ranch Owner's Manual* (1881) is an impersonal professional, a technician and "researcher," the Hernández of *The Poem of Martín Fierro* is the poet, sensitive to all "the environmental and historical circumstances in the life of the rustic in our country" (I, 403). I have spoken in Chapter 3 of Martínez Estrada as a Hispanic American thinker in the "cold-blooded" tradition described by Count Keyserling, in psychological affinity to the world around him and obsessed with those particular circumstances of national history that would lead ultimately to a system of concrete (never formal or abstract) values.

In José Hernández—or more precisely, in the representative gaucho who assumes the autonomy characteristic of all vital fictional creations—Martínez Estrada found the literary embodiment of his own "cold-blooded" philosophy. The philosophy itself, however, was in large part Scheler's; Martín Fierro, as seen by Martínez Estrada,

---

[22] Cf. Miguel de Unamuno's concept of "intrahistoria" in *En torno al casticismo* (1895) and elsewhere.

possessed "that open-ended, metaphorical knowledge which sensed and conformed with the truest elements of life" (I, 403) and which was the heart of Scheler's phenomenology. The hero represented concrete values in opposition to abstract values (matching, for example, his will to personal freedom against a totally abused conception of abstract justice). As a basically collective feeling of the underdog, the hero's *resentment* of his fate in the world colored his outlook, causing him to interpret in emotional terms all reality. The hero was part of a "total personality" beyond individuals, the figure driven by the anonymous forces of pampa life.

Martínez Estrada adapted these philosophical tenets of Scheler (shaded with Kafka's fatalism) to *The Poem of Martín Fierro*, influences that contributed much to his consideration of that work as the proper point of departure for "an essay of interpretation of Argentine life." Martín Fierro, to put it briefly, was "transfigured" by an eager student of phenomenology who could accept neither the deductive conclusions of logic nor the empirical evidence of history. This does not mean that Martínez Estrada was either irrational or unaware of nineteenth-century history; it means that he was struggling always to find the evasive human motivation behind literature and life. In his view, reality was more valuable as symbol than as evidence; for him the physical world had only metaphorical significance. The components of the tragic perspective in which he interpreted the *Poem* were collective resentment, the will to power, and social fear of the individual (the three influential aspects of Nietzsche's thought mentioned at the beginning of this chapter); fatalism gleaned from Spengler and Schopenhauer; Scheler's phenomenological (i.e., metaphorical) system of knowledge; and Franz Kafka's idea of the anonymous persecution of a man who has committed no crime, with the resulting frustration, indignity, and death (*The Trial*).

Death and Transfiguration of Martín Fierro is Martínez Estrada's most ambitious work. Not only is it an extensive analysis of the most celebrated work in Argentine literature; it is also "an interpretation of Argentine life," as well as the expression of his own "world view." The neo-Marxist critic Juan José Sebreli attacks him for his romantic

interpretation (in *Death and Transfiguration, The Head of Goliath,*
and *The Marvelous World of William Henry Hudson*) of Argentine
history,[23] for having accepted the idyllic interpretation of life on the
pampa of Hudson, Cunninghame-Graham, and others, and for condemning the advances of urban society since the industrial revolution.

One need not be a Marxist to agree that Sebreli has spotted a basic
flaw in Martínez Estrada's sociological thinking, for, in the three
works just mentioned, Don Ezequiel consistently emphasizes the destructive nature of modern civilization and recognizes no significant
change for the better from Hernández's time to the present. From
his reading of Kafka he develops the idea that the despots in society
are "provoked" and incited by their victims. "The condemned men
themselves, like Martín Fierro, Cruz, and Picardía, beget the injustice that they suffer" (II, 287). "The despot is a deification of the
slavish spirit" (II, 288). For Martínez Estrada civilization in *any*
country is little more than window dressing.

The theory of "invariable" elements in Argentine history, developed in an important essay on Sarmiento's *Facundo*,[24] is presented
in *Death and Transfiguration* as universally valid:

If we accept the proposition that once the force initiating certain characteristics in a race or national history has disappeared, the invariable
factors which over the centuries give form to every country also disappear,
then history would be an agglomeration of shifting substances impossible
to organize into a system. The contrary is the case. As great as individual
variation has been in the inhabitants of England, Spain, France, Holland
or any other nation that has undergone the most unbelievable changes in
its historical evolution, all these specific traits understood to constitute a
nationality keep alive the elements we recognize as basic to their formation as peoples and states (II, 166).

For Martínez Estrada history is not the continual creation of new
problems, but the progressive complication of the same one or two
fundamental problems that have always afflicted a particular na-

---

[23] *Martínez Estrada: Una rebelión inútil,* Chapter V ("El paraíso perdido"),
pp. 61–71.
[24] *Los invariantes históricos en el Facundo.*

tional community. If, in his anarchistic denunciation of Western civilization, he shares the romantic naturalism of Rousseau as expressed in *Emile*,[25] it is not an illusory lapse into pastoral pipe dreams, but rather a form of poetic discontent with modern industrialized life. The "paradise lost" formula in William Henry Hudson's *Far Away and Long Ago* and *The Crystal Age* was sufficiently appealing for him to accept it subconsciously if not logically. In *X-Ray of the Pampa* he made very clear his disbelief in any form of better life in the past. But Hudson impressed him as an exemplary life, as a man in nearly perfect harmony with nature who took inspiration and knowledge directly from nature. Hudson, though well read, was not "studious." "In that precocity of artistic feeling he has only one attribute of the scientific mind: the desire to observe well and to record his observations in writing."[26]

Although Martínez Estrada rated Hudson, as a writer, superior to Hernández and as one much more sensitive than Hernández to the natural life of the pampa, Hernández did produce *The Poem of Martín Fierro*, which was the candid revelation of life that he had been searching for. In it he thought he discovered the historical reality of his country.

The title *Death and Transfiguration of Martín Fierro* suggests the end of an era that was to repeat itself in new ways. The author's purpose is to describe the permanent factors of Argentine history. Martín Fierro and the other characters in the *Poem* express the scorn, melancholy, and inhibition that Martínez Estrada considers basic to the Argentine personality. The two-volume work is divided into four parts, two of them in the first volume, "The Poem" and "Its Values," and two of them in the second, "The Frontier" and "The World of Martín Fierro." Volume I is primarily concerned with an analysis of the *Poem* itself. Volume II is primarily concerned with an interpretation of the social and historical background of the *Poem*. The author thus moves from the particular to the general, toward a justi-

[25] Such is Sebreli's belief; see *Martínez Estrada: Una rebelión inútil*, pp. 63–64.
[26] "Estética y filosofía de Guillermo Enrique Hudson," *Sur* 10, no. 81 (Buenos Aires, 1941). Reproduced in *Guillermo Enrique Hudson: Vida y obra, bibliografía, antología*, pp. 67–74.

fication of his fatalistic philosophy of the "invariable" element of history.

Martínez Estrada: Reader of "Martín Fierro"

Martínez Estrada sees the *Poem* in terms of a psychological duality. Martín Fierro is the primal urge, the instinctive energy, the subconscious existence of José Hernández. José Hernández "himself," Hernández the social critic, reacts consciously to the outside world comprising the objects of Fierro's instinctive concern. Martín Fierro is the id, Hernández, the ego, of a composite personality. For this reason there is, as discussed earlier, a "twin-brother" relationship between the author and the protagonist of the *Poem*. But the essayist does not accept Hernández's role as legitimate and accuses him of moral oversimplification, of treating his improverished characters as "domestic servants," and of adopting the viewpoint of these superficial readers who have taken the *Poem* as a rather sophomoric criticism of gaucho indolence and a paean to honest work (I, 451). He attacks even "the most studious of the critics" (Eleuterio F. Tiscornia)—also editor of the best-known edition of the *Poem*—for assuming that the central theme of Part II is the "assimilation" of the gaucho into "normal, democratic life," through an alleged repudiation by the gaucho himself of his "sterile individualism."[27] Literally, of course, that is the meaning of Martín Fierro's advice to his sons and Picardía at the end. But there is no assurance that the advice is taken; on the contrary, the undisclosed pledge among the four, followed by their immediate separation and departure, strongly suggests that an acceptance by them of normalcy is still impossible.

For Martínez Estrada the *Poem* is an exhibition of the civic scorn and the distrust of human motivation that he believes to be typical of the Argentine mentality. He accuses the twentieth-century reader of the work of a kind of spiritual cowardice, of fearing to discover the emptiness of many commonly cherished values. He does not see the possibility of a truthful evaluation of the best works in nineteenth-century Argentine literature, for the average reader is afraid, as was Don Quixote in ruling out a second test of his helmet and visor, "that

[27] Eleuterio F. Tiscornia's prologue to his edition of *Martín Fierro*, p. 12.

everything true and false, the cardboard as well as the steel, might crumble together." Thus, Martínez Estrada conceived of life for modern Argentines as a kind of dream that must not be plunged into the ugly revelation of wakefulness. "We do not put our reality to test, nor our spiritual works either, because secretly we believe that no God protects them and that they are inherently fragile" (I, 453). In part, this dream is preserved by the uncritical praise of all that has been classified as sacred, including *The Poem of Martín Fierro*; in part, also, the dream is preserved by a blanket acceptance of one's customary values and way of life: a form of Freudian "defense" that is psychologically harmful. Hernández himself—"Hernández against Himself," as the next-to-last chapter of Volume I is entitled—shares equally in the blame for self-delusion with his latter-day readers. His simple moralizing obscures the true problems of human life, the history within history, that constituted the substance of the *Poem*.

Despite the rather temperamental and somber coloration of his meditations, Martínez Estrada is persistently and consistently analytical, examining the work and its social and historical background in several perspectives. The completeness of *Death and Transfiguration* is due to his observations not only on what Hernández wrote but also on what he left unwritten. Like Cervantes, Hernández produced what could be called the culminating work in a historically significant literary tradition. *Don Quixote* was to the chivalric novel, approximately, what *Martín Fierro* was to gaucho poetry. The rich dimensions of psychic and external reality so evident in *Don Quixote* are missing in the ingenuous style of Hernández. But there is more than what meets the eye. Martínez Estrada wrote *Death and Transfiguration* on the principle that it is unjust and unwise to interpret a psychologically complex work as a simple one only because its author happened to be a simple man with simple intentions. Hernández himself was not aware of what he had wrought.

The intellectual insecurity of Hernández is Martínez Estrada's point of departure. The first section of Volume I is an analysis of characters, with emphasis on the protagonist. That protagonist is to a great extent the result of a "transference"[28] of the author's char-

[28] A psychoanalytical term: "a. reproduction of emotions, especially those ex-

acter. "They are, if not the same person, the same being." Hernández and Martín Fierro are not novelistically comparable, but they are complementary in a psychological way. In Hernández's life the essayist finds the loneliness, the "physical rather than spiritual restlessness," and the declamatory tendency, which are all reflected in the portrayal of Martín Fierro. Martínez Estrada also points out that Hernández, who lived in a period of significant cultural progress in Argentina, had no interest in culture (I, 49). Furthermore, his political opposition to the generally liberal policies of Mitre and Sarmiento revealed his affinity for the more anarchistic gaucho caudillos, such as Urquiza and López Jordán. Accordingly, his protagonist takes form not as an autonomous fictional creation, not as a "human personality," so much as an allegorical figure who in his virile, emotional, and generally antisocial conduct, represented the collective destiny of the gaucho. Martín Fierro is little more than a "reminiscence," but despite the vagueness with which he is depicted, "he is destiny itself, the configuration of a forlorn existence, in the anagogic manner in which Dante created his complete world in order to dramatize his quest of perfection" (I, 53).

The poet further developed the composite, allegorical nature of Martín Fierro by portraying him in relationship to Sergeant Cruz (I, 79–94). He designed Cruz as an auxiliary gaucho, who, through his surprise intervention in support of Fierro and his subsequent companionship and death, would lend dynamism and magnitude to the protaganist. But actually—as Martínez Estrada points out—the moment of Cruz's intervention in Fierro's furious fight against the police marks Fierro's loss of initiative in the action of the *Poem* and of his autonomy as a character. Up to this point Fierro's bravado and energy predominate; from this point on, Fierro is totally passive. "It is as if Martín Fierro had died for Cruz's sake," and what Martín Fierro proposes, as if "paraphrasing the invitation of an unknown person who has become his inevitable friend, is taking refuge in In-

---

perienced in childhood, toward a person other than the one toward whom they were initially experienced. b. displacement" (*Random House Dictionary of the English Language,* unabridged edition, 1967, p. 1504).

dian territory, definitively renouncing his past, his world" (I, 80). The only occasion on which he recuperates his former vitality is in the fight with the Indian (Part II, Canto 9). Cruz is Fierro's "double," but also his "caricature" and his "sterilization" (I, 89). Unable, indeed, to distinguish between right and wrong, it is Cruz who unwittingly induces Martín Fierro's every thought and act after his encounter with the police (Part I, Canto 9); and the death of Cruz from smallpox causes such anguish in Martín Fierro (by contrast, the news of his wife's death caused only sad resignation) that the reader can only assume that in Cruz's death Fierro has subconsciously lost part of his own identity.

Martínez Estrada does not make such a conclusion explicit, but he has suggested it in all he has written about the two gauchos, particularly in stating that "Martín Fierro and Cruz are the same person" (I, 88). Further on, Martín Fierro's younger son and Picardía (Cruz's son) are considered in the same way as their respective fathers, one complementing the other (I, 102).

Vizcacha ("rodent," a species of burrowing animal native to the pampas) is, as Martínez Estrada says, the only *complete* character in the Poem, and the most vital force in Part II. Loquacious, philosophical in his cynical way, and described in impressive physical detail, Vizcacha "creates his own atmosphere around him" (I, 95), something that can be said about no other character in the work. Vizcacha is appointed by a corrupt judge as guardian of Fierro's younger son and is everything a guardian should not be: vindictive, slovenly, misanthropic, dishonest, and miserly. His only friends are his dogs, and after his burial even these friends eat one of his hands, which is projecting from his slipshod grave. Hernández seems to be telling us that Vizcacha is a dramatic example of the kind of man a corrupt society engenders, and a dramatization of the social problems an underdog of society (such as the underdog Martín Fierro's underdog son) must face. But in his perverse way Vizcacha is a great teacher in the school of general experience. As a violent pessimist who carries out his philosophy in action, he gives strong resonance to the lower-keyed futilitarianism of Fierro, Cruz, and their sons:

The world reflected in Vizcacha's mind is an inferno embellished by man, but it is not a simplified world like that of Leibniz or that of Comte. It is an inferno, a mass of human reptiles and alligators stretched out in the sun and gently devouring one another. That philosophy, which might or might not have a logical basis, is part of the person, body, and life of Vizcacha, and it gives force—as does no physical trait nor any anecdote— to his gloomy personality. He is indisputably the maximum creation of the *Poem* (I, 97).

In a later chapter ("Vizcacha, filósofo moralista") Martínez Estrada finds important analogies between Vizcacha's cynicism in a little world of corruption and the more universal cynicism of Machiavelli, Hobbes, and Sir William Hamilton. He says that the "perverse spirit" of these practical political philosophers had shown the world "how to perpetuate the status quo (a social status constitutively and organically corrupt) by taking advantage of it . . . converting it into a lucrative enterprise stimulated by intelligence and energy" (I, 412). Once again Martínez Estrada has supplemented intuitive criticism of Hernández with his own moral philosophy.

Martínez Estrada completes his observations on the characters by remarking on their anonymity—none of them except the protagonist has more than a nickname. Cruz has only a last name. Martín is so named because Saint Martin is the patron saint of the township in which Hernández was born (I, 110). The names and nicknames of the more important characters are, of course, symbolic: Fierro suggests the resistant and durable qualities of iron and the valor and agility necessary to wield the knife effectively; Cruz (cross) connotes sacrifice and, in Martínez Estrada's opinion, a new burden of misfortune and solitude that Fierro assumes when, at the end of Part I, he breaks his guitar and decides to follow Cruz ("his cross") into the wilderness (I, 89);[29] Vizcacha looks and acts like the animal for which he is named; Picardía (*pícaro*) has lived as a rogue, and so on.

Ironically, Martín Fierro, the only personage with a first and last

[29] "Cruz is a gallows for Martín Fierro, the instrument of his crucifixion" (I, 89).

name, has the least concrete personality of all, and Martínez Estrada compares him with Kafka's Joseph K. in *The Trial* (1925), who, like his unknown gaucho ancestor, was the constant victim of a vast and baffling bureaucracy. Like Joseph K., Martín Fierro was the predestined and "necessary" defendant (I, 111). It seems logical to assume that Martínez Estrada's whole interpretation of the *Poem* was strongly influenced by Kafka, because his emphasis in describing Hernández's presentation of characters is always on the portrayal of continually defeated people, ingenuous gauchos unable to understand the complexities of social injustice destroying their will and their happiness, particularly in the case of the protagonist. Joseph K., of course, is completely degraded and frustrated and, finally, killed. Fierro, on the other hand, begins a new life that is a total question mark. But the structure and the sentiments of each work do suggest similiarities. Joseph K. was a mask for Kafka (the autobiographical sense of the initial is obvious) and Fierro was a mask for Hernández. Like Joseph K. in *The Trial*, Martín Fierro lives from one test of his endurance to another; the continual testing is what gives the succession of anecdotes and episodes coherence.

Hernández's formal purpose is an analysis of the evils of Argentine society. But the results of his creation transcend that purpose. In *Martín Fierro* the didactic and moralistic elements are submerged in the bleak resignation of the characters and the sterile atmosphere in which they live. Like *The Trial*, *The Poem of Martín Fierro* impresses the twentieth-century reader more as a lament for the human condition than as a call to moral restitution. This is precisely the reason why Martínez Estrada wrote his two-volume interpretation. As a reader of Kafka he took the fatalistic view and applied it to the *Poem*: all judges are corrupt; all gauchos destitute; all learning is through adversity; all men induced to kill are the victims of circumstance and temperament. Considered in the light of his fated existence and that of his sons, Cruz, Picardía, the captive woman, and Vizcacha, Martín Fierro's fatherly plea for prudence, diligence, and tolerance is far from convincing. The suggestion at the beginning of the final canto that Fierro, his two sons, and Picardía (who all change their names) have "guilt to conceal" is also a statement of the inevitability of human guilt—a major theme in Kafka's work.

Of course, these rather general analogies do not signify analogous intentions, viewpoints, or psychologies. Hernández wrote still within the romantic tradition; Kafka, in the existentialist tradition. Hernández's world was local, Kafka's universal. Hernández's spirit was melancholy, Kafka's tragic. Hernández was an anti-intellectual; Kafka, an intellectual. But the important point for the purposes of this study is not so much the fact that Martínez Estrada interpreted Hernández while under the influence of Kafka, but the fact that Martínez Estrada himself was a dynamic snythesis of the two spirits.

From the characters of the *Poem*, the author passes to an analysis of its "morphology" which is, for the most part, a rather technical examination of Hernández's style as revealed in his preference for the six-line stanza, his rhyme schemes, his attempts, through special spelling and syntax, to reproduce authentic gaucho speech.

In his discussion of structure Martínez Estrada attributes the unity of the work to a unity of style and the predominance of intuition over logic (I, 153). He believes, on the other hand, that its structure—"a la manera homérica"—is characterized by digressions and by various parts (such as the fight with the rural police and the *payada*) conceived in isolation, which nevertheless contribute to the "harmonic whole" of the work.[30] Another important unifying element is the perspective *through memory* of the entire work. He suggests that in the second canto of Part II there is a transition from lyric to narrative style and from the lyrical self-centeredness of Martín Fierro to his awareness of the complexities of life around him (I, 163). The last and most dramatic phase of that awareness is the *payada*, or encounter in song, between Fierro and the Negro, in which the theme of

---

[30] Martínez Estrada did not have access to the original manuscripts but he recalls that Carlos Alberto Leumann (an editor of the *Poem* and author of *El poeta creador*) had stated that the episodes of the fight and the *payada* do not appear in "the Manuscript." Presumably he means the manuscripts for the first editions, respectively of 1872 and 1879 (I, 154).

Martín Fierro's guilt is made explicit. Here (Part I, Canto 7) the brother of Fierro's victim reminds the protagonist of his crime, adding to the latter a psychological dimension that otherwise would have been missing. As Martínez Estrada claims (I, 168–169), the appearance of the dead Negro's brother at the end of the work is an important "bridge" between Parts I and II.

Part II ("La Vuelta" or "Return") also acquires symmetry as the protagonist ultimately falls back upon the same solitary, indecisive, and inconclusive state in which he had found himself at the beginning of Part I. "In the last cantos he turns to his solitude, for the advice he gives is in the manner of meditations and soliloquies. No one is in dialogue with him, and thus, as the *Poem* ends, he is once again the axis of its action, but in full deterioration, returning to the situation he had identified at the beginning, when, like a solitary bird, he had consoled himself by song" (I, 185). Martínez Estrada believes the "true ending" of the *Poem* occurs at the end of Part I, and that the addition—seven years later—of Part II was essential to the reader but not to Martín Fierro himself, clearly resigned to his destiny of loneliness and oblivion (I, 226). Actually, however, Part II is a reaffirmation of Part I; once again the protagonist (with three other characters) drifts into the unknown. The conclusion is therefore a *continuation*. Its message: life is a problem without solution, an unending purgatory. Or, in the essayist's own Kafkian terms, the vaguely biographical and testimonial nature of each of the characters gives "the impression of a world from which the defendant (*el procesado*) cannot escape" (I, 305).

The second and briefer part of Volume I discusses the "values" (I, 319) in the *Poem*. Despite the fact that "characters and objects are nearly abstractions" (I, 319), the author is convinced that in all Argentine literature only *The Poem of Martín Fierro* reveals Argentine life in the sense that Homer's epics and Shakespeare's plays revealed life in primitive Greece and Elizabethan England (I, 325). The *Poem* is an open invitation to critical analysis, mainly because it is, "much more than any other great work of literary significance, a work of omissions—incomplete, carried out in such a way that no form of action or psychology is conclusive; it is up to the reader to fill in what is missing" (I, 326).

In accordance with this very basic notion of the incompleteness of the *Poem* (possibly the most important stimulus he had for writing *Death and Transfiguration*), Martínez Estrada has outlined no less than seven "reader's attitudes" with which to confront Hernández's work (I, 328–335):

1. A superficial and literal reading by students, foreigners, and big-city dwellers.

2. A more attentive and detailed reading, which recognizes the collective and representative character of the protagonist, and which accepts Hernández's premise that Martín Fierro represents a dispossessed class. Like reading no. 1, this is a simplification. It is the favored approach of most Hispanic Americans and of "sociologists and ethnologists" in other countries.

3. A reading which, like the traditional reading of *Facundo*, gives first importance to the external forces of geography, race, and climate, unrecorded history, and national destiny. It emphasizes the the adjectival quality that Martínez Estrada ascribes to the world of the *Poem*, the importance of all that remains after the *substantive* elements (people and events) disappear.

4. The best and most complete reading. It requires cautious and sensitive complementation by the reader; the intervention of his own experience, intuition, and intelligence. As in the case of the *Divine Comedy, Don Quixote, Hamlet,* and *Faust,* this requirement for *The Poem of Martín Fierro* suggests the presence of a spiritual richness and depth of meaning that *Facundo*, for example, does not have to a comparable degree. Hernández brought his intimate experience and his familiarity with the gaucho's character and environment into the *Poem*. However, that experience and familiarity are sometimes barely insinuated, sometimes guarded in total silence, and it is up to the resourceful and knowledgeable reader to discover them.

5. A literary reading, by cultured persons, which seeks poetic values beneath the tough exterior of regional country language and Hernández's own syntactical and idiomatic inconsistencies. Careful

readings of this type reveal the essential harmony between Hernández and the world he describes.

6. The most defective and biased reading: by "justices of the peace,
army officers, commissioners, sentinels, politicians, statesmen." Such
a reading interprets Martín Fierro, his life, and surroundings as
concluded history, written in the tone of a quaint caricature for the
amusement of the thoughtless. These self-interested readers think of
Martín Fierro as a kind of curio doll, "which is what they are themselves" (I, 334).

7. An incomplete reading by women, whose failure is understandable. The work is totally "masculine." Women are forgotten in the
circumstances that have led to their abandonment; their fate is even
more desolate than that of the solitary, widowed, and virtually
celibate men. Nevertheless, women seem unaware of this stark reality
when they read the *Poem.*

In addition to this classification of reader types—objective by intention, critical in its expression—Martínez Estrada recommends
to every serious student of Argentine culture a series of three readings of the *Poem.* Such readings are a progression from the literal to
the symbolic, a progressive discovery, that is, of the hidden and
transcendental meanings of the work. He quotes Wilhelm Dilthey's
"Poetica"[31] to support his contention that the poetic value of the
work is due to its presentation of "living experience" (*vivencia,* a
favorite word of Martínez Estrada's), that is, experience transformed
into feeling. The form and the technique of *Martín Fierro* are simple,
unmusical, graceless, unpoetic. Yet there is poetry in the *existence*
of the characters—in their loneliness, their frustrations, and their
sadness "recollected in tranquility." In structure and substance the
work is a song, for like most songs, it is a remembrance, a reliving of
the past in the framework of the present. As Martínez Estrada puts
it, composing the work was a question of "feeling and understanding life which is lived and (at the same time) observed" (I, 341).
This is the great gift with which he believed Hernández was endowed.

[31] I, 340. *"Poetica"* is probably a reference to *Das Erlebnis und die Dichtung*
(Experience and Poetry).

Volume II is divided into two general topics, "The Frontier" and "The World of Martín Fierro." Actually, both sections deal with Martín Fierro's "world" as the basis for analyzing the problems of national culture. However, Volume II is less unified than Volume I. The material is more varied, because the topics discussed extend beyond the literary limits of the *Poem* to the social and historical spheres of Argentine life.[32] Again and again, Martínez Estrada launches his basic attack. Afflicted by a persistent psychological self-censorship and entangled in an intricate maze of social taboos, the Argentines have grown accustomed to deceiving themselves, to the point of believing that there is no important difference between what is authentic in life and what is simple affectation (II, 402–403). In this sense *Death and Transfiguration* is clearly a sequel to *X-Ray of the Pampa*. Volume II is an enumeration of themes, all of which are problems: the frontier, the Indian, the gaucho, the country vs. the city, poverty, political injustice, smallpox, and others. Many of these problems, the author feels, stemmed from the average Argentine's lack of sensitivity to his surroundings. Hypersensitive to the problems themselves, he was for the most part insensitive to the natural, psychological, and social realities that produced them. So, at least, thought Martínez Estrada.

It would be up to William Henry Hudson (1841–1922), in the essayist's opinion the most accomplished literary artist in nineteenth-century Argentina, to discover the landscape. Although Hudson abandoned his native land at the age of thirty-three and emigrated to England, in spirit he remained an Argentine. Having been born with both the outdoor naturalist's instinct and the story-teller's intuition of human motivations and having lived in close harmony with his environment, he offered the reader a much more complete interpretation of life in the countryside than did Hernández. Obsessed with the problematical themes discussed by Martínez Estrada in Volume II of *Death and Transfiguration*, Hernández passed over the beauties of his surroundings; his *vivencia*, limited to loneliness

---

[32] Symbolically, one section devoted to the description of customs of pampa life is a series of short chapters entitled "Miscellany" (II, 359–380).

and frustration, was not open to the meditations and sensitive relationships that those surroundings inspired in Hudson.

In Martínez Estrada's view, the stage across which the characters
of the *Poem* move is a no man's land of invisible forces.[33] Figuratively
and psychologically, Hernández himself was a gaucho, *the* gaucho,
on the defensive against those forces. As such, he retreated into the
cheerless allegory of *The Poem of Martín Fierro,* concerning himself
only with the gaucho's predicaments. But Martínez Estrada does not
condemn him for that retreat. On the contrary, he recognizes Hernández's somber message as a legitimate complaint, and he directs
his attack at readers of every generation from the 1880's to the
present for having taken it so lightly, for reacting as if the evils described had been limited to the *Poem* itself. Actually, "that which
among the wretched people of *Martín Fierro* was no more than petty
plunder and thievery was carried out on a grand scale by the State
with public and private lands" (II, 19). He directed his accusation
not only at the average reader but at such scholarly literary historians
as Eleuterio F. Tiscornia. Tiscornia interpreted Martín Fierro's abandonment of a nihilistic and anarchic life—abandonment that is
thrown open to very serious question by the enigmatic conclusion
of the work—as his gentle transformation into a first-class citizen
about to reap all the benefits of "the democratic reorganization of
the country." But neither Martín Fierro himself nor Martínez Estrada
accepted such a euphoric view. The fictional hero and his twentieth-
century interpreter saw no important transformation, no "democratic
reorganization," but only a grand illusion (II, 211).

On the other hand, the essayist refers disdainfully to the "pastoral
structure" of modern Argentina, showing that he has not accepted,
after all, the romantic naturalism and individualism of Hudson. In
the vast enumeration of national institutions, problems, and customs
that fills the second volume (the cow, the horse, the corral, the Indian
camps, the psychology of the gaucho, the general-store society,
smallpox, etc.), Martínez Estrada deplores the low esteem in which

[33] "As in Kafka's works, there are hierarchies or echelons of power that set
things in order, or disorder, similar to the fateful divinities of the Greeks" (II,
211).

the human being is held, "that lack of respect for one's fellow man" characteristic of those accustomed to thinking of "voters, tenants or subordinates as cattle" (II, 56). *Dehumanization* (not in the sense that Ortega y Gasset uses the term with reference to literature and art, that is, in the context of an aristocratic spirit in things aesthetic) was for Martínez Estrada the root of all evil and the principal inducement for his combative critical attitudes; dehumanization, that is, in the sense of deprivation, of the abasement of individual man, of cruelty and crime elevated to the level of social order and constitutional legality, of barbarity in the trappings of civilized life.

If dehumanization was the root of evil, chaos was the root of dehumanization. With abundant quotations from nineteenth-century historians, journalists, and travelers, he attempts to show the psychological consequences of a turbulent life in which Indians, gauchos, cattle, and horses drift like lost asteroids in space. His point seems to be that Indians, gauchos, cattle, and horses were considered basically the same: ideologically indistinguishable one from the other, for they were mere physical configurations of the "primitive forces" described in the third section of *X-Ray of the Pampa*. At any rate, the gaucho conscription that made so many gauchos fugitives, the civil wars and the Indian wars, the close association between man and beast, and the lack—even in the towns—of social cohesiveness, all had permanently divisive effects on the nation.

The main heritage was that of scorn and distrust. Violence was inbred for too long. Charles Darwin, whose *Diary* Martínez Estrada read with attention,[34] described in this way the plight of a group of Indians near the Chilean border in September 1833:

The Indians are now so terrified that they offer no resistance in body, but each escapes as well as he can, neglecting even his wife and children. The soldiers pursue and sabre every man. Like wild animals, however, they fight to the last instant. One Indian nearly cut off with his teeth the thumb of a soldier, allowing his own eye to be nearly pushed out of the socket. Another who was wounded, pretended death, with a knife under his cloak, ready to strike the first who approached. . . . This is a dark picture; but how much more shocking is the unquestionable fact that all the

[34] See *Death and Transfiguration*, II, 84, 130, 272, 334.

women who appear above twenty years old are massacred in cold blood. I ventured to hint that this appeared rather inhuman. He [Darwin's guide] answered me, "Why, what can be done? They breed so!" Every one here is fully convinced that this is the justest war, because it is against Barbarians. Who would believe in this age in a Christian civilized country that such atrocities were committed?[35]

More involved yet less sensitive than Darwin, Hernández made "ambivalent" appraisals of life on the pampa only a few decades later, "because he belonged to what, since 1880, was called the oligarchy, and he was a man of such vehement political passions that he could even resort to those expedient attitudes which, deep down, repelled him" (II, 137). Like the Martín Fierro of Part II, fresh from his victorious combat with the wild Indian, Hernández deceived himself, thinking that the final defeat of the Indians in the late 1870's signified also the end of all that was evil in public life.

The wretched Indian, of course, was not the only object of moral ambivalence. The gaucho too was to become the source of a literary admixture of light-hearted disdain and romantic compassion. The most probable etymology of *gaucho*, writes Martínez Estrada, is *haucho* ("orphan" in the Quechua Indian language), and orphan is the image that has stuck ever since. Steeped as he was in that negative tradition, the gaucho developed from generation to generation a strong feeling of inferiority and resentment. Essayists in other countries, including the Mexican liberal Samuel Ramos (1897–1959) and the nonmaterialistic Communist José Carlos Mariátegui of Peru (1895–1930), have also been concerned with this psychological phenomenon in writing about Mexican and Peruvian culture. Briefly, it can be said that the resurgence of interest in the native in several Hispanic American countries is part of a strong emergence of cultural nationalism. In the spirit of this nationalism the Spanish and indigenous origins are agonizingly reappraised. Curiously, the psychology of the downtrodden and the pariahs (the Indian, the cholo, the mestizo, the gaucho) finds new, articulate expression in the writers, intellectuals, and politicians of the mid-twentieth century.

[35] *Charles Darwin's Diary of the Voyage of H.M.S. Beagle,* ed. Nora Barlow, p. 171.

Martínez Estrada and his pessimistic disciples, H. A. Murena and Julio Mafud, have a double perspective. These men are objective in their analytic view and in their rejection of the facile glorifications of gaucho valor and independence. They are subjective in their assimilation, as if by infection, of the gaucho feeling of the dispossessed— extending their psychological image of the gaucho as the archetypal pariah to the whole political and social structure of the nation. Constantly on the outlook for excessive idealization, asserting that William Henry Hudson was the only nineteenth-century writer to use the truly "historical" gaucho as a literary model (II, 160), Martínez Estrada went to the other extreme, pointing out grave insufficiencies in the national character, all of which he thought were based on patriotic delusions of grandeur. He pleads for more continuity in historical thinking; one can not rightly consider the many testimonies of rural barbarism in the past century (Sarmiento, F. B. Head, Hernández, Hudson, Mansilla) as a closed book. In mid-twentieth century, the Argentine problem was not a new one, but the complication of an old one. (II, 178). "Formerly, the gaucho served in the ranks of tyranny and war against the Indian, without uttering a word of protest against his master, the ranch owner; he now serves the same tyranny, fighting against his master in the name of a hard-core organization of governmental and military caciques" (II, 185).

Martínez Estrada is also particularly subjective in adapting from Hernández and Hudson their aversion to cities and "civilization," insofar as civilization has come to mean to him the sacrifice of all natural virtues to a dehumanized commercial world. He reminds us that *The Poem of Martín Fierro* was born of the "inverse idea" of Sarmiento's *Facundo*. For Hernández—and for Martínez Estrada, as we shall see in the next chapter—Buenos Aires was not civilized man's outpost against rural barbarity but an overgrown den of iniquity, injustice, and discord (II, 207). However, the author of the *Poem* was too much immersed in the miseries of his world. Throughout *Death and Transfiguration* Hernández suffers by contrast with Hudson. As spokesman for "wild characters" born of a "wild society" and living in a "wild world" (II, 221), Hernández had no basis for evaluating them in the light of ideal standards. His poem was morally evasive; the half-truth of small-time criminality was offered as a substitute for facing the whole truth: the civil wars, the systemized robbery by government officials, the tacit acceptance by Martín Fierro and all Argentine society of the social evils that would regenerate and thrive in the modern period beginning in 1880. The ominous specter of Vizcacha, "the correct and well-adapted citizen" (II, 221), but also the model of amorality, is the personality of the future. Martín Fierro, the absolute solitary, fades into oblivion; Vizcacha, *maestro* in persuasion and deceit, leaves his monumental testament of defensive and selfish living to future generations. He is the embryo of Argentina's participation in the "industrial civilization" of the West so consistently denounced by Hudson and Martínez Estrada. The nation has remembered Vizcacha's advice as "the best attuned to the nature of things" (II, 222).

In the extensive section entitled "The Historical Sphere" (II, 196–292), the longest in the book, Martínez Estrada supplies what Hernández has left unsaid, commenting extensively on politics, caudillos, life in the *pulpería* or general store, the gauchos and Indians as underdogs, the popular disdain of everything indigenous, and what the author considers to have been "the natural state of injustice" in gaucho society (II, 278), simple prelude to the complex "organized banditry" he presents as the essence of the twentieth-century state. In the pampa society of Argentina, as in contemporary Western society as a whole, he believes with Kafka that "the victims of the law themselves, like Martín Fierro, Cruz, and Picardía, beget the injustice they suffer" (II, 287). Referring directly to Kafka on the following page, he states that it is natural for the victim to provoke the aggressor, and "the despot is a deification of the spirit of slavery." Injustice, in the most universal sense, is in his opinion the fundamental theme of the *Poem* (II, 283) and, we could add, the theme that links it with some of the great works of Western literature, particularly those of Kafka, Rousseau, Dostoyevsky, Thoreau, and Cervantes. Ironically, however, Hernández was no seer or prophet. Blindness to justice is presented in the *Poem* as "a normal state," a reason for which Martínez Estrada's expansive two-volume essay was especially necessary. Hernández *revealed* what he could not *see*.

"The Frontier" comprises about two-thirds of Volume II. The title suggests a demarcation of thought, as well as of geographic areas. Hernández and the characters of his poem lived in a "frontier world," which was also a crucial point in historical time. Martín Fierro's farewell, his separation from his sons and Picardía, and their common decision to change their names did not signify the end of a way of life but a transformation.

The second and final part of Volume II is "The World of Martín Fierro." It begins with an enumeration of themes in the *Poem* that had previously appeared in Spanish, gaucho, and world literature. Negative themes (fraud, torture, death, marital infidelity, punishment—human and divine) predominate, as one might expect, over the positive (companionship, courage, consistency in character and purpose). Martínez Estrada thinks that there is probably an influence of Lope de Vega's narrative poem *Saint Isidro of Madrid* (1599) on *Martín Fierro*. In the passages quoted from Lope's work (II, 301–303), one can see that the expression of the popular spirit, the simple philosophy of life, and the lamentations on the past misfortunes are stylistically quite similar to those in Hernández's poem. Most important, however, is the picaresque tradition—that of Cervantes' *Rinconete y Cortadillo*, or Francisco de Quevedo's *Life of the Sharper*. The author stresses (II, 304) the solitary aspects of picaresque life (restlessness, the antisocial feeling, the orphan complex) as more influential, in the long run, than the moralistic aspects (vice, fraud, aggressiveness, disdain of human values). Nevertheless, Vizcacha is more the product of Hernández's own experience than of any combination of literary antecedents. Martínez Estrada is right in calling this unforgettable rogue unique in literature (II, 309). As he points out in the first volume (I, 411–412), Vizcacha is the only character thoroughly adapted to the adversities and corruption described in the *Poem*. Vizcacha thrives on the ubiquitous degeneracy of which he forms an integral part, "perpetuating the system by taking advantage of it."

Martínez Estrada finds special significance in the characters' almost complete lack of nobility and generosity of spirit. Their vital experience can be summed up, in the essayist's apt phrase, as oscillating between "the attitude of the attacker and that of the attacked" (II, 322). Thus, he dwells mostly on those themes which, in his mind, explain the permanent problem of Argentine society, such as poverty, mass Indian attacks, counterattacks by whites, knife duels between gauchos, and captive women. Life was a school of violence. In the endless struggle between the civilized and the savage, historians and chroniclers partial to the "civilized" were seldom defenders of "justice and decency" (II, 349). The only nonviolent theme, "The Golden Age" or nostalgia for an idyllic past, was not developed by Hernández as it was by Hudson, but it was repeatedly implied. The continuing antagonism with which the urban dwellers and inhabitants of the provinces consider each other is traceable to the total separation (ideological separation) between city and country in Martín Fierro's time. But neither the city dwellers nor the country people seemed to realize, says Martínez Estrada, that barbarism permeated the cities while the most corrupt aspects of civilization spoiled the country (II, 320–321).

Conclusion

Death and Transfiguration of Martín Fierro is without doubt the most sensitive, exhaustive, and thoughtful study that has been written on the *Poem*. But, beyond a study, it is a memorable testimony of the author's own poetic despair turned into meditative discourse. As in *X-Ray of the Pampa*, Martínez Estrada has approached his subject in a seemingly clinical manner and used Hernández's silences and omissions as well as his affirmations in order to round out the analysis. The characters of *The Poem of Martín Fierro* are solitary, unambitious, self-pitying, dispossessed, mere shadow-pictures of what might have been full and dynamic lives; but the poignancy of their obscure existences is nevertheless felt. The special eloquence Martínez Estrada adds through his pessimism and subdued desperation increases that poignancy. Although the following passage refers to Martín Fierro's life and times, it seems obvious that it also is an expression of the essayist's emotional philosophy: "In this poem the love sentiment is perhaps very great, but it is lost in the void, spilled out like tears over missing persons and the dead of the past.

We see how a family is destroyed by the mechanical action of things, events and persons that contribute to the work no more than an unequivocal yet hidden will to destroy" (II, 389). The whole panorama of national life he sees reflected in the *Poem* constitutes a tragedy, for the characters are the unknowing agents of "dissolving and destructive forces" (II, 408). As in Kafka's "The Great Wall of China," Martínez Estrada points out, the inhabitants of the pampa portrayed in the *Poem* work for a distant and archaic authority, no longer even existent. Nevertheless they follow orders like automatons. Each person could be replaced by another, and the replacement would act and react in the same way. "That is the most intensely tragic note of the *Poem*" (II, 409). Although José Hernández never consciously adopted such a philosophy, his interpreter believes that, through some kind of intuition, he tacitly expressed it.

First published in 1948, though composed over an eight-year period, *Death and Transfiguration of Martín Fierro* has stirred less controversy among the author's compatriots than *X-Ray of the Pampa*. If the world-view in *Death and Transfiguration* is just as bleak as that of *X-Ray*, the general tone is less combative. Skepticism and resignation have increased with age, and with the violent course of events from 1933 to 1948. Some readers had begun to sense, by the time *Death and Transfiguration* was published, a meaningful relationship between the dire prophecies of *X-Ray* and current history. Others had simply seen the author's ambitious attempt to "interpret Argentine life" through the looking-glass of *Martín Fierro* as but one more chapter in his continuing chronicle of bitterness. With or without his readers' approval he was not disposed to recant. The last sentence of the epilogue to the 1958 edition of *Death and Transfiguration* ("When we know what country we live in and with whom we live, we shall know what we are and what we must do") has the same meaning as the last sentence of *X-Ray*. Hernández and Hudson, each in his own intuitive way, began the work of national self-discovery. Martínez Estrada felt the need to continue and adjust their candid undertaking to twentieth-century circumstances.

5 · Homo Urbanus

Ultrahumanity

"A large city is a thing against nature," wrote Rilke, and Martínez Estrada used that opinion as an epigraph for *The Head of Goliath*.[1] This book is an idealistic rejection of Buenos Aires, the mammoth metropolis, a diatribe against the modern city. But it is also a poetic

---

[1] *La cabeza de Goliat: Microscopía de Buenos Aires.* "Buenos Aires, with its suburbs, sits on the banks of the Río de la Plata as a rough half circle whose radius measures some 18 miles. Here live 30 percent of the Argentine people. . . . Few cities so dominate a country as does this sparkling 'Paris of South America.' Fifty-five percent of the nation's imports and 40 percent of its exports funnel across Buenos Aires docks. Railroads and highways radiate from the city to tap the countryside. Within the metropolitan area are half the nation's industrial plants, employing three-fifths of all its workers and producing seven-tenths of all its products" (Jules B. Billard, "Buenos Aires, Argentina's Melting-pot Metropolis," *National Geographic* 132, no. 5 [Nov. 1967]: 664–665).

appreciation of the Argentine capital. As such, it is one of the finest examples of the author's prose. The eighty-seven meditative essays that make up the work are widely varied in subject matter, unified in emotion and attitude.

Like *X-Ray of the Pampa*, *The Head of Goliath* is a serious pretext for writing on the all-pervading solitude of contemporary man. Society, architecture, music, dress, and modern conveniences all bear the stamp of this solitude. Man lives out his life paying the interminable debt of his own idiosyncracies. According to Martínez Estrada, man is not so much the mirror of his environment as is his environment the mirror of himself. In essential agreement with Marshall McLuhan's concepts of "the extensions of man," the Argentine essayist sees the human life process as a universal transformation of the individual's basic psychological impulses into the collective circumstances that we commonly call society or environment. Thus, man is not—as most naturalists would have it—the product of his surroundings so much as he is the victim of his media or peculiar modes of expression: his telephone, his automobile, the façades of his buildings, his music, and the political structures to which—at least formally—he adheres. To put it still more simply, he is the victim of himself magnified.

Although Martínez Estrada scorns almost every aspect of city life, he finds a basic similarity between city and country environments. The man of the plains, like the urban inhabitant, is the victim of his primitive past. Far from solving the problems of modern man, the highly organized city complicates them; the city, in a far more expressive way than the country, is the cumulative synthesis of his past and present aberrations. If a large city is, as Rilke believes, "a thing against nature," it is so because it is *excessively human.* History is not lacking in examples of the "inhuman" and the "dehumanized." But one can easily see that in the most extreme examples—the most terrifying massacres and the most frightful cruelties—a strictly human ingenuity or perversion, characterisic of no animal, machine, or cosmic force in nature, is at the heart of the matter. The illusion of the "inhuman" is surely due to the collective neurosis that has transformed individual traits and desires into strange and incomprehen-

sible social and economic phenomena. The urban tempo, urban over-
crowding, the inharmonious variety of urban sights and sounds, the
sense of aggressive competition that one encounters in urban social
and professional life all contribute directly to the neurosis.

Only because of this special tempo, disharmony, and aggressiveness does one feel alienated by the city. Martínez Estrada observes, however, that the inhabitant of the provinces who arrives in
Buenos Aires recognizes quite easily the fact that Buenos Aires "is
the sublimation—in the form of dreams, one might say—of all that
[i.e., life in the provinces]; that it is the great capital of the south, for
even though Buenos Aires is the decapitated head of that immense
body, it still is anatomically and physiologically related to it."[2] Like
Lewis Mumford, he has seen the evolution of modern industrial cities
as a series of large social miscarriages. It is the decay, the blind struggle for individual survival, the dissipation of individual endeavor, and
the resultant aimlessness of life in the city that has most impressed
him. Mumford shares his impressions with the same propensity to
convert the real into the symbolic. Consider, for example, the North
American's bleak view and his tragic implications for the future:

> Circle over London, Buenos Aires, Chicago, Sydney, in an airplane, or
> view the cities schematically by means of an urban map and block plan.
> What is the shape of the city and how does it define itself? The original
> container has completely disappeared: the sharp division between city and
> country no longer exists. As the eye stretches toward the hazy periphery
> one can pick out no definite shapes except those formed by nature: one
> beholds rather a continuous shapeless mass. . . .
> Failing to divide its social chromosomes and split into new cells, each
> bearing some portion of the original inheritance, the city continues to grow
> inorganically, indeed cancerously, by a continuous breaking down of old
> tissues, and an overgrowth of formless new tissue.[3]

Like life in the country, city life produces its archetypes. But the
country archetypes are in generally simpler circumstances, as far as
their *human* relationships are concerned, and they live in generally

[2] *Cabeza*, p. 95. The author had already referred to Buenos Aires as "a decapitated head" in *X-Ray of the Pampa*, p. 67.
[3] Lewis Mumford, *The City in History*, p. 543.

better harmony with their surroundings than do their city counter-
parts. The city is not "inhuman" but ultra-human. Aggression, crime,
vice, and neurosis are aggravated wherever humanity is heavily
concentrated—a principal theme of "The Deluge," an important short
story by Martínez Estrada to be discussed later. Sensibilities are
exacerbated, frustrations unexplainable, ambitions unsatisfiable.
Martínez Estrada thus speaks of the country archetype—the gaucho,
Martín Fierro—as a "transfigured" being, one who has brought his
primitive manner, his animal-like, instinctive defensiveness, his antisocial attitude, his personal pride, and his solitude, to the alien environment of the city.

In the city things are inevitably worse, a conclusion anticipated by
William Henry Hudson and later confirmed by a wide variety of
Argentine authors, including Manuel Gálvez, Eduardo Mallea, Julio
Mafud and Raúl Scalabrini Ortiz. "The man at the corner of Corrientes and Esmeralda," the archetype of Buenos Aires characterized
by Scalabrini Ortiz, is the Argentine mass-man who inhabits the
spirit of each of his compatriots; in a sense, he is the gaucho transfigured. Like Martínez Estrada, Scalabrini Ortiz enumerates the defensive and narcissistic qualities of the modern *porteño*. Like the
plainsman, the man of Corrientes and Esmeralda "recognizes no landscape around him," and the four adjectives that best describe the
gaucho ("idle," "taciturn," "long-suffering," and "arrogant") also
characterize the *porteño*, for Buenos Aires is "again the capital of
the countryside."[4] But like the gaucho, his urban descendant has
been portrayed by these authors as a man notably lacking in will and
self-respect.

Eduardo Mallea has defined contemporary man's dignity in the
terms of his capacity for "resistance" to his circumstances: "I admire
only those who *resist* in the wilderness of life, in the cities, in villages,
in uninhabited places, those who refuse to let themselves decay.
What I've been telling you about is the process by which one acquires
a taste for struggle."[5] Martínez Estrada recognized no such strength

---

[4] Raúl Scalabrini Ortiz, *El hombre que está solo y espera*, pp. 50–51.
[5] The words are those of Lintas, Mallea's protagonist in *Fiesta en noviembre*,
p. 129.

in the men of his time. Those few earnest ones whom he admired, such as Leopoldo Lugones and Horacio Quiroga, who took their own lives, were destined to fail. No man could thrive, he believed, in the city, for the city was like an infinite multiplication of oneself transformed into enemies. The city was a long and complex metamorphosis of primitive man that slowly and painfully had acquired the label of civilization.

The Head of Goliath

The world was a prison for Martínez Estrada, as it was for Kafka. He associated Buenos Aires, where he so reluctantly spent the most productive part of his life (1916–1947), with the drudgery of his job in the Central Post Office, with the confined atmosphere of apartment living, his economic worries, and the chaotic political life of his country since the late 1920's. Buenos Aires was a prison, full of movement, but the centripetal movement of individual and social frustrations. Hudson in *The Purple Land* and *Far Away and Long Ago* had added to his historical nostalgia for country living and his aversion to city life. Dostoyevsky and Balzac had increased his sensitivity to the hardships of city life. Yet it cannot be emphasized too much that Martínez Estrada, in continually criticizing Buenos Aires, was denouncing an allegedly very serious void in Argentine cultural life—not so much the hardships as the false fronts, the human malice, and the self-delusions with which Buenos Aires seemed to him to have infected Argentine culture. "The same phenomenon which in the political sphere causes the country to revolve around the metropolis like a nearly-extinguished satellite has also occurred in literature; because our literature is, in every sense, metropolitan, urban and bureaucratic. One cannot fail to consider Buenos Aires as a literary work—magnificent perhaps—in which we exhibit somewhat as in a store window our riches, our culture and our well-being."[6] The author goes on to say that this "metropolitan" literature fails to deal with the underlying conflicts of national life and history, that the Argentine critical sense is limited to the art of parody and a rather simplistic

[6] *Para una revisión de las letras argentinas*, p. 84.

didacticism, and that "our eternal tendency to deify some figure"[7] has consistently evaded reality.

Martínez Estrada began his extensive treatment of the Buenos Aires theme—one of the three or four basic themes of his life work— in Chapter IV of X-Ray of the Pampa. However, in that famous book Buenos Aires was an integral part of his general thesis of historical degeneration: the city without a historical past, a place for the collective adaptation of "primitive forces" to modern civilization, the most monumental symbol of what Julio Mafud, as an attentive reader of Martínez Estrada and Simone Weil, was later to call Argentine "uprootedness." In one sense, The Head of Goliath is a continuation of that thesis. In another less systematic and more artistic sense, it is a series of meditations in which the sensitivity and creative power of the writer is more strikingly apparent. The subtitle, Microscopía de Buenos Aires, contrasts with the X-Ray of the previous work, suggesting a less theoretic and more intimate and realistic approach to the raw material about to be recreated. Less shadow-picture, more concrete detail. In X-Ray of the Pampa one has the impression that the author is overwhelmed by his subject matter, or rather, his thesis. In The Head of Goliath the author is a free agent, and we feel that the atmosphere he describes and his own sensitivity are much better coordinated.

The sense of artistic freedom in these meditations makes them literarily superior not only to X-Ray of the Pampa but to every other essay that he wrote. This is not to suggest that a central thesis is lacking; on the contrary, it is stated and restated, like the recurring motifs of a Beethoven symphony, and is succinctly summed up in a sentence of his 1946 prologue to the second edition: "Buenos Aires is the first obstacle to understanding our history, and our history is the most formidable of all obstacles for understanding our reality."[8] Ten years later, in the aftermath of the recently overthrown Perón regime, he attaches new political significance to the book: "every po-

---

[7] Ibid., p. 88. This tendency is particularly evident, according to Martínez Estrada, in The Poem of Martín Fierro—a point I have tried to make clear in Chapter IV.

[8] Cabeza, "Introducción a la segunda edición" (May 1946), pp. 9–10.

litical party is a cancerous outgrowth of a big city."[9] In these prologues and in the text itself Buenos Aires is subjected with cruel repetitiveness to the role of a Protean monster, always different in its self-revelations, always the same in its effects on the sensitive inhabitant.

But it is not this concept of monster-city and victim-inhabitant that gives Martínez Estrada's work its deepest unity. Rather, as in the case of his best poetry (e.g., *Humorescas*, 1929), it is the somber personal view, the radical solitude, and the obsession with death that hold the eighty-seven inspired essays together. Together they constitute a *meditatio mortis*, and the writer's tragic vision seems to infect with the force of a plague everything he contemplates.

The Head of Goliath is the ideological continuation of Chapter IV of *X-Ray of the Pampa*, in which Martínez Estrada initiates his sustained lament for metropolitan Buenos Aires. It is there that he presents for the first time the theme of collective solitude in city life: the tango as the urban dance of solitaries, in which each partner is absorbed in a kind of narcissistic trance; the annual carnival festivities of the city, actually a way of covering up, with masks and contrived gaiety, the true desolation of the Argentine spirit; the prison-like aspect of the closely spaced buildings and narrow streets, and so forth. In a cogent critique of Martínez Estrada's personal philosophy, Ludovico Ivanissevich Machado underscores his apparent refusal to consider *himself* part of the world and the universe that he so nihilistically interprets:

> The intellectual chastity of Don Ezequiel has made him the archetype of the autonomous man of our time. Autonomous as far as his corrupt fellow men and God are concerned. But this autonomy may have taken consistency from his thought. Doesn't man consist of re-ligation [*re-ligación*], of religion, as Zubiri believes? Isn't our being inevitably a being in God? Isn't it possible, as Toynbee believes, that civilizations are simply provinces of theology?[10]

In justice to Martínez Estrada, however, it must be said that this

[9] Ibid., "Prólogo a la tercera edición" (June 1956), p. 11.
[10] "El puritanismo en Martínez Estrada," *Ciudad* 1 (Buenos Aires, 1955): 23.

cruel autonomy or unfraternal independence of spirit so prevalent in *X-Ray of the Pampa* is for the most part absent in *The Head of Goliath*. His whole work, from the poetry and the unpublished treatise on the art of chess of the 1920's, to the essays and fiction of the 1940's and 1950's, is a steady gravitation from the metaphysical to the real, a progressive humanization. In *The Head of Goliath* the author continues to subject reality to preconception, but he has broken the theoretical barrier that makes his world-view such a partial one in *X-Ray*. In the skillful essays on Buenos Aires, the great city comes alive with its own sights, sound, and tempo; Martínez Estrada is dealing directly with *people* and their habitat. If Ernesto Sábato is right in saying that Martínez Estrada should have been a novelist,[11] there is substantiation for his judgment in the presentation of human types and situations throughout *The Head of Goliath*; for here, much more than in any previous work, the author lives in the atmosphere and with the people he describes. Had he devoted more of his efforts to narrative fiction *The Head of Goliath* might well have been subtitled "A Novelist's Notebook"; not a notebook in the relatively erudite sense of Eduardo Mallea's *Notes of a Novelist*, but rather in the Balzacian sense of scenes and experiences recollected—festivals, soccer games, life on Florida Street, the author's domesticated sparrow, the description of representative types of Buenos Aires, and life in a hospital ward. Martínez Estrada's image of Leopoldo Lugones, the great Argentine poet who committed suicide in 1938 and who served many years as director of the Library of the National Council of Education, is worth quoting at some length, for it strikingly reveals the essayist's novelistic talent:

Lugones worked there for many years. In his little office, without waiting rooms or clerks, without a car, without family help, without special authority, he passed the greater part of his luminous life. In the afternoons a few friends would visit him, in search of the great gift of his spoken word. Sometimes his conversations were interrupted by the sound of the buzzer by which his superiors summoned him. Lugones would then leave to receive orders and instructions from those above. Once I found him, in

<hr />

[11] From an interview between Sábato and the writer in Buenos Aires in August 1966.

a typical season of our bad climate, rubbing his hands by the heater, his
hair almost entirely white, his suit scrupulously clean but threadbare from
his sedentary chores. Cold, old age and poverty. Within me I felt the sorrow and shame of 12 million human beings together, and a strong desire
to throw myself on the floor and to scream.

On the wall behind his desk a large portrait of W. H. Hudson, with his
noble and saintly visage of a bird of prey, watched over the imprisonment
of that other bird, the most brilliant and melodious of all our history: his
poor captive son. In the desk drawers, a few pages of manuscript written at
home so as not to steal time from his job, nor to contaminate his dutiful
activity with the bureaucrat's ink. Verses among booksellers' bills.[12]

The Head of Goliath is divided into four parts, but, unlike *X-Ray*
and *Death and Transfiguration*, it is not systematically organized.
Roughly, it can be said that the twenty-five essays of Part I deal with
the city itself—in its more physical aspects—and the symbolic meaning that the author finds in those aspects. Buenos Aires, the giant's
head attached to an undersized and sickly body, was not originally
a giant's head; it has grown to its present proportions by "absorbing
the life blood of the body" (p. 29). The giant's head is also the head
of an octopus, and the eight railroad stations in Buenos Aires extend
their "tentacles" out into the provinces of the nation in search of food,
"the only real and positive contact between Buenos Aires and the
Republic." Finally, "the spider also has eight legs" (pp. 38–39). The
city is the vortex of a continuous and futile circulatory movement
of pedestrian, cyclist, automobile, and subway, and the driver of
automobiles, taxis, and buses is a degenerate descendant of the
gaucho horseman. The city is "an immense apartment house in which
no one is interested in anything" (p. 63), a theme developed later
in the short story "The Stairway."[13]

"Borremos las huellas" ("Let's Erase Our Footsteps") is probably
the most representative essay in Part I. It stresses the provisional
and temporary quality of all activities and projects in Buenos Aires.
"We had a past without art, without substance and without dignity,

---

[12] *Cabeza*, p. 250. Subsequent references in the text to this edition are by
page number only.
[13] Included in *La tos y otros entretenimientos*, and in *Antología*.

for things were not built, as in Rome, to last forever, but only to remain the short time that our adventure would last" (p. 75). In place of constructiveness, there existed a "desire to mutilate." Martínez Estrada discerned no progress—only mutilation—in the constant destruction or defacement of the old in the name of the new. The "spectacular grandeur" of new buildings, streets, and monuments was purely "fictitious" (pp. 80–81). His conclusion is the basic conclusion of the whole work: "In reality, Buenos Aires is a great machine which produces income but works neither with nor for the nation. Brutally and blindly it absorbs the wealth of the interior, devours incredible appropriations and eats as if to feed an entire giant through the mouth of its severed head. It feeds on misery and backwardness, ignorance and loneliness. Buenos Aires is a wall on the urban horizon which prevents one from seeing the rest of the country" (p. 81).

Part II, the longest, consists of twenty-eight essays. Together with Part III, it is the most novelistic and the most intimate in its view of human beings. In addition to admirable sketches of the postmen, drivers, policemen, car watchers,[14] street cleaners, and poets, the author describes the *tilingo*, a strange social species of large cities, particularly Buenos Aires. The *tilingo* is a dilettante, dandy, and parasite, the first to arrive at a party and the last to leave. He dresses well, sings, recites poetry, and knows the latest news. Despite his charm, however, he is an idiot who simplifies the complex and complicates the simple. "He would be an interesting person in a world that was not worth living in" (p. 176).

Recalling Alexis Carrel's judgment that man tends always to prefer the weak to the strong (p. 153), including the sick, the criminal, and the mad, the author comments on some of the "representative men" in the history of Buenos Aires. Only one (Hipólito Irigoyen, president of the Republic) was a man of some stature. The great majority—General Eusebio, Juan Manuel de Rosas' court jester; *el Negro Raúl*, an emancipated slave ("last vestige of colonial servi-

[14] The car watcher (*cuidador de coches*) is a well-known figure in most Latin American cities. His function is to protect parked cars, for which the driver pays a small voluntary fee.

tude") who became the fashionable adviser for many political personages and whose popularity was due to "the stupidity of his protectors" (p. 154); Carlos Gardel, the tango singer; Roura, an insignificant bank teller who became an embezzler of distinction, among others—came into prominence from the obscure regions of society and contributed little or nothing of positive value to history. True idols are not men of achievement and virtue but rather those who appeal to the hidden subliminal desires of the rest of us. Accordingly, Martínez Estrada remarks, few proper persons, or even such quasi-proper persons as politicians and popular writers have achieved the fame of John Dillinger in New York, Al Capone in Chicago, or Scarfó in Buenos Aires (p. 158).

Repeatedly the author reminds us that the agglomeration of people, customs, and private interests in Buenos Aires has made the city chaotic rather than systematic in its social structure (p. 148). Whatever unity that may exist is not voluntary but circumstantial. The combination of urban economics and special situations ("stadiums," churches, professional meetings, processions, political gatherings") brings people inevitably together. If humanity is a unity, biologically or socially speaking, it is not a unity in any ideological or spiritual sense: "What is lacking among these heterogeneous masses of varied backgrounds and inclinations is an ideal adaptable to reality, a reality meaningful enough to influence them, and those ideals cannot exist without love, love for the people and things that constitute the world in which we are rooted" (p. 148).

In one of the beautiful essays on birds in Part III[15] Martínez Estrada deplores the lack of free birds in Buenos Aires. The "ant-like farmers" among the colonists and, later, the immigrants, steadily destroyed the Argentine bird population. Quoting Hudson's The Naturalist in La Plata at length (pp. 231–233) he contends that man's inherent destructiveness has revealed itself in the average Argentine's indifference to nature and cruelty toward birds. His point

[15] "Birds" ("Pájaros"), pp. 230–234. Others in the same section are "Nests of the Birds of Paradise" ("Nidos de aves paradisíacas"), pp. 224–230; "Sparrows" (Gorriones"), pp. 234–238; "Pigeons and Swallows" ("Palomas y golondrinas"), pp. 238–240. The influence of William Henry Hudson is noticeable throughout.

here and in all other parts of the book where he comments on the forgotten world of Argentine nature is that the Argentine has consistently failed to recognize that world as his most authentic reality, preferring to build for himself the false world of illusions embodied in modern Buenos Aires. The *porteños* are indirectly portrayed as victims of anonymous forces in the ghoulish chapter on the nineteenth-century epidemics (pp. 194–198); in the chapter on the radio ("la voz del diablo") as a form of collective masochism ("la vocación natural del hombre es la mortificación tanto como el placer" [p. 200]); and in the last chapter of Part II (pp. 203–208), where sexuality in its infinite sublimated forms is identified as the atrophied vital force behind city life. To add to his general picture of tragic frustration the author reflects Freud's influence in concluding that "every great city is a neurosis of anguish caused by frustrated sexual activity," and that civilization can be defined as "the measurable distance between the initial sexual impulse and the total satisfaction of the same" (p. 207). For Buenos Aires no possibility of anything like "total satisfaction" exists, for Buenos Aires, we are reminded, does not express the forceful and free sexuality of Wagner, but the suppressed, anxious, and sublimated sexuality of Nietzsche (p. 207). Sexuality plus neurosis equals urban civilization.

Parts III and IV are considerably shorter than Parts I and II. The essays on birds contained in Part III are written under the influence (which borders on fascination) of William Henry Hudson. The sparrow, "of all birds, the most natural inhabitant of Buenos Aires," hops about "with a hereditary distrust, after so many years of persecution" (pp. 234–235). The sparrow reflects the human being's nervousness and skepticism and, like man, has attuned its existence to the humdrum rhythm of city life. By contrast, the graceful swallow, having nothing but the beauty of its flight to show humanity, has found no home in Buenos Aires. Only on one occasion, in 1932, did the city experience the miracle of thousands and thousands of swallows on its horizon, soon to disappear "when man's eyes began to focus upon them, and the fascination of contemplation began to change into an urge to shoot" (p. 240).

City life is a tragic experience, whether it is seen in the perspective of its birds, its buildings and streets, or its forlorn and forgotten souls. Without doubt, the most poignant and depressing essay in the book is "Descent into Hell" (pp. 251–254), in which the author describes a hospital ward for patients with incurable ailments. Although he is not mentioned by name in this particular piece, the friend visited by the author over a period of five months, "one of the dearest and perhaps most indispensable persons in my life," was Horacio Quiroga, who committed suicide in February 1937. Martínez Estrada's recollection of those visits is concentrated into a literary nightmare of four pages, a tragic vision of hospital beds, the occupants of which appear with different faces but with the same fate, united in the same unnatural purgatory. "A hospital is a nightmare, just as an idyll of love is a dream" (p. 252). Their only individuality consisted in the grotesqueness or deformity caused by their illness.

The twenty essays of the fourth and last part constitute the shortest section (forty-seven pages) of the book. Notwithstanding the loosely organized character of the work as a whole, Part IV is a fitting conclusion, because it is the gloomiest, a finale of despair that is a logical epilogue to the rest. Parts I, II, and III are the author's imaginary pilgrimage toward death. Part IV is the image of death itself. Death, in the most flexible sense, is not devoid of a certain entertainment value, and Martínez Estrada in most of *The Head of Goliath* has referred to it consistently if indirectly. Aside from the cemetery, the plagues, and hospital and funeral scenes, which are a direct contemplation of the other world, he has almost invariably chosen variations on the theme of extinction—people and things that used to be: birds, flower girls, public urinals, flophouses, reminiscences of a more genteel age along the tree-lined lanes of Palermo Park;[16] or people and things that are ephemeral to the extent of almost not existing, such as the young *porteño* dandy, buildings and streets that are razed to make way for new buildings and streets, large and opulent government offices, and the elevation to the status of temporary idols of the dubious personalities previously mentioned (embezzlers, clowns, and tango singers). But, most of

[16] "Palermo is still a fiesta with guests who have forgotten the purpose of their visit" ("Visitas al ausente," Part I, p. 91).

all, death is insinuated in the agitated tempo, the aimlessness and the pathos of little lives: the dying patient with a tumor on his back the size of a set of bagpipes (p. 254); the young office girls who eat alone in cheap cafeterias, remaining there a little longer than necessary, reading or applying lipstick, because there is no place to go for the rest of the lunch hour (p. 116); the traditional lack of dignity in the suicides of Buenos Aires compared with those of the Japanese and the classical Romans (pp. 302–303).

Part IV is an account of the anxious spirit of a city in which everything is described as if it were part of a universal catharsis of that city's inhabitants. The sports stadiums on Sundays become the scene of collectively, almost ritually, released passion. Soccer fans go to their games with the same "cathartic need" as the religious who attend church or—in another time—as the Greeks who participated in Dionysian rites:

> The passion that boils in soccer stadiums releases all the integrating forces of personality: religion, nationality, rancor, political persuasion, revenge, frustrated ambitions, love and hate—all on the verge of a delirium —in a molten, burning mass. Progressively the players set free, or exacerbate or hold back those igneous liquids, as if guiding them toward the dikes, ditches and channels within which the torrent finally takes form (p. 287).

The ways in which *porteños* continually try to remove themselves from reality in carnivals, at the movies, in stadiums, on weekends, and at spectacular but generally unemotional funerals—all of this against a background of vague sadness—is the central theme of the most representative essays in Part IV: "The Return" (the return home of vacationing families on late Sunday afternoon, riding trains, buses, and trolley cars); "Turning Over in Bed" (i.e., "renewing oneself"—"Renew thyself or perish," said D'Annunzio and Rodó—by doing something over the weekend, even though the novelty of weekend experiences is mainly illusory, and the restless celebrant returns basically unchanged to the usual grind on Monday); "The Pomp of the Dead" (the most insignificant person can count on one luxury for sure: his funeral); "Stadiums" (see above); "The Race

Track" (on the addictive ritual of betting, now devoid of all sporting and aesthetic appreciation of that once semidivine creature among Argentines, the horse).[17] With the years the hectic movement and the sound and the fury of the metropolis increase, and the overall situation adds up to a panorama of civilization in steady yet unending ruin. An anecdote from his chapter on dogs and cats in Buenos Aires reflects quite well the author's skepticism on city civilization: "The director of a government office bought a lot of cats some years ago to defend the archives against rodents. Later on, since additional funds were not forthcoming, he decided to sell the archives in order to feed the cats" (p. 308).

Fiction

The panorama of steady yet unending ruin is also the underlying theme of Martínez Estrada's fiction, written between 1943 and 1957 and published in four volumes.[18] With the exception of "Juan Florido and Son, Printers,"[19] started and completed just before and just after the author's four-year illness (1951–1955), and the material included in *The Cough and Other Divertissements* (1957), which he wrote after his recovery, the stories were written between 1943 and 1949. These seven pieces are clearly his best fiction, produced in the decade of the 1940's, when Martínez Estrada was at the peak of his literary power. Little attention has been given to his stories,[20] more because of his very justifiable fame as an essayist than because of any factor, positive or negative, of the stories themselves.

[17] The essays, in order mentioned, are: "Regreso," pp. 290–291; "Una vuelta en el lecho," pp. 292–293; "La pompa del muerto," pp. 293–297; "Estadios," pp. 286–290; and "Hipódromo," pp. 284–285. Three of these ("Hipódromo," "Estadios," "Regreso") were published for the first time in the second edition of *La cabeza de Goliat* (1946).

[18] *Tres cuentos sin amor* (includes "La Inundación," first published by Emecé, Buenos Aires, 1943); *Sábado de gloria*; *Marta Riquelme*; and *La tos y otros entretenimientos*.

[19] "Juan Florido, padre e hijo, minervistas." This story is included together with "Sábado de gloria" in the volume of that title, pp. 81–121.

[20] Juan Carlos Ghiano, while acknowledging their power and the significance of their author's philosophical attitude, is generally critical of these stories ("vitalmente truncas"). He finds too much adversity presented with such persistent regularity that it wears down the reader's sensitivity ("Martínez Estrada, narrador," *Ficción* no. 4 [Nov.–Dec. 1956]: 139–148).

However, it is in the stories that Martínez Estrada best combines his sensitivity to the world around him with the cosmic, pessimistic philosophy he began to elucidate in his poetry from 1918 to 1929. As well as a revelation of intimate preoccupations, the stories are a travesty on the feeble patterns for living evolved by contemporary civilization in the face of an aggressive world. The most visible influence in the stories is that of Franz Kafka. Man is portrayed, in essence and in circumstance, as a victim. In almost every one of these narratives the protagonist begins and ends his existence in absolute solitude. The universal truth of failure and permanent suffering was first dramatized in the myth of Prometheus. Myth, in Kafka's definition, is the attempt to explain the unexplainable: "As it comes out of a ground of truth, it must end again in the unexplainable."[21] In Martínez Estrada's fiction, myth (the "unexplainable") again finds expression; invariably his stories end in permanent dilemma—disaster, desolation or suicide—with no possibility of solution. What Martínez Estrada criticizes has, in his judgment, no possibility of reform, not because man is originally evil or corrupt, but because man can never decipher the riddle of life. He is the cork on the ocean wave, the automatic and permanent victim of the "anonymous forces" of which Martínez Estrada first spoke in some detail in X-Ray of the Pampa, and which are ominously present, though invisible, in everything that Kafka wrote.

Kafka has taught the literary generations succeeding him the art of the ambiguous, for the ambiguous is what Kafka has painstakingly and systematically presented as the essence of reality. His ambiguity extends to every phase of life: causes and purposes, identities and functions, time and space. Who can explain the appearance, or purpose, or identity, or the dramatic relationship with others, of K. in The Castle? The sense of bewilderment and suffering is as strong as in any of Dante's or Milton's visions of Hell, or Dostoyevsky's exploration of deteriorating minds. More so, because Kafka endowed the existentialists who followed him with a concept of infernal experience without end, in a total fusion of dream and wake-

[21] From the third Notebook, quoted by Walter Kaufmann in Existentialism from Dostoevsky to Sartre, p. 122.

fulness. As in Kafka's narratives and parables, life is a lesson that is always learned too late. In the shortest of Martínez Estrada's three plays, the one-act *Shadows* with only two characters ("He" and "She"), "He" observes that "one always learns the facts of life with some delay, just late enough so that there is no chance of straightening oneself out. In every case it's the same. To live is to discover that one has been mistaken."[22] And "She" concludes, toward the end of the dialogue in which the couple reflects on twenty-three years of marriage, "Nothing is left to keep us together, nothing except an understanding of our unhappiness."[23]

The Kafkaesque atmosphere of Martínez Estrada's stories is evident in four ways: (1) the inconclusiveness of the lives portrayed; (2) the allegorical and microcosmic nature of the communities described; (3) the complex process of spiritual isolation in all the protagonists; and (4) the fascination with the unexplainable, the "mythical" basis of life.

But in some of the stories there are elements of the grotesque and the perverse that are not nearly so prevalent in Kafka. One of Martínez Estrada's pieces, "The Explosion,"[24] is a good example of his inclination to the grotesque. It begins with the explosion of a large boiler in the basement of a factory, resulting in the death of three workmen and extensive damage throughout the plant. Blas Brass, the mechanical engineer responsible for the mishap, goes home for lunch with an understandably troubled conscience. After lunch his elderly mother assures Blas that she will take care of everything while he takes a nap. She then leaves the house. Too uneasy for the nap, Blas follows her at a distance. They enter the half-destroyed factory, which appears bigger and stranger than ever; and while Blas sets to work in his office designing a new boiler, his mother begins to clean up the rubble, lifting large pieces of wood and twisted metal and sacks of lime and sand. She is assisting hundreds of workers and firemen in this task, which appears to her son to be too much for her. As she brings out a cadaver on her shoulder, Blas

---

[22] *Sombras*, in *Tres dramas*, p. 81.
[23] Ibid., p. 86.
[24] "La explosión," in *La tos y otros entretenimientos*, pp. 59–63.

tries to stop her, and she knocks him down. Witnessing this, many of the workers shout, "Lynch her Lynch her! Let the rats loose on her!" The workers then attack the mother, but she defends herself with amazing strength, beating them all off. Finally, the son decides to help her with her work, but just as he begins, hordes of large, aggressive rats—until then lurking and quarreling in the rubble—rush upon him. "They ran up his legs, climbed agilely all over his body and arms, got up on his shoulders and head, nuzzling him with their little snouts and tickling him with their tails, on the neck, nose and ears." As the rats start to tear at his clothes and to bite him, Blas Brass awakes from his nightmare, realizing that "all had been a dream, including the explosion and the mangled workmen."

The scene of "Juan Florido and Son, Printers"[25] is a dirty tenement house that occupies an entire block on the site of what was once a Protestant cemetery in a Buenos Aires slum. The house ("Leap-Year Palace"), it is said, was once a viceroy's fortress. Now, symbol of the human race in hopeless degeneration, it is infested with cockroaches, centipedes, uncollected garbage, and delinquent children; murder on the premises is frequent. "Juan Florido and Son" is grotesque in a more complete, farcical, and realistic way than "The Explosion." It is an obsessive and sadistic treatment of death. Juan Florido, tenant of Leap-Year Palace, has died at the age of sixtytwo, forty years after his arrival in Argentina from his native Seville. Among his few possessions brought from Spain were a seventeenthcentury lute, a suit of clothes, and a large jar of formaldehyde containing the body of his first son, who died at birth and who ever since has adorned a shelf in the living room, beneath the image of the Virgin of Carmen. In this story Martínez Estrada gives us his most vivid character portrait, a rogue whose alias for the week is Braulio (cf. the Braulio described by Mariano José de Larra in "El castellano viejo" ["The Old-Time Castilian"]), a destitute, opportunistic, and dishonest neighbor of the Florido family. Characterized in a style reminiscent of Quevedo, Larra, and José Hernández (cf. Vizcacha), Braulio ("don Baltasar, don Basilio, don Blas, don Benito") intro-

---

[25] "Juan Florido, padre e hijo, minervistas," in *Sábado de gloria*, pp. 81–121.

duces himself to the widow and son as they mourn Juan Florido, Sr.'s death in their apartment. Braulio eagerly accepts their offers of food and drink and loquaciously tells of his adventures and misfortunes, including the bizarre account, by a woman he once picked up, of a funeral wake in which the floor of the parlor gave way, depositing the cadaver, casket and guests in the flooded cellar below.

For two pesos Braulio offers to go to the pharmacy and buy some incense to neutralize the increasingly powerful stench of the remains of the deceased. He also suggests that the family take the fetus out of its jar and place it in the casket with Florido. Although after forty years the fetus—"little angel of God"—has become a family and neighborhood tradition,[26] the widow thinks this is an excellent idea. As a mass protest against the frightful odor emanating from the casket begins to be heard throughout the tenement, Doña Carmen (the widow) takes the fetus from its customary place on the shelf and begins to empty the formaldehyde into the sink, "slowly, because the body seemed about to fall apart. In spite of her precautions, the extreme care with which she proceeded, that's just what happened; a little arm and the remainder of the umbilical cord fell out. The little angel was left with only one arm and with the most delicate part of his little body badly mutilated, for the forty-year soaking in formaldehyde had converted the latter to a slimy paste, though of fairly firm consistency."[27] After this unsuccessful operation, she closes the jar again and places it in the casket, between the cadaver's legs. Soon the room is invaded by cockroaches and the cockroaches begin to nibble at the cadaver's face. Juan, Jr., suffers the terrible migraine headache that has been "a family tradition," and the headache reaches the intensity of a nightmare in which Juan, Jr., finds himself in his father's print shop, many years before, in the midst of violent labor agitation. When he awakes, the funeral carriage is at the door. As the casket is being lifted onto the carriage the cover opens part

---

[26] "Thus, some of the women, especially the young ones, would come to pray before the fetus in the jar; for some, the little angel had miraculous powers, even if it was true that nearly all directed their prayers to it in order to bring about the harm, illness or death of some careless enemy or lover." (Ibid., pp. 89–90).

[27] Ibid., p. 111.

way and the fetus slips out of its jar, making the funeral of Juan Florido, padre, the most memorable in the history of Leap-Year Palace.

"Abel Cainus," as one might guess from the Old Testament title, has to do with the problem of guilt. Abel Cainus, a once-wealthy engineer from Rumania, escaped from his country during the Nazi occupation and emigrated to Argentina. One morning when Cainus was away from home, the invaders executed his wife and two small children. Several months later Cainus shot to death a money lender in Buenos Aires over an argument about some jewels in hock. His guilty conscience and his solitary life in the boarding house become unbearable to him. He is afflicted with visions of how the bodies of his wife and children must have looked in the community grave in his native town in Rumania, but still more is he afflicted by the blood on his own hands. He plans suicide but he cannot go through with it. The newspapers report one morning that another suspect, immediately after being arrested, killed himself. Telling his boarding house companions that "there are now two innocent victims instead of one," Able Cainus goes up to his room and shoots himself in the head.[28]

In his most important stories—"Holy Saturday," "The Deluge," "Examination without Honor," and "Marta Riquelme"—the atmosphere and setting are markedly hermetic, and the protagonists move feebly about their little lives as in a labyrinth or extensive prison. The government office building in "Holy Saturday," the unfinished cathedral in "The Deluge," the mammoth hospital in "Examination Without Honor," the country estate that has grown into a city in "Marta Riquelme"—not to forget the tenement house in "Juan Florido and Son, Printers"—are all presented to the reader as complete environments, worlds in which absurdity is synonymous with reality and in which each man's life is by definition a problem without solution. The thoughts of the narrator-protagonist of "Forget-me-not" apply to all Martínez Estrada's protagonists: "Judging by my own case, which does not seem unique, I have often thought that

---

[28] "Abel Cainus," in *La tos y otros entretenimientos*, pp. 37–50.

there is a destiny against which it is useless to struggle. I've read many stories and legends that I'm just beginning to understand and I'm convinced that reason and justice have nothing to do with what happens in the world and in the society of men."[29] This is the case of most of Martínez Estrada's forlorn heroes and heroines. He uses the grotesque freely in both his depressing "A Widow's Lot" and his pointedly aburd "Examination without Honor" in order to stress the futility of all personal endeavor.

"A Widow's Lot" is appropriately included in the collection entitled *Three Stories without Love*.[30] If the reader were to guess the author's favorite writers on the basis of this story alone, he would probably name Francisco de Quevedo, the Marquis de Sade, Ramón del Valle Inclán, and the motion-picture director Luis Buñuel. After "Holy Saturday," it is Martínez Estrada's longest story, and the one that comes closest to being a novel—mainly because of its loose structure and the sense of an unending, suffering existence, despite the fact that the action is confined to a period of about a day and a half.

The tone is effectively set in the first sentence: "Only three people went to see Doña Rosa Inés, and that was because of obligation." Doña Rosa Inés, with four children from three to twelve years of age and a long accumulation of unpaid rent on the farm, has lost her husband. The cause of Simon Albert's death is unknown; there are only rumors in town and, from the police, no explanation of his quick burial. The story enumerates Rosa Inés' incredible legacy of misfortune. One of the three people expressing condolences is her husband's main creditor. Due to the drought, the family's livestock is steadily dying off. Rosa Inés' greedy brother-in-law, with whom Simón had rented the farm in partnership eight years before, wants her to sign over to him all her personal property and rights to remain on the farm. Don Luis Cederio, her most prosperous neighbor, denies her help. After her day-long futile search for help, Rosa Inés and her twelve-year-old daughter are accosted on the road by a satanic masked man dressed as the Indian leader Calfucurá, armed with

---

[29] "No me olvides," ibid., p. 98.
[30] "Viudez," in *Tres cuentos sin amor*, pp. 61–118.

dagger and revolver. Insinuating that he knows something about the death of Simón Albert, he offers Rosa Inés two hundred pesos for her daughter, whose underpants he pulls down as he forces her into the back of the wagon together with the mother. To distract the masked man from amorous advances toward her daughter, Rosa Inés begins caressing and kissing him and immediately accedes to his lust. Late in the afternoon Rosa Inés and her daughter finally return home. At dusk the relatives and friends who had offered no condolences the day before appear in carnival costume and begin a raucous, nightmarish celebration with beer and accordion music. Calfucurá reappears, laughing madly, and throws beer in Rosa Inés' face. As the party goes on Rosa Inés desperately tries to haul water from the nearly dry well for the dying livestock. Suddenly the carnival guests leave, expressing no concern for the widow or her awesome problems, and thus the story ends.

Structurally it is the poorest of Martínez Estrada's narratives; the plot gets out of hand. He develops it on two parallel planes: the formidable, aggressive reality in which Rosa Inés and her children are doomed to suffer—corruption, treachery, adverse climate, death— and the intense emotional state of the heroine herself, ranging from absolute depression to moments of exalted but illusory hope. The portrayal is slipshod and, for the most part, unconvincing. Rosa Inés is a small by-product of the infernal machinery of decadence that, in this narrative and the major portion of Martínez Estrada's other stories and essays, overwhelms the individual characters. The author expresses his penchant for the decadent not only in the sex scene with Calfucurá but also in many of his normal and physical descriptions, such as that of the cadaver in the police station, awaiting the return of the examining physician, who is out of town, and its official identification by the police chief, who is busy celebrating at the carnival. "With astonishment they saw stretched out on a bench the still body of a clown: rigid, dead, on its back, with a bloody face. A swarm of flies struggled in and out of the nostrils and the partly open mouth, tumbling over the moustache. What most impressed the two astonished women was the rapidity with which those flies went in and out of the nose and mouth without the slightest reaction on the part of the dead man; it was like the beehive opening where they had often watched the laborious activity of drones."[31]

Little did Cireneo Suárez suspect ("Examination without Honor"[32]) that when he visited his company manager in the hospital he (Suárez) would himself become a patient the next day. The pattern of the story is an ingeniously ironical contrast between the protagonist's intentions, or more precisely his lack of intentions, and his fate; between his absolute desire for noncommitment and his total enmeshment in the maze of personal and impersonal interests that constitutes the life and substance of the world around him. "Examination without Honor" narrates a series of errors and consequent discoveries on the part of its hero, an insignificant and passive man whose basic principle has always been to mind his own business. Cireneo Suárez did not *intend* that morning to visit Benegas (his company manager), but in the first visit the preceding afternoon Benegas had been unusually cordial and unnaturally interested in Suárez's affairs. It turns out that the company manager is not a patient at all, though Suárez is made to believe he will be operated on, but rather the instigator of a complex conspiracy to lure Suárez into the hospital and have a fibroid or tumor (which Benegas has been watching grow for ten years) removed from his head.

Every staff member, doctor, nurse, and even construction worker in the immense hospital participates in the conspiracy, which is similar to others that take place daily. Cireneo Suárez is given a green card with enigmatic instructions and directed through innumerable hallways and patios to an operating room. Like Buenos Aires itself, the hospital is described as a growing city. It has thirty-five buildings built over a period of fifty years. Much of it is rat-infested, "giant rats that wail like cats and many of which are as big as dogs." At night there are ferocious battles between the rats and cats. "There are nights when as many as twenty die on each side. The rats are the more warlike. Everybody comes to watch the battles and some doctors bring chairs. It's barbarous."[33] Among other points of interest,

---

[31] Ibid., p. 96.
[32] "Examen sin conciencia," in *Marta Riquelme*, pp. 49–99.
[33] Ibid., p. 56.

Suárez passes an "aerium solarium," where patients are suspended from under their arms on wires, in different colored smocks ("according to illness and the type of solar rays to be filtered").

Suárez's treatment is considerably quicker than that. On his arrival in the operating room, he is brusquely shaved, strapped to the table and given a local anaesthetic. He is further dismayed to discover that his surgeon (Gregorio Cáceres) is an intern who has failed eleven examinations over a period of eight years and that this operation is his last chance. It was scarcely a consolation to him that the odds on the betting among students and physicians in the gallery are three-to-one against Cáceres' passing this time. Against all sorts of adversities Cáceres completes his operation: insufficient light, improperly administered anaesthetic, and dishonest judging on the part of the examining board. Luckily, at least, Suárez (by lottery) had been ticketed for a head operation, instead of one on his lung or kidney, and the head operation happened to coincide with the company manager's purpose. There is a twenty-minute rest period during which the anaesthetic wears off and the second half of the operation is an "inquisitorial torture" in which Suárez's hair-raising screams are echoed by the gallery's cheers. As Suárez at last makes his way dizzily out of the hospital, with a bandage on his head in the form of a cross, he is congratulated by Benegas, the company manager, for acceding to the indispensable medical treatment, but scolded by Cáceres, the student surgeon, for having screamed during the operation, thus giving the examining board their pretext for flunking the perennial student for the twelfth and last time.

Suárez has finally made his way out of the labyrinth, with a very understandable feeling of relief but with no feeling of freedom. Martínez Estrada's protagonists never achieve freedom. "Cireneo realized that he had not reached the end, but only the beginning of something that for a long time had been plotted against him. . . . He understood with absolute clarity that nothing that had happened to him was absurd, but perfectly logical and in accordance with his fate."[34] That reality and absurdity are essentially the same, and that

---

[34] Ibid., p. 99.

absurdity is therefore logical is one of Martínez Estrada's main philosophical contentions.

"Marta Riquelme" is the most original of Martínez Estrada's stories, mainly because it is more than a story.[35] It is more than a story not simply because it is a prologue to a long (1,786 pages), intimate journal by an imaginary writer (Marta Riquelme), but also because the imaginary manuscript is lost, and it is the imaginary editor's task to reconstruct parts of it from memory and also to explain some of the peculiarities and ambiguities of the hand-written text. In doing all this, Martínez Estrada makes informal commentary on the problems and idiosyncrasies of the creative process and develops, through mere suggestion, a character more convincing than any other in his fiction. Ironically, Marta Riquelme is not presented as a homogenous human being, but as several *possible* personalities. Her atrociously bad handwriting can often be interpreted in two or three different ways, and the character of Marta—through the abundant but frequently vague insinuations of the diary—oscillates between the angelic and the diabolical. Much of this ambiguity is reflected by the acts and attitudes of other persons commented on by the mysterious authoress; for example, her sister Margarita who, after a quarrel with Marta, commits suicide; and Marta's uncle, Antonio, married to a nervous and jealous woman ("jealous because she couldn't stand the happiness of others"). Marta has sentiments for Antonio that range erratically from maternal compassion and filial devotion to erotic attraction. Marta's character is rounded out by her account of the mysterious relationship with these and other characters, including the young Mario, considered a "trophy" of sorts by both Marta and her cousin Amelia, and Marta's mother. There is a most equivocal quotation about Marta and the mother near the end of the story.

Following the general pattern of other representative stories by

---

[35] "Marta Riquelme," ibid., pp. 9–45. "Marta Riquelme" is also the title of one of William Henry Hudson's four tales in the collection *El Ombú*. This is why Martínez Estrada writes, "the name was known and even familiar to me," in the first sentence of his story ("Marta Riquelme," p. 9). Hudson's tale is about a beautiful young girl who, after losing her husband and children, goes mad and is transformed into a horrible vulture.

the author, "Marta Riquelme" aspires to collective and universal meaning in addition to the spiritual intimacy of a few private lives. Marta Riquelme is a good historian as well as an interesting confessor. "La Magnolia" was originally a country estate, established in colonial times by Marta's great-grandfather. Her grandfather converted the estate into a hotel, and remote relatives, in addition to the already numerous family, began to fill the rooms. Finally, the estate property surrounding the hotel became the town of Bolívar. It is a large two-story hotel with three patios, and in the middle of the main patio the symbolic magnolia tree (remindful of William Henry Hudson's *ombú*) still stands. Marta writes:

> I always repeat without tiring, almost in the same words, that the gigantic magnolia tree in the middle of the main patio had human personality, that it was a member of our family, full of branches, twigs and leaves, a family relationship so distant that it could be justified only by the trunk shared with preceding generations. For we too were related by a common origin, and then divided into innumerable independent groups which, nevertheless, lacked the freedom to move closer or to separate further, joined, as we were, to an invisible trunk.[36]

The analogy is clear. The magnolia tree, the hotel, and the surrounding property of the former estate now transformed into a small city (Bolívar) are symbols of the Argentine nation with Buenos Aires as its nucleus. For the nation is also a "family," like that of La Magnolia with its "eight branches and 120 people." The eight branches, or families, we are told, have lived in almost continuous discord. "In the city or town of Bolívar they say that the magnolia tree holds them all together, and that a feud over property rights has gone on for eighty-five years without settlement" (p. 15). Among the steadily growing family are many children and several lawyers. The great house, like any city which imposes its characteristics on its inhabitants, has seemingly become the protagonist of a complex story. Marta writes, "The home was a tragedy, and all we did was to act it out" (p. 25). The peculiar pattern of development of Buenos Aires is reflected in Bolívar, the small city that eventually grew up around

---

[36] Ibid., p. 26. Subsequent references in the text to "Marta Riquelme" are by page number only.

La Magnolia. "If, as a general rule, communities are formed by the overflow of the inhabitants of a house into outlying areas, in our case the opposite has occurred: the outlying areas moved in, and finally the house became a whole community on a small scale, condensed."[37] Martínez Estrada first expressed this theory of evolution from country estate to town to city in *X-Ray of the Pampa*; regarding Buenos Aires he wrote, "Everywhere the city is invaded by the pampa; the large estates that have been sold and the farms rented for high prices are transformed into city buildings."

The originality of "Marta Riquelme" is largely due to the circumstances of its imaginary composition. Marta Riquelme herself has disappeared, and since the manuscript of the imaginary *Memoirs* is also lost, Martínez Estrada—as editor—takes great pains to reconstruct it and explain its idiosyncrasies. What we have at hand is reputedly the prologue to the *Memoirs*, and the prologue includes a quite meticulous account of how the editor and his collaborators did their work. Arnaldo Orfila Reynal, editor and publisher in Argentina and Mexico and in real life a close friend of Martínez Estrada (who also appears as a character in the prologue), is said to have given the original manuscript to Martínez Estrada. With the assistance of four other literary scholars, the author of the prologue has spent three years conferring with his colleagues on the manuscript in almost daily seminars, placing the misplaced pages in order, deciphering the handwriting, interpreting ambiguous passages in much the same way that expert chess players might discuss a problematical move by thinking out the consequences of each possibility. A consideration of several alternative character traits of Marta Riquelme—innocent, angelical, passionate, treacherous, maternal, licentious—is at the heart of the prologue. We are told, for example, that "the authoress often reaches the edge of the abyss of obscenity, and just as often she attains the mystic bliss of the purest of souls" (p. 19).

[37] Ibid. I have translated *pueblo* as "community" ". . . y al fin la casa vino a ser todo el pueblo resumido, condenado."), since in this context Martínez Estrada seems to be referring to the formation of cities rather than nations or peoples. *Pueblo*, of course, can have any of these three meanings.

But the main difficulty is one of interpreting specific dialogues and scenes. The editor cites the case of a conversation between Mario and Marta in which Mario confesses a feeling of shame for something that has happened, and in which Marta replies, "Why? I too have enjoyed it infinitely. I doubt that any one has seen us and at least our pleasure has been intense, which is what we wanted; and everything turned out perfectly" (p. 38). The editor's problem is one of placement. If the conversation is situated in the dining room *after* the two lovers have met at dusk in the barn, where they are found seated on a harvesting machine, the reader is led to assume that there has been love-making in the hayloft. If, on the other hand, the dining-room conversation partly quoted above *precedes* the meeting in the barn and refers instead to an idyllic berry-picking session in the morning, then innocence and chastity are well preserved. The more we read about Marta Riquelme the more firmly inclined we are to suspend judgment because her testimonies and the expression of her emotions lead us not toward one general conclusion but to Martínez Estrada's exposition of several possible (and quite feasible) personalities, each with its respectively logical plot.

Actually, then, "Marta Riquelme" is not a story but an account of what may have happened, with only a minimal admixture of what indeed can be assumed as fact. Thus, for reasons quite different from those set forth in my commentary on *The Head of Goliath* (novelistic raw material, descriptive elements appropriate for inclusion in novels about life, the hospitals, streets, carnivals, apartment buildings, and other obscure locales of Buenos Aires society), "Marta Riquelme" may also to a large extent be considered a "novelist's notebook." The reasons, of course, are more compelling and more specific than in the case of *The Head of Goliath*; for in Marta Riquelme as a protagonist we have, in potential form, not just a unique woman but *the* woman in her most fundamental and vital aspects. We are told that Marta began writing her *Memoirs* at the age of twelve, a moment in her life Martínez Estrada compares to "the shock of awaking one morning in somebody else's bed," or the first serious awareness of the complexities of human existence. By internal evidence he supposes that the *Memoirs* cover a period of eight years and that at the time of the writing of the prologue in 1942 (four years after the completion of the manuscript), Marta must have been twenty-four. The editor considers this information important, because Marta's nostalgic sentiments and the intensity of her emotions suggest a much longer period of time. In this sense, the eight years, he says, are the equivalent of an entire century, "because of the intensity with which she has already lived her life, relishing it in all its details, with the feeling that one gets while closing one's eyes in the midst of a dizzy spell" (pp. 21–22).

From beginning to end there are unsubstantiated, but also unrefuted insinuations. Marta Riquelme, who lived in a cloister until she was ten, becomes increasingly involved in the maelstrom of life at "La Magnolia." But this involvement brings only disorder, loneliness, and frustration. Marta's sister commits suicide; her father loses his money and succumbs to drink; Uncle Antonio's marriage is a failure, and Marta—notwithstanding her adolescent infatuation with Mario—experiences a steadily growing affection, compassion, and, finally, love for her uncle. The last quotation we are given from the *Memoirs* suggests that Marta and Antonio go off together but that their union is not necessarily a good or enduring one. "He also lived in solitude, torn, like me, from the bosom of his family. I was alone, completely alone, in the world. He was the sword I needed to defend myself with. His love could not have changed, I supposed, since my love for him had grown and intensified with absence. For me he would now have to be like a fortress and protect me against the worst misfortunes of my sad life. My mission would be to console him to the limit of my feeble strength, and with the help of God" (p. 45). Martínez Estrada's last sentence ("Everything that follows is simply stupendous") not only eliminates every possibility of a conclusion but also adds to the force and impenetrability of Marta's character.

It is important to note that the author of the prologue suggests three possible ways to read the *Memoirs*. The first—when all is considered, not the most convincing—calls for a totally angelic heroine. The second sees Marta as a female Satan. Martínez Estrada is quick to point out that his editorial committee's opinion was evenly divided as to these two possibilities. Although he assures us that Marta's passions ("those of a child, those of a woman, those of an old woman —even those of men") were, because of their very intensity, free of all sin (pp. 42–43), it is easy to see how in actual fact he has her continuously poised on the razor's edge between glory and total perdition. It is precisely this precarious balance that seems to compel him to mention the third interpretation, which is the Freudian view. This would necessitate portraying Marta "as a hysterical or a perverted woman." In the same breath, Martínez Estrada says that this might well be the "most interesting" interpretation, even if it would be a "sacrilege."

In this multiperspective presentation of his heroine the author has endeavored to show us that the reader who cannot suspend moral and spiritual judgment, thereby attributing to the author ideas and attitudes that in reality exist only in his own mind and reflect his own prejudices, automatically falsifies both the writer's intention and the reality of the world that, consciously or unconsciously, is revealed in the author's completed work. As we have seen in the chapters on Sarmiento and *Death and Transfiguration of Martín Fierro*, this is precisely the accusation Martínez Estrada directs at those whom he considers to be soft-minded and gullible patriots in the face of the harsh realities of Argentine history.

"The Deluge" was Martínez Estrada's first and best-written story, completed in 1943. As Juan Carlos Ghiano has remarked, it is a description of "the unredeemed world of the Old Testament."[38] That is pretty much the world of all Don Ezequiel's stories; in no case is there a suggestion of salvation or even of the partial efficacy of faith. The only certain conclusion to be drawn by the characters—and by the reader—is that the suffering they have undergone is endless. In this sense Ghiano includes these characters in a tradition begun with *Martín Fierro*, for they all end "with that same indecisiveness of persecuted men, which is the essential motivation in *Martín Fierro*."[39] The scene of the intensely unified action is a large, unfinished church on a hill in the remote provincial town of General Estévez. Before the

---

[38] Juan Carlos Ghiano, "Martínez Estrada, narrador," p. 143.
[39] Ibid., p. 144.

flood, which caused twelve hundred people to take refuge in the church, the pastor, Father Demetrio, had been unable to attract more than fifty faithful on a Sunday. The rains came after a three-month drought.

If there is monotony in Martínez Estrada's fiction it is largely due to the gruesome succession of major misfortunes without relief. If, on the other hand, there is indeed a counteraction to that monotony, it is largely due to the author's talent for the grotesque and the farcical, a vision that has as much in common with Quevedo, Valle Inclán, and Baudelaire's *Flowers of Evil*, as with the suffocating realism of the Spanish *tremendistas* of the 1940's. All his main characters have the suffering, if not the patience, of Job. The church on the hill is a repetition of Noah's Ark, with the important difference, of course, that the salvation of contemporary humanity—a last generation—and not that of all creation, is at stake. The rains came and the rains continue. As a last resort, the people have forced their way into the church, and with each passing day, their impatience, their irritability, their sickness and hunger increase.

Little by little, the social structure of the refugee community disintegrates (or integrates, depending on one's point of view). On the third day the male and female sections of the group begin to mix; until then they have been divided—the women on the right, the men on the left—as has always been the custom at mass. Some two hundred hungry dogs outside the church have skinned and eaten a horse. The children are crying and the dogs howling. As the general desperation grows, a demented young man—whose grandmother claims he is a prophet—has a tense confrontation with the pastor, Father Demetrio. Each, indeed, accuses the other of being possessed by the Devil; and the author stresses the diminishing effect of each on the disillusioned members of the refugee community. Even the seventy-year-old priest, unmoveable in his faith, "had the impression that he was achieving no more than a meaningless sham" in saying mass.[40] As time passes, the refugees begin to feel that "all had known and detested one another for ages" (p. 208). The words of the priest and

[40] "La inundación," in *Antología*, pp. 200–222. Subsequent references in the text to this story are by page number only.

the efforts of the Spanish doctor (who dies of the epidemic that takes
the lives of several children) are futile. The only consolation—and
it is no more than momentary—is the music the priest plays on the
organ. "The music extended over every thing and every being like a
balm, purifying the fetid and sinful atmosphere, and infusing the
murky evening shadows with a delicate luminosity that gave life to
every solid and inert form" (p. 216). Father Demetrio's last sermon
is a single phrase, the basic lesson from the Book of Job: "My children, God tests us right up to the end" (p. 220). The reader is not a
witness to the end, but the conclusion of the story is unmistakably
tragic. For a moment there is a clearing in the sky and the people
rejoice. But, as if in answer to a final reaffirmation of faith by one of
the congregation ("God will perform the miracle of saving us; he
will not let us die in this way"), the sky darkens once again, and once
again "the rain let fall its large drops on the uplifted faces" (p. 222).
The end has not come, but it is imminent, and the impossibility of
salvation is stressed anew in the terse phraseology of the last paragraph. The futility of all hope is also emphasized in the refusal of
a Rumanian couple to give up their dead child, wrapping the body
in all available garments and rags and zealously defending it from
the hordes of hungry dogs that have finally been admitted into the
church.

While on the surface it appears that "The Deluge" is the story of
man defeated by nature, the deeper meaning of the narrative is
man's total helplessness compounded by his total misunderstanding
of his fellow human beings. The people forced together in the church
misinterpret and distrust one another; and *as a community* they are
portrayed as more helpless than as individuals. It is utopia in reverse.
The spiritual leader (Father Demetrio), the physician, and the
prophet (the idiot boy) can give them no strength. By their own
nature, as well as by circumstances, the people are condemned to an
infernal existence. They are condemned, above all, because of their
lack of love. ("The Deluge" is another of the stories in the volume
with the subtitle "Three Stories without Love.") It is a dramatic
demonstration of the author's belief, adapted from Raner Maria
Rilke, that "faith" is meaningless and that "love" is everything, for it

is only through love that God and one's fellow human beings assume vital importance.[41] In "The Deluge," ironically, only the nearly starved dogs, kept out in the rain by their indifferent masters for many days, are capable of any affection.

The Chorus of the Dispossessed

The dispossessed are variations of the *homo urbanus* of the nineteenth and twentieth centuries. Martínez Estrada's masters in interpreting the dispossessed are William Henry Hudson, Balzac, Nietzsche, Horacio Quiroga and—as I have suggested in my opening remarks on the stories—Kafka. Hudson, whose *Purple Land* Martínez Estrada included among the works of great poetic depth "that have documented the fall of man,"[42] portrayed his protagonists (including himself) as part of a generation living out its last years amidst the beauties of nature; for Hudson, like Nietzsche, foresaw the defeat of human beings by human civilization. And as if to underline his profound misgivings about a progressively more industrialized humanity, Hudson wrote almost all his books on his experiences in nature—some recent, more of them "far away and long ago." Hudson represented for Martínez Estrada the highest degree imaginable of personal freedom—both as an artist and as a man. Hudson also wrote, he thought, about nineteenth-century life in Argentina with far greater candor and perceptiveness than any of the "classic" Argentines, including Sarmiento, Echeverría and José Hernández. Hudson believed in "civilization" even less than in progress. Don Ezequiel was convinced that William Henry was not, to begin with, "civilized" at all.

[Hudson,] without being a primitive plain and simple—a savage—has not assimilated nor, perhaps, understood the fruits of cultured knowledge and of the power of civilization. His works could have been read without surprise by an Athenian of the age of Pericles or by a Saxon at the time of the Norman conquest of England. . . . But possibly that Greek and that Saxon would not have understood them so easily as a treatise on physics

---

[41] The quotation from Rilke is in Martínez Estrada's "Montaigne, filósofo impremeditado," in *Heraldos de la verdad*, p. 65.
[42] *El mundo maravilloso de Guillermo Enrique Hudson*, p. 193.

or a Baedecker [European travel guide] . . . because the Baedecker and the treatise would have fit into their world, already described, measured, weighed and mastered. On the other hand, concerning nature, which before Petrarch had not been interpreted as such, Hudson's sensibility would have created preposterous problems for them. Because all the culture and civilization that Hudson could assimilate had not influenced his mind but his sensibility.[43]

In *Idle Days in Patagonia* Hudson himself tells us of the moment when he became fully aware of his disenchantment with the political world and his definitive embrace of the world of nature.[44] He had spent several weeks in solitude on the southern plains of Argentina and, on seeing his first newspaper since before his isolation, he realized that civilization for him was only something to be avoided as an unnecessary distraction. Hudson's tragic view of modern life is based mainly on the belief that man has sacrificed his instinct to reason, and that reason untempered by feeling is man's most dangerous weapon.[45] Martínez Estrada has found support for this view in Bergson's judgment that intelligence is essentially destructive while instinct is constructive.[46] Not primitive men but wars, political and economic systems, and various restrictive taboos lead us astray from the righteous paths of nature. Wars, systems, and taboos have contributed not to man's quest for knowledge but to "his secret urge to deny and to annihilate" (p. 261). In order to fortify his anti-civilization stance, the essayist cites Lewis Mumford (*Technics and Civilization*) and Arnold J. Toynbee (*A Study of History*), who, he thinks, substantiate his belief that human beings have not improved over the centuries but, rather, have simply increased their capacity for getting into trouble (p. 264).

Bergson tells us that intelligence and instinct are two methods of "innate" knowledge. Instinct implies the concrete knowledge of material and "things." Intelligence implies the hypothetical knowledge of forms and "relationships." If the intelligence is destructive, it is so

[43] Ibid., pp. 267–268. Subsequent references in the text to this edition will be by page number only.
[44] *Idle Days in Patagonia*, p. 70.
[45] See Chapter I of *A Hind in Richmond Park*, especially pp. 6–7.
[46] Henri Bergson, *L'Évolution créatrice*, pp. 147–164.

because through intelligence man extends his function from that of *homo sapiens* to that of *homo faber*; that is, he devises and creates artificial objects—*instruments inorganisés* in the terminology of Bergson—which Hudson and Martínez Estrada feel he is likely to use inadvertently toward his own destruction. Bergson recognizes that there has been "progress" punctuated by the invention and manufacture of an increasing abundance of "instruments." Bergson says we have failed to take seriously into account the fact that "the modifications in humanity ordinarily take place considerably later than the transformations in his machinery."[47]

The longest and most important section of *The Marvelous World of William Henry Hudson* is the chapter devoted to "Ideas" (pp. 251–339). The aspect of Hudson that most interests Martínez Estrada is his sensitivity not only to his immediate environment but to the separate worlds of nature and civilization, and to the problem of the future of man. Innocent of all formal philosophy, Hudson was nevertheless able to see people and the world in terms of their natural evolution, and he foresaw the inevitable imprisonment of man by his own inventiveness. Don Ezequiel understood this clearly and, beyond that, made it one of the first principles of his own philosophy: "Within his blindly realistic materialism—open, that is, to the possibility of the marvelous and the supernatural—he formulated skeptical opinions on the destiny of urban man, caged in a machinery of living and thinking that artificially replaced the natural forms of sustenance without which he is doomed to degeneration and death" (p. 269).

"All Hudson's books," wrote John Galsworthy in 1915, "breathe this spirit of revolt against our new enslavement by towns and machinery, and are true Oases in an Age so dreadfully resigned to the 'pale mechanician.' "[48] Like Herbert Spencer, Hudson considered phenomena as manifestations of "the unknowable." Unlike Spencer, he recognized no utilitarian connection between morality and physical

---

[47] Ibid., p. 150. Martínez Estrada quotes this observation in *El mundo maravilloso*, p. 261.
[48] Foreword to Hudson's *Green Mansions*, p. viii.

well-being. Like Martínez Estrada, Hudson clung always to the premise that natural freedom is life and civilized systematization is death. To justify this premise, Martínez Estrada did not rely—as one might logically suppose—on the support of Bakunin, Kropotkin, or any other anarchist, but rather on John Dewey's interpretation of Rousseau in *Democracy and Education* (pp. 272–276). We must make, of course, an important distinction between Dewey's glowing hope that man in the eighteenth century had taken the first step— in intimate accord with nature—in the long process of his liberation "from his internal chains of false beliefs and ideals" (p. 276), and the Argentine's closed-end view that by the early twentieth century man had not been able to see the process through and had already succumbed to civilization. For this *final* defeat of man, it was necessary for civilization to move from a primitive stage of "passion" to an advanced stage in which it has achieved its own "philosophy" and its own "religion, morality, laws, economy and social psychology," all to be meticulously codified and actualized by the various totalitarian systems of our era (pp. 277–278).

If nature is life and civilization is death, man takes refuge in whatever form or pseudoform of nature he can find. One such refuge is music, to which Hudson and Martínez Estrada were both fully devoted. Hudson's philosophy of music goes a long way toward explaining his aversion to civilization and his deep romanticism. If Martínez Estrada was born too late to partake of the experience in nature that it was Hudson's good fortune to enjoy, if his alienation and irate involvement in his own unnatural century permitted him only a kind of romanticism-in-restrospect, he surely appreciated music for basically the same reasons here set forth by Hudson:

We may say then that music is essentially a refined and beautiful expression of all emotions common to all men in all stages of life; that because of this origin its appeal is universal, its hold on us so powerful. Beethoven, speaking of his own music, said that those who listened to it were lifted above this earth into a higher sphere and state. It may be so: I do not know; but I do know that it takes me back; that it wears an expression which startles and holds me, that it is essentially the "Passion of the Past"

—not of mine only, my own little emotional experiences, but that of the race, the inherited remembrances or associations of its passionate life, back to a period so remote that it cannot be measured by years.[49]

One is impressed, in reading *The Marvelous World of William Henry Hudson*, by the author's repeated rejection of abstract thought and all its practitioners. Accordingly, he includes Hudson in the company of Giordano Bruno, Tolstoy, Goethe, and Thoreau, discoverers all of the fact that absolute truth is undiscoverable, that no abstract thought yet devised can adequately explain the mysterious forces that determine our lives, and that (especially Bruno) our view of the world is circumstantial, contingent on the place and moment from which we perceive things. All found ecstatic pleasure in their particular relationships with nature. It is significant to note that Max Scheler (1874–1928), one of the most important phenomenologists, strongly influenced Martínez Estrada's interpretation of Hudson and the writers just mentioned, as his long quotation from *Essence and Form of Sympathy* shows (p. 256). Scheler here refers to the contrast between Western man's persistent efforts to dominate and direct the forces of nature and the harmony that the people of India have traditionally found between those forces and their own aspirations.

Whereas Western man, *homo faber* and *homo urbanus* par excellence, is the "superior" being who sets out to control and utilize nature, Eastern man strives to live in intimate harmony with nature, allowing no kind of separation between "spirit" and "life." As Barry Commoner has forcefully demonstrated in an age in which all humanity trembles before a terrifying orgy of the physical sciences, "the real question is not *whether* we should use our new knowledge, but *how* to use it." [50] The great theme on which all Martínez Estrada's works are symphonic variations is the contention that *homo urbanus* does not know how. Hudson did know how, he thinks. In contrast to *homo faber* Hudson extracted his knowledge directly from his own surroundings, and, on the basis of that always vital educational experience, he extended his attention to the world of

[49] *A Hind in Richmond Park*, p. 249.
[50] *Science and Survival*, p. 25.

books and civilization. In his fiction and in his essays, observes Don Ezequiel, "place and human beings complement one another in a broad vital harmony, because each person is interpreted in the light of everything around him. He sets the individual—man or animal— in an ecological context, and gives him dynamic meaning through some vital situation, through a 'being placed' in an order of relation- ships in which life is the clue to every event" (pp. 314–315).

Together with Hudson, José Martí (1853–1895) and Horacio Qui- roga (1878–1937) form Martínez Estrada's trinity of uncorrupted manhood. He considered them all as pragmatists, but with none of the utilitarian implications of that term. In each of these men Mar- tínez Estrada admired the transformation of experience into a phi- losophy of living by which man as a free agent made no compromise with a society more subservient to its technological means than to its ideological ends. In each he appreciated a most noble affinity to nature, and in each he lamented the ultimate failure of the free person as a victim of "civilization."

In his last and longest work, the biography of Martí,[51] he stresses the Cuban patriot's importance as a teacher through experience and example. "His political and social doctrine is his philosophical credo. Martí is not a philosopher but a thinker in action who prefers chang- ing the world to understanding it."[52] In the very next sentence, as if in quick amendment of that rather brash judgment, the biographer adds that Martí was, in any case, "according to the distinction made by Max Scheler, a man of culture more than of knowledge." While the treatment of the Cuban leader's political and social thought in the two volumes so far published is the most complete that we have to date, the work is also, and perhaps more importantly, the final expression of Martínez Estrada's tragic sense of life. Like Sarmiento, Martí is portrayed as a man of aspirations unmatched by his capaci- ties. But the author does not qualify his characterization of Martí as he does that of his own compatriot. Whereas he blames Sarmiento

[51] *Martí revolucionario.* This is the first of a projected three-volume work, the third of which was actually published first (*Martí: El héroe y su acción revolucionaria*). Volume II had not been published at this writing.

[52] *Martí revolucionario,* p. 531. Subsequent references in the text to this work are by page number only.

for several of Argentina's most fundamental weaknesses and for failing to fulfill his political mission in accordance with his educational principles, he praises Martí for his constant growth of spirit and his total sacrifice. The temporal failure of Martí was due more to his unlimited will and anachronistic heroism than to his limited political strength, because already in 1895, the year of his death in hopeless revolutionary combat, history had passed beyond the last era of those whom Martínez Estrada classifies as "Great Men" (pp. 447–456).

Martí the magnanimous, the courageous, and the just, could not have survived much longer, even if his life had been spared on that fateful day of May. That is because, at least so Martínez Estrada would have us believe, magnanimity, courage, and justice expressed by one man addressing himself to other men no longer constituted a significant historical force. With absolute romantic conviction, the Argentine biographer assures us that "from Antiquity to the Renaissance" men were taken for what they were, "and not for what they possessed or represented" (p. 451). One would judge from the abundance of references to Carlyle's observations on heroes in this section of the book[53] that Martínez Estrada had been overly influenced by Carlyle and (from a longer time back) by Nietzsche, as far as their concepts of the superior man were concerned. At any rate, his romanticizing of the individualism of times past made his view of contemporary *homo urbanus* more dramatically antithetical than ever. For Martínez Estrada, Martí was the legendary mythological hero, a Cuban Ulysses in triumphal return. Notwithstanding the futility of the patriot's abortive revolution, his epic legend was established, and his immediate tragedy could serve as an enduring hope for future revolutionaries.

But the point is, of course, that while Martí will always be a libertarian inspiration to Cubans and all the other nationalities of the New World, within the context of the various oppressive twentieth-century sociopolitical systems there can never be another Martí. Although the revolutionary fervor surrounding the Castro revolution is

---

[53] Part V, "El hombre biológico y mítico," pp. 447–545.

obviously in the background of this work, Martínez Estrada limits
his doctrinal discussion to observing that the worlds of the property
owner and the wage earner are incompatible (p. 531), that Martí
was in thought "open, free and progressive," therefore defending the
right of any country "to seek the most convenient markets and ex-
change their products without serving the interests of the great
powers" (p. 532). Surely the critical condition of the Cuban sugar
trade in the early 1960's had something to do with this "revisionism"
of Martí's democratic ideology; although we are reminded on the
same page that Martí was an enthusiastic admirer of the American
economist Henry George (1839–1897), whose ideas on natural
wealth (land as the legitimate source of wealth for all) constituted
a basic part of the nineteenth-century economic utopianism which
Martí and Martínez Estrada happened to share and which, in turn,
had a great deal in common with Rousseau.[54]

Bit by bit, in this long, loosely constructed work, José Martí is
resurrected in the biographer's own idealistic image. Needless to
say, this is the universal temptation of all biographers; but it is
especially a temptation when the biographer wishes to make a historical justification, not only of his subject in his subject's time, but
also, by extension, of himself in his own time. For Martínez Estrada,
Martí—the last heroic, natural man—was both a tragic and utopian
figure: a man too good for his own era, to say nothing of the 1950's
and 1960's. Thus, Martínez Estrada portrays him as a kind of equali-
tarian with a faith in eventual human perfection that was imbued
with "the positivistic and transcendentalist philosophy of Darwin
and Marx" (p. 107), but not with Marxist-Leninism, which condones
revolutionary violence and vengeful reprisals. He portrays him also
as a "Christian," but "the Christianity of Martí is humanitarianism
rather than speculative religion." Not faith and obedience but "purity
of soul, righteous behavior and self-sacrifice for the love and benefit
of one's fellow man . . . natural religion" (pp. 107–108). A natural
and ingenuous religion, that is, which Martínez Estrada thought was

[54] See especially Rousseau's *Discours sur l'origine de l'inégalité des hommes*
(1754).

a perfect reenactment of the deistic and unrestrained experiments by Rousseau's Vicar Savoyard's experiments in *Emile* (p. 108).

Finally and most important, Martí was, above all, a revolutionary in his conviction "that it was not possible to institute a rule of law within a system of injustice" (p. 119).[55] The remarkably strong emotional element in his revolutionary thought led him to a form of political "priesthood," of wisdom through suffering, of solitude and exile. In his country he came to be known as "the Apostle," stimulated, in his biographer's words, by "a kind of humanitarian fanaticism" (p. 145). To reduce Martí's missionary zeal to the category of patriotism would be to slight him, because that mission, though carried out for the homeland, was individually and uniquely heroic, the result of "an irrational, mystic and fanatical love, like that of Dostoyevsky, Whitman and [Charles] Péguy" for their respective countries (p. 153). The form and intensity of Martí's nationalism, we may conclude, was psychologically very similar to the agonizing nationalism of his Argentine biographer. Each was a herald and prophet strongly imbued with a tragic sentiment of life. Each felt that he was a natural man in unnatural circumstances.

If José Martí was the last hero, he was not the last dissenter from civilization. Possibly Martínez Estrada's most intimate literary acquaintance, Horacio Quiroga—"Brother Quiroga"—lived in a nearly continuous state of alienation. Quiroga lived out a series of frustrations in love that Henrik Ibsen's *Brand* ("the only book I have reread five or six times")[56] seemed to exemplify. For just as the uncompromising idealist of Ibsen's poem sacrificed not only himself but also his family to his "Church of Life," Quiroga sacrificed the happiness and the psychological stability of his first wife and first two children by exiling himself and them from civilization. Many of his stories reflect their hardships in the wilderness in the Misiones area of northeast Argentina. But it was their emotional disposition and

---

[55] The words are Martínez Estrada's. It should also be mentioned that he applies them not only to Martí but to the nineteenth-century Mexican leader and president, Benito Juárez.

[56] See Letter no. 26, dated July 25, 1936, from Quiroga to Martínez Estrada, in *Cartas inéditas de Horacio Quiroga*, I, 124.

their personal philosophies much more than their habits or activities that brought Quiroga and Martínez Estrada together. "The words from Quiroga to Estrada [in the collected letters] have the naturalness of one who senses that he is addressing an identical spirit," writes one critic.[57] Martínez Estrada recalls that Martín Fierro had said of his new companion in adversity, Sergeant Cruz, "Now I see that the two of us are splinters from the same stick."[58] and he applies the words to himself and Quiroga. *Brother Quiroga* is Martínez Estrada's account of his relationship with Quiroga, from about 1928 to February 1937, when Quiroga, afflicted with cancer and hopelessness, committed suicide in his hospital room. They were united by mutual comprehension and a similar temperamental disposition of character that made life particularly difficult for both, and both always felt a strong inclination to solitude and a deep disdain for urban society and the professional world of writers.

There were, of course, fundamental differences between them. Martínez Estrada never heard the call to the wild regions of nature that had always so enchanted Quiroga. Quiroga "lived" the fiction he produced; Martínez Estrada hypothesized reality on the basis of his meditations and his vast readings. Quiroga was essentially a materialist who, against one and all, strove for freedom and self-sufficiency; Martínez Estrada was essentially an abstract moralist, a mystic humanitarian who was driven to distraction and finally to resignation by the realities—*all* the realities—of a "technocratic" civilization. But they were kindred spirits in their total rejection of the social and political arbitrariness that characterized the history of the Western world in the 1920's and, especially, the 1930's. It must not be forgotten that Quiroga, seventeen years older than the author of *X-Ray of the Pampa*, exercised a strong personal influence on him, and that much of the pathos and tragic sentiment found in the stories I have discussed in this chapter came from Quiroga. Martínez Estrada saw in the eccentric and anachronistic hero that was Quiroga

---

[57] Arturo Sergio Visca in the prologue to *Cartas inéditas*, I, 12.
[58] "Ya veo que somos los dos / astillas del mismo palo." *El hermano Quiroga*, p. 7. Subsequent references in the text to this book are by page number only.

the only legitimate form of *homo faber*, recognizing, at the same time, that such a concept of work was valid only for a man in complete isolation.

Notwithstanding his tragic existence, the Uruguayan lived just about as he wanted to live: uncomfortably but independently, working for no one but himself. "For Quiroga work was a kind of Benedictine asceticism by which he could withdraw from the world and from himself" (p. 59). He was a Robinson Crusoe on an imaginary island in the middle of the ocean of civilization. Quoting Ibsen in a letter to Martínez Estrada in September 1935, he wrote, "Isolated man is the truly strong one."[59] Nearly a year later he recommended to his correspondent Thoreau's *Walden*,[60] being deeply impressed by the extent to which the North American naturalist had reputedly done and made things on his own. In spite of Quiroga's frustrations—domestic, economic, and professional—Martínez Estrada's admiration for him surpassed his compassion. Quiroga did ceramic work on an old Victrola turntable, bound books, made a canoe out of a tree trunk, built his own dwellings—both in the jungle land of Misiones, where he had an impoverished eight-hundred-acre estate, and in Vicente López, a suburb of Buenos Aires—and darned his own socks. He did all the repair work on his Model T Ford, which he drove with wild abandon until demolishing it in Buenos Aires in 1928. His nautical acrobatics in an outboard motor boat were, in Martínez Estrada's words, "a form of psychic self-flagellation."[61] Whatever Quiroga did, or made, bore the indelible stamp of his personality. His "chalet" in Vicente López, recalls Martínez Estrada, "was a kind of bungalow in a shambles with rural furnishings, and the garage-woodshed-livingroom was an antique shop in which a helicopter and a dinosaur's skeleton would have gone together quite naturally" (p. 39).

[59] *Cartas inéditas*, p. 87.
[60] Ibid., p. 140.
[61] *El hermano Quiroga*, p. 34. Martínez Estrada was quite logically convinced that Quiroga had a "death wish." Not only did Quiroga take his own life, but his father shot himself by accident; his stepfather committed suicide; his first wife and first two children also committed suicide—she in 1915, they in 1937 (?) and 1950 (?) respectively. Their half-sister, María Elena Quiroga, gave me these "approximate" dates (1937 and 1950) in an interview in July 1966.

In city or country Quiroga was a misfit, precisely because of his unique role as a *creator*, that is, as one who insisted on creating everything. He was a self-sufficient and inimitable *homo faber* who was adaptable neither to nature nor the urban life. Far out in his own luminous orbit, equidistant from the slave-to-custom or the work-for-work's sake, and the exploiter or the oppressor (the two types who appear in various symbolic forms in Martínez Estrada's stories), Quiroga traveled majestically alone. Although he never rested, neither did he toil or serve; work for him was an exercise in perfection. "He gave to work the same meaning that all great men have given it, considering it a natural, necessary and moral duty. Of course, as far as Quiroga is concerned, all the rhetoric and defenses of work—the commonplaces of demagogues and urban sybarites—have nothing to do with his love of disinterested and ritual action. I have said that he worked as he wrote: conscientiously, as a good artisan, *con amore*" (p. 61). Free men are alone, free men suffer, free men create. This is the teaching that Martínez Estrada believes his three greatest masters—Hudson, Martí, and Quiroga—offered to the world.

6 · The Poet

It has commonly been assumed that with *X-Ray of the Pampa* Martínez Estrada set off in a new direction in his literary life. "The brave and generous poet, Ezequiel Martínez Estrada," wrote Waldo Frank, "sets aside the lyre for the scalpel; and in his *Radiografía de la pampa*, excoriates the moral bankruptcy of his people."[1] "In the three decisive years of 1930, 1931, and 1932," believes Juan José Sebreli, "Martínez Estrada is silent; then he reappears with *Radiografía de la pampa*, totally transfigured. Not only has he exchanged poetry for prose, but optimism for pessimism, harmony for chaos."[2] In this same first chapter of his book ("Situation of the Argentine Writer in 1930") Sebreli stresses the disoriented feeling experienced

[1] *South American Journey,* p. 73.
[2] *Martínez Estrada: Una rebelión inútil,* p. 19.

by most Argentine intellectuals after 1930. It was not coincidence, he points out, that three of the most prominent writers, and three lesser-known ones, all committed suicide by 1940.[3] Sebreli rightly states that changes in literary form and style follow or accompany socioeconomic changes.[4] The dissolution of the elitist group of poets and critics (the *Martinfierristas*) who had issued their vanguardist proclamation the same year that André Breton made his surrealist manifesto (1924), and the return to historical and social preoccupations by the great majority of Argentine writers with the political crisis of 1930, is confirmation enough of Sebreli's appraisal of the general tendency of that period.

Martínez Estrada, however, did not, from the beginning, follow the general tendency. He was never a *Martinfierrista*, and he was a pessimist from the time of his first published essay (1917).[5] Furthermore, not only was there no hiatus ("in the three decisive years of 1930, 1931, and 1932") in the writer's production, but rather an intensification of his essay writing from 1928 on.[6] In addition to publishing a number of short essays in this period, he devoted most of his time from 1930 to 1932 to writing *X-Ray of the Pampa*. There is an important revelation in *Brother Quiroga*: "He [Quiroga] initiated me in unpleasant readings . . . and extinguished in me the sickly lamp of poetry that had illuminated the gloomy pathways of my youth."[7] It is interesting to note that the "unpleasant readings"—the work of

[3] Horacio Quiroga, Uruguayan-born but a resident of Argentina most of his life (1878–1937), Leopoldo Lugones (1874–1938), and the Swiss-Argentine poetess Alfonsina Storni (1892–1938) were the prominent ones. Of the lesser-known (Enrique Méndez Calzada [1898–1940] is listed in Anderson-Imbert's *Spanish American Literature*. Cf. Sebreli, *Martínez Estrada*, p. 18.
[4] Sebreli, *Martínez Estrada* p. 20.
[5] "Tesoros velados," *Nosotros* 27 (Oct. 1917): 193–199.
[6] Martínez Estrada was a frequent contributor to *La Vida Literaria, Síntesis*, and *Babel* from 1928 to 1932. Possibly taking his clue from Sebreli, Martin S. Stabb also believes that Martínez Estrada "from 1929 till 1933 . . . wrote virtually nothing" ("Ezequiel Martínez Estrada: The Formative Writings," *Hispania* 49, no. 1 [March 1966]: 55). The truth is, of course, that in addition to the periodical contributions just mentioned, the essayist was intensively engaged from 1930 to 1932 in writing *Radiografía de la pampa*. On the other hand, Stabb rightly maintains "that despite the apparent ambivalences in his work, the comparison of his earliest writings with those of his maturity reveals a remarkable consistency of personality and outlook" (Ibid., p. 58).
[7] *El hermano Quiroga*, p. 70.

"geniuses of the literary underworld"—are all those of North Americans (O. Henry, Bret Harte, Dreiser, Jack London, Sherwood Anderson, Hemingway). Undoubtedly, the friendship with Quiroga, which began in 1928, was one of the principal factors in bringing about the substitution, in Waldo Frank's words, of the "lyre" by the "scalpel." Quiroga was alternately inspired and despondent, a "difficult" person for virtually all his acquaintances, but his relationship with Martínez Estrada appears to have been continuously good. This was due, more than to anything else, to a spiritual and intellectual affinity between two men who were able—following Simone Weil's principle—"to preserve untarnished their own solitude."[8]

Quiroga was influential, as his friend and admirer himself testified, in transforming the poet into the essayist.[9] But it should be noted that Martínez Estrada's best poetry was published in 1929, and that Horacio Quiroga had a large part in its inspiration. One of the best poems in *Humoresca*, indeed, is "Humoresca quiroguiana." It was *Humoresca*, not *X-Ray of the Pampa*, that most clearly marks a point of transition from poet to essayist; and the transition was much more gradual and natural than Sebreli assumed. There were seeds of deep discontent in some of the poetry of the earlier volumes and in the second part of *Argentina* (1927), a volume which, possibly because of a careless reading of the first part only, has generally been dismissed as an epic-toned exaltation of the Argentine countryside. We recall, also, that due to his extensive readings in preparation for the literature classes he began giving at the University of La Plata in 1925, a trip to Europe in 1927, and the professional encouragement of Leopoldo Lugones, Rafael Alberto Arrieta, Enrique Espinoza, and Horacio Quiroga, the young poet was fast emerging into the world of ideas. The essay, more and more, was becoming his natural form of expression.

The essay is, besides, psychologically and esthetically very close to lyric poetry. Like the essayist, the poet is an interpreter of himself in the light of his circumstances, and Martínez Estrada wrote prose after 1929 not because the lyric spirit abandoned him, but because in

8 Ibid., p. 9.
9 Ibid., p. 8.

the essay he was able to widen the circle of his experience and to develop his natural power of moral criticism. On the other hand, more than a decade of poetry writing—three volumes of it before he was thirty, three more before he was thirty-five—gave his spirit and his stylistic technique their necessary development. Like many other serious poets, he was to live out an existence in which his psychological half was at war with his intellectual half, a situation that made his idealistic aims in life impossible to realize. Anderson-Imbert states the case this way: "The demon of conscience made him conceive rationally of an order which dignified man through the ideals of freedom, well-being, justice, beauty, and truth; but that same demon had worked his way up to the conscience from the orgiastic depths of the jungle, with a tragic urge for survival."[10] There is little satisfaction with the sweet mysteries of life in the lyrics of this uneasy prophet. We could consider the period from 1918 to 1929 as Martínez Estrada's progressive awakening, in which the conscience supplemented by consciousness multiplies the mirrors of itself. That is the essence of the complete poet—to see oneself in every object of one's attention. At first, the youthful Ezequiel's mirrors are cosmic and abstract. Then, as feeling permeates the abstract vision and the ravages of doubt replace the poet's contemplation of fleeting celestial bodies, the mirrors become the concrete circumstances of life in this world. Little by little he has taken cognizance of those circumstances; there is now room in his universe for history, the society of the pampas and the cities, the distant rumblings of strife on other continents, the subdued desperation of individual men and women. In his first works Martínez Estrada is scarcely tasting life; from the second part of *Argentina* (1927) on, he is experiencing it fully.

However, in the earliest poetry a pattern had been set. It consisted, mainly, of a symbolic interpretation of all things, which was to find new vigor in his later writing. Like the young poet, the mature essayist read voraciously, always seeking fresh confirmation of his doubts and forebodings. Whereas Spengler, Nietzsche, and Schopenhauer were already molding his spirit in the early 1920's, it was not

[10] Enrique Anderson-Imbert, "Martínez Estrada en 1926," *Sur*, no. 295 (July–August 1965): 51.

until after 1930 that he conscientiously applied his readings of Spengler, Nietzsche, and Schopenhauer to the most serious contemporary events. Accordingly, in discussing the poetry I shall attempt not only to give the reader an idea of its style, but also to indicate in which ways Martínez Estrada's poetic thought of the 1920's, his emotional prelude, influenced his thought as essayist from 1930 until his death—the great opera of his literary fulfillment.

Restless Harmony: The Early Volumes

The "subtle fevered fantasies" described in the first poem of Martínez Estrada's first book (*Gold and Stone*, 1918) bear some of the sensuous qualities of Hispanic American modernism, a poetic fashion that quickly declined after Rubén Darío's death in 1916. But in addition to being fashionable, the fantasies were this young poet's natural way of awakening to creative consciousness. Like most other beginning writers uncertain of what their definitive style might be, Martínez Estrada represented a flexible compromise between two concepts defined by Northrop Frye in *The Well Tempered Critic*: the "classic temper" (aesthetic; art as artifact) and the "romantic temper" (psychological; art as expression). In the author of *X-Ray of the Pampa* the compromise grew steadily into a violent mental struggle in which the romantic temper emerged victorious. While there was a persistent structural harmony throughout most of his poetry, there was an increasingly strong emotional undercurrent also. The dramatic tension resulting from these two conflicting tendencies has not been taken sufficiently into account by most critics to date.[11]

---

[11] Alfredo Veiravé sees in Don Ezequiel's verse an expression of everything in the perspective of "a cerebral harmony" ("La poesía de Ezequiel Martínez Estrada," a lecture on Aug. 2, 1966, at the Sociedad Argentina de Escritores in Buenos Aires). Juan Pinto believes he was more an "aesthetic" than a "sentimental" poet (*Diccionario de la República Argentina*, Editorial Mundo Atlántico, Buenos Aires, 1950, p. 436). Julio Fingerit, writing about *Argentina* (1927) shortly after its publication, asserts that Martínez Estrada was not interested in confessing "his intimate emotions." His four books up to then, says Fingerit, are "for the most part intellectual adventures of a poet stymied by modesty" ("La poesía de Martínez Estrada," *Babel* 8, no. 27 [Buenos Aires, March 1928]). Although these judgments find confirmation in some individual poems, they are generally misleading because of their superficiality, or because of their respective authors' failure to take into account Martínez Estrada's poetic production in

This tension differentiates his verse from that of his admired Leopoldo Lugones (1874–1938), a memorable verbal gymnast and leading Argentine modernist. Lugones' decorative style had an obvious impact on the intellectually inclined Martínez Estrada, but little by little the fatalism and the melancholy of the younger poet prevailed over the elder poet's persistent virtuosity. Lugones had reverently practiced a cult of the literary that Martínez Estrada, according to his own confession, had himself indulged in at first. *X-Ray of the Pampa*, he assures us, represented the cancellation of his "mental adolescence," of the phase of his life "devoted to the sport, speculation and cult of letters,"[12] and Lugones had been his stylistic model during that phase.

However, a close reading of the six volumes from 1918 to 1929 leads one to the conclusion that Martínez Estrada in retrospect was over-dramatizing the change from poetry to prose. In an adversely critical essay, "Gold and Stone Forever" ("Oro y piedra para siempre"), one astute and sensitive reader portrays a poet unable to free himself from his purely bookish influences, a victim of his own "infallible method," which is scarcely concealed beneath his candid yet forced spontaneity.[13] In sum, it is the work of a laborious eclectic, feeling his way through a pedantic labyrinth of disparate sources. Adelaida Gigli's judgment, to be sure, is closer to the truth than Martínez Estrada's almost flippant dismissal of his formative period. Whereas Don Ezequiel attributes to himself a kind of experimental light-heartedness ("sport, speculation, and cult of letters"), Miss Gigli is impressed by his resolute enchantment with himself as an

---

its totality, and to perceive the pessimistic spiritual undercurrents beneath the forced *virtuosismo* of many of the poems. Still more misleading is Horacio Armani's statement that "there are not many connections between the work of Martínez Estrada the prose writer and that of Martínez Estrada the poet, because in him the poetry constitutes a previous phase, only fleetingly renewed toward the end of his life" ("La poesía de Martínez Estrada," *La Nación* [Buenos Aires], 4a sección, April 27, 1969). The present chapter is designed to show that Martínez Estrada's poetry is actually quite intimately connected (ideologically and emotionally) with his prose.

[12] From "Prólogo inútil" ("Useless Prologue"), in *Antología*, p. 12.

[13] Adelaida Gigli, "La poesia de Ezequiel Martínez Estrada: Oro y piedra para siempre," *Contorno*, no. 4 (Buenos Aires, Dec. 1954): 17–19.

artist. It is precisely this self-centeredness—more entertaining and more profound than his alleged addiction to "sport, speculation, and cult of letters"—that makes his poetry significant. If the self-centeredness is more immediately noticeable in the stylistic embellishments of the poetry, it is no less a part of the nervous pathos of his prose. Instead of curtailing his narcissism after 1930, he sublimated it; by giving it a more humanitarian orientation, he also gave it more power. Juan Carlos Ghiano probably comes closest to an objective synthesis in calling the young poet's work "an extremely personal intellectualization of what he sees and feels."[14] "A certain asceticism, a grimly gay whole-hearted renunciation," wrote Nietzsche in a passage that Martínez Estrada could not have missed, "is . . . one of the most favorable conditions for the highest intellectualism."[15] Martínez Estrada, whom Nietzsche would not have hesitated to call one of his "priests of the serious," began working out that "whole-hearted renunciation" in his first work and continued it until the last. It is alienation rather than playfulness that best characterizes his poetry. Men, diseased as they are with civilization, can offer no solace comparable to that of the stars.

While there is a good measure of intellectuality in *Gold and Stone*, sentiment and imagery seem to be the two main preoccupations of that brief first volume. But sentiment too often lapses into a rhetorical form of sentimentality; the poet addresses death, his youth, his soul, a rose garden, and "humanity" with uneasy self-consciousness; he accumulates philosophical platitudes ("A supreme reason governs all things") throughout and loses touch with life in a tedious "Requiem Mass" in which "Love," "Joy," "Desire," "Hate," and "Sorrow" all sing their prosaic parts.[16] The inspiration is abstract, as are the themes, and many of the metaphors are strangely mixed: "I praise the powerful and silent stone / its mystery and calmness. / Over it

[14] *Poesía argentina del siglo* XX, p. 18.
[15] Friedrich Nietzsche, *The Genealogy of Morals,* trans. Horace B. Samuel, p. 114.
[16] *Oro y piedra* (1918) in *Poesía,* pp. 9–45. The five other books are also reproduced in this volume: *Nefelibal* (1922), *Motivos del cielo* (1924), *Argentina* (1927), *Humoresca,* and *Títeres de pies ligeros* (1929). Subsequent references in the text to this edition of *Poesía* are by page number only.

the tonics pour / from the udder of eternity" (p. 10). This is only
a prose translation, of course, but the reader may be sure that the
tonics-udder-eternity context is just as grotesque in the original
Spanish. Disillusionment over his vanishing youth and painfully recalled adolescent love, a Virgilian exaltation of life in his grandiloquent "Panegyrics and Odes to the Four Seasons" (pp. 18–26), and
the enigmas of death and human destiny constitute the bulk of the
themes in *Gold and Stone*. If imagination, perception, and sensibility
may be considered the three principal requirements of the poet (i. e.,
creative power, clarity of expression, and feeling), one may conclude
that Martínez Estrada demonstrated more of the last than of the first
two in his first book. Not a great deal more can be expected of a be-
ginner.

There is, however, evidence of genuine ability in two of the
poems: "Welcome to the Magi" and the last piece in the book, "Ecce
Homo." The re-creation of the quiet journey of the Magi has both
power and tenderness. His portrayal of the "three vague visionaries"
and his magic transformation of the land and sky into a holy atmosphere are very fine. The last of the three stanzas is a prayer for the
Magi's safety and comfort as they realize their part of the miracle of
the Nativity:

> Que la tierra se aduerma, como en sopor de luna,
> bajo la maravilla de un fulgor estelar;
> que no turbe los cielos pacíficos ninguna
> nube; que ningún viento los sorprenda, al pasar;
> que se aplane y florezca la montaña y la duna;
> que el silencio les guarde, y el mar sea como una
> laguna, por si tienen que atravesar el mar (p. 30).[17]

The reader disposed to believe Martínez Estrada's own testimony
that the period of his poetry writing was merely "sport, speculation,

---

[17] "May the earth sleep, as in a lunar lethargy, / beneath the marvel of the
starlight glow; / let no cloud disrupt the peaceful heavens; / let no wind dis-
turb them [the travelers] on their journey; / may mountain and dune stretch out
into a flowering plain; / may the silence protect them, and the sea become / a
lagoon, if they have to cross the sea."

and cult of letters" would do well to consider the lasting sense of fatalism that begins to express itself with "Ecce Homo." The human being, "privileged," sensitive, heroic in his aspirations, is nevertheless only "the shadow of a dream." "Tomorrow a cold blast will extinguish the embers / that fired his lust, his virtues and his wars" (p. 45). But the important thing about this fatalism is not the mere ephemerality of man; rather, it is his inevitable corruption. Life is not in vain just because it is a dream, but also because it is an inherent malignancy. The poet's youthful readings of Shakespeare and Goethe convinced him that man's fate is not separable from man's character.

> Ama, cree, sufre, piensa. Exigente y astuto
> engaña y el engaño de los demás lo indigna.
> Envidia la inconsciente vitalidad del bruto
> y su vitalidad le parece maligna.
> Ayer vivió el espanto de un niño entre las fieras
> y por salvar su vida ensangrentó sus manos;
> hizo casas, iglesias, puentes y carreteras
> pero siempre con sangre de sus propios hermanos (p. 45).[18]

In this quick but conclusive portrayal in "Ecce Homo" appears the basic pattern that will be expanded and elaborated, but never changed, in the later essays and fiction. Modern man is still "the naked ape," as Desmond Morris affirms.[19] As his character is inseparable from his fate, his ideals are inseparable from his aggressions and deceits. Martínez Estrada seems to have sensed this not only before anthropology became the great unifying science it is today but before reaching his own intellectual adulthood.[20]

[18] "He loves, prays, suffers, thinks. Exacting and astute, / he deceives, though the deception of others makes him indignant. / He envies the unconscious vitality of the beast / and his own vitality seems to him malignant. / Yesterday he lived the terror of a child amidst the beasts / and to save his life bloodied his hands; / built homes, churches, bridges and highways / but with his own brother's blood."

[19] "Behind the façade of modern city life there is still the same old naked ape. Only the names have been changed: for 'hunting' read 'working,' for 'hunting grounds' read 'place of business,' for 'mate' read 'wife,' and so on. . . . It is the biological nature of the beast that he has moulded the social structure of civilization, rather than the other way around" (*The Naked Ape*, p. 84).

[20] Martínez Estrada's fatalism from the very beginning seems to have been based on his reading of Schopenhauer, who inspired his first published essay

The enthusiasm and transcendent spirit of his second volume has led some to think that the author of *Gold and Stone* had definitively emerged from his adolescent gloom to become the exuberant singer of odes in the 1922 collection, *Nefelibal* (*Inhabitant of the Clouds*). Indeed, the ecstatic joy of description, the vision of a world literally saturated with love (pp. 55–70), the fervent praises of nineteen heroes of Spanish civilization (pp. 83–92), all reflect the sensuous jubilation and virtuosity of Leopoldo Lugones, then his principal stylistic model. The inspiration for *Nefelibal*, as well as for *Heavenly Motives* (1924) and *Argentina* (1927), comes from Lugones in the sense that Lugones impressed Martínez Estrada as a creative rather than an ornamental poet, and as a master craftsman whose guiding principle was precision.

In the image I recall he was always standing, pacing the floor, continuously building cathedrals of metaphors and reflections. An urgent need for wakefulnesss, for living in the zenith of lucidity, power and exactitude gave coherence to his evasive personality. Correct in dress and speech, without carelessness or error, he constructed his phrases as if he were materially exhibiting them; and he poured out with the naturalness of breathing or walking the great wealth of his lexicon, his skillful feats of thought and emotion, the almost industrial accuracy of his expression. His constant lesson was responsibility to the language, which is not an instrument of approximation but of precision, like a weapon and a violin. With agility he created, through the evangelical magic inherent in the word, beings of unfading life and beauty. For his word was not simply an ornament, rhetorical and grammatical, but the creative word, *logos espermaticos*, language as a plastic force. He himself, as restless as his own ideas, seemed to be moved by it.[21]

"Tesoros velados," *Nosotros* 27 [Oct. 1917]: 193–199). Schopenhauer's idea of only one will manifesting itself ("objectification of the will") in all the creations of nature from the lowest forms of cellular life up to man is basic to Martínez Estrada's thought, especially where Schopenhauer's pessimistic conclusions are concerned, such as, "the will to live everywhere preys upon itself, and in different forms is its own nourishment, till finally the human race, because it subdues all the others, regards nature as a manufactory for its use. Yet even the human race . . . reveals in itself with most terrible distinctness this conflict, this variance with itself of the will, and we find *homo homini lupus*" (*The World as Will and Idea,* [Book II, Part 27], trans. R. B. Haldane and J. Kemp, p. 163).
    21 "Quiroga y Lugones," in *Cuadrante del pampero,* p. 188.

Precision, discipline, is what Martínez Estrada acquired from Lugones. Secretly, I believe, the younger poet aspired to the older
poet's virtuosity as well. The nineteen Spanish heroes praised in
Nefelibal—including the Cid, Hernán Cortés, Cervantes, Velázquez,
and the violinist Pablo de Sarasate (1844–1908)—were all, in their
respective fields of endeavor, virtuosos. The young writer's interest
in poetry as a precise art was deep and enduring. In the 1920's he
began as yet unpublished writings on the "Philosophy of Chess," in
which he makes many comments on aesthetics. Another of his unpublished manuscripts is devoted to the life and works of Niccolò
Paganini, part of which was probably written during his own intensive study of the violin from 1933 to 1940. In 1934 he delivered a
long lecture, "The Meaning of Paradox,"[22] in which he stressed that
the relatively new consciousness of paradox in poetry and the criticism of poetry had added a new dimension to poetic reality: the
vision of the subconscious, which, he believes, has raised jokes,
dreams, and the illogical to the level of delicate art. His lecture, in
fact, is a rejection of the classic spirit (or, at least, the classic spirit
as he understands it) for which he had felt no aversion in his early
poetry. Man feels a strange uneasiness as he contemplates the
"architectonic" excellences of a classical work of art, because that
work (the object) as a product of logic and conceptual symmetry is
basically incompatible with him (the subject): the man, who is a
mysterious embodiment of sensuality and atavistic prejudices. This,
we may suppose, is the basis of all paradox—the incongruity between a real subject and an idealized object.

The importance of this viewpoint cannot, in Martínez Estrada's
case, be overemphasized. On it is based the projection of his lyric
sensibility into all the areas of national and universal concern that
he deals with in the essays. That projection began long before his
1934 lecture on the paradox.

The first evidence of the youthful poet's transformation from an
intellectual virtuoso into an emotional prophet can be seen in "The
Poem of Love" in *Nefelibal*. The inspiration is Dantesque in its

---

[22] "Sentido de la paradoja" (June 1, 1934), in *Anuario del Instituto Popular
de Conferencias de "La Prensa,"* pp. 45–61.

cosmic view of love and Freudian in its sense of the power of Eros. There is also a mystic satisfaction in nature which, instead of giving tranquility to the poet, makes more dramatic his sensitivity to the aggressiveness of man. In the opening poem of the book ("Nefelibal"), an invocation, he pleads for spiritual release.

> Vuela, nefelibata,
> en espiral inmensa
> sobre el hombre que piensa,
> que procrea o que mata.[23]

The awkward allegorical structure of "The Hours" (pp. 50–53), "The Poem of Love" (pp. 55–70), and "Poem of the Several Moons" (pp. 76–78) need not obscure the fact of his despair over the human condition. In "The Machines," a brief part of "The Poem of Love," he states that man was made not in God's image but in that of the ant or the beetle, "absorbed in war and toil, / full of hate, fear and fatigue." It was only after he perfected machinery, levers, gears, and axles as extensions of himself, that "he made himself over" in the image of God. He was still, for all that, a *man* of ant-beetle characteristics. The closing "Hymn" of "The Poem of Love" expresses fervent hope that universal love may unite "the brothers of every hierarchy" ("men, snakes, plants"), but here, as in "The Hours," there is a strong preoccupation with "the murderous hate that binds our hands" (p. 70). In commenting on the festive sublimation of sex and violence in "Carnival" (an unmistakable anticipation of "Carnival and Sorrow" in Part IV of *X-Ray of the Pampa*) he speculates on the possibility that everyday life was predestined to be sadder than the cruel deceptions of the annual carnival that precedes the Lenten season.

But it is in "The New Pure Reason" (pp. 80–81) that Martínez Estrada most forcefully expresses his pathos, which permeates too much of the glimmer of anarchic hope at the end of the poem. ("He who shows the way is our enemy, / and he who conceals it is our true brother.") This is the "Theorem" with which he concludes; it follows a "Thesis" of absolute stoicism. The soul is beautiful in contrast with

---

[23] "Fly up, cloud-spirit, / in a widening spiral / above the man who thinks, / who procreates or who kills" (p. 50).

the world; life is ephemeral and senseless; only the soul's capacity for love—that in itself—makes human existence worthwhile against our background of total futility. The "Hypothesis," the first and longest of the three parts, not only sets the tone for this composition but also advances the subjective philosophy that will become the basis of all his essay writing. By this philosophy "the entire cosmos" is subjoined to his personal life, and as they are bound together in fateful relationship, cosmic time and psychological time—the objective time of the clock and the subjective time of the poet[24]—seem to coincide absolutely. Mentioning Fichte and Schelling, he claims that everything outside the visible sphere of the self (*el No-yo*) is actually "the projection of ourselves into heaven or hell." From there, he proceeds to his fundamental philosophy: each of us creates the reality he lives in or, at least, the perspectives and circumstances of his existence.

> Da pena, pero es cierto que creamos las cosas,
> que el mar o que la estrella son sólo una emoción,
> y que entre este tumulto de cosas misteriosas
> somos la única realidad de las cosas.[25]

The next stanza describes the climax, the end of the illusion, when the "delicate crystal" of his soul will share its death with the universe, simultaneously destroyed. That universe, as it turns out, has no existence independent of the poet's existence, for "we are the only reality of things." Many years later, in one of the numerous aesthetic digressions of *Death and Transfiguration of Martín Fierro*, the author reiterates the poetic principle that, from the time of *Nefelibal* (1922) to his latest writings, is to be more intimately and more forcefully his. The principle is adapted from the *Poetics* of Wilhelm Dilthey: "lived experience," not the world or reality as such, is the

---

[24] Martínez Estrada does not mention Bergson's duality of an impersonal and abstract *temps homogène* and a personal and concrete *durée héterogène* that makes life dramatic (and tragicomic). But Bergson's influence (*L'Evolution créatrice*) seems possible.

[25] "It is sad, but the truth is that we create all things, / that the sea and the star are but an emotion, / and that amidst this mysterious pandemonium / we alone are real."

theme of every true poet.[26] Like the philosopher and the politician, the poet creates the stage on which he is to perform, his own "circle of experience," as Dilthey put it. Then with time the circle widens, and the "transformations of the representations of life" (Dilthey) grow more complex. But Martínez Estrada, untempted by the surrealistic displacements of the self that were essential to so much of the vanguardist poetry of the 1920's, remained even more resolutely at the center of his circle. Absorbed with the enigmas of history and the ironies of personal existence, he took little interest in the beauties of the unreal, beyond, that is, the unreal that he identified with the illusory thought of the not yet disillusioned: hopeful adolescents, Spanish explorers of the New World, exalted progressives of the nineteenth century, and political and social humanitarians of the twentieth century. Increasingly, he became the poet of the visible, the witness of specific situations. His power grew as he moved away from the aesthetic ideal of Leopoldo Lugones, toward the natural ideal of William Henry Hudson. It was in his book on Hudson that he wrote, "Poetry is not so much the expressive need of one who has understood beauty as the need to be exact and worthy of confidence."[27] This belief was the strongest link between the author's poetic and essayistic functions, which constituted no basic conflict, but rather two complementary means to the same end—art as the revelation of self.

   Heavenly Motives (1924) is the third and last of the "early" books. It is dedicated both to Emanuel Swedenborg, the scientist and mystic to whom heaven "opened" in 1745, and to Johann Sebastian Bach, the religiously inspired composer. *Heavenly Motives* produced little heavenly expression, however. Readers have tended to take the third line of the introductory poem ("for there is a harmony which is only cerebral") as a fundamental characteristic of all Martínez Estrada's poetry. The four lines with which the same poem ends do not confirm such a view. They reveal an admiration of Verlaine's and Darío's ideal ("art is blue"), as well as the young poet's quest of true lyricism:

[26] *Muerte y transfiguración de Martín Fierro*, I, 340.
[27] *El mundo maravilloso de Guillermo Enrique Hudson*, p. 230.

porque no hay flor que tenga menos de cien mil años;
porque un teorema es flor y música y ser vivo;
porque llamamos cielo al azul que no vemos;
porque el arte es lo azul y azul es lo infinito.[28]

But that quest has not yet been realized. *Heavenly Motives* marks the end of a poetic adolescence, but with a whimper, not a bang. The author has simply played himself out as the formalistic singer of cycles and seasons, and it is quite possible that more than a few readers who used *Heavenly Motives* as their first sampling of Martínez Estrada's poetry quickly decided to make it their last. The volume contains more than a little intellectual name-dropping—classical, mythological, and contemporary—which shows clearly how proud the author was of his rapidly growing general knowledge. So far as the knowledge was concerned, that pride was justified; so far as the poetry was concerned, it was not. Noticeably more than in *Nefelibal*, there is exaggerated emphasis on eternity, infinity, and cosmic spaces, and the poet is adamant in his refusal to replace thoroughness with suggestiveness. In this regard he shares with his seventeenth-century predecessor Luis de Góngora and his illustrious compatriot of the modernist age, Leopoldo Lugones, a mania for the total vision. His concern is not, at this point, "to see a world in a grain of sand," but to display all of creation's grains of sand together, as if they formed part of God's own panorama and the poet had simply transcribed it.

To write about "The Zodiac" he required a learned introduction and a separate poem for each of the twelve constellations (pp. 115–124). It is a carefully constructed piece, bringing together in a strange fusion erudite references to Descartes, Darwin, and Hesiod; an intermittent lament on the fatality of all existence; stoic resignation inspired in Confucius and Buddha; epic praise of friendship, form, liberty, and love. "Poem on Human Lunation" ("Poema de la lunación humana") is the cumbersome title of a cumbersome

---

[28] "because no flower is less than a hundred thousand years old;
because a theorem is a flower and music and a living being;
because we call 'sky' the blue that we do not see;
because art is everything blue and blue is the infinite" (p. 99).

composition on the four phases of the lunar month. He uses it as a sorrowful allegory on the life of man (pp. 128–131). "Cycle of the Day," as one might readily suppose, is divided into morning, noon, afternoon, and night (pp. 136–139). The four sections represent a transformation from sunlit hope to black pessimism.

The Return to Earth

Rafael Alberto Arrieta's first, very enthusiastic, impression of young Martínez Estrada's poetry was not without some reservation. In *Gold and Stone* he found "the calculating cerebration of a chess player."[29] But this friendship, which began with Ezequiel's visit to the editorial offices of the prestigious cultural and literary review *Nosotros* in April 1918, was to stimulate a remarkable literary progress from the first to the last two volumes of poetry in 1929. Arrieta's reminiscent essay discloses a growing friendship that came to a mysterious end, apparently through the initiative of Martínez Estrada in 1930, and which would be renewed with only a part of its former intimacy in 1948. From Arrieta's testimony, and from the fragments of Martínez Estrada's letters accompanying it, the reader gets a quite vivid impression of the seriousness with which the young poet began to fulfill his literary mission after 1925. This was when he began his teaching duties at La Plata (where Arrieta secured for him a chair in world literature) and diminished for a time his poetry writing.

The time was ripe for self-appraisal and for a change of orientation. From a letter in January 1926, in which he comments on his reading of Goethe, we can sense a spiritual situation that will be suggested many times and in many forms in his later writings: the feeling of absolute independence that was both exhilarating and somberly fatalistic. Of Goethe's unique intelligence he says:

He has been able to free himself *completely* from the Christian conception of the world, including the Judaic, usually the last thread to tie the various Western ways of thought to that extremely complex mechanism (he nevertheless lived in and for a Christian world). He achieved complete

[29] "Ezequiel Martínez Estrada o la amistad discontinua," in *Lejano ayer*, p. 179.

imperviousness, definitive detachment, absolute dehumidification, from everything Christian (granted: the Gothic is really Christian) and, consequently, from everything anti-Christian (because there is an essentially Christian anti-Christianity, like that of Strauss and Nietzsche). The secret of Goethean sublimity lies in the fact that *he was denied the grace of the Lord*; and in the fact that he devoted himself neither to God nor the Devil. His only concern was for Man.[30]

It was also in 1926 that, according to Arrieta, Martínez Estrada confessed in a moment of great despair that he had "lost" his ability to write verse. Arrieta reminded him of an ode to Argentina for which he had won a prize from the Patriotic League, persuading him that it could be the basis of a new volume, his definitive return, no less, "from the heavenly spheres to the earth, our Argentine earth."[31]

By the end of the year the book was finished, and for *Argentina*, published in 1927, he would win the First Municipal Prize for Poetry in Buenos Aires in 1929. One fears, on beginning to read the first long and quite declamatory poem in the book, that Arrieta's hope for a return "from the heavenly spheres" had been in vain. Although I have been unable to find the first published version of the poem, which earned Ezequiel his prize from the Patriotic League, I judge from the textual evidence of *Argentina* itself and from the information provided by Arrieta that it is identical—as a whole or in part—with Part I of the 1927 edition. Part I comprises ten numbered sections followed by a "Hymn" in six stanzas to the nation. It is all very grandiloquent, panoramic, and unspeakably reverential: still the work of an uneasy experimentalist trying to produce simultaneously the image descriptions of Virgil and Whitman and knotting it all up with erudite references.

But Part II, which seems to be the part written under the guidance and encouragement of Arrieta in 1926, is fortunately a different matter. The flowery epithets and clarion calls to eternal glory are replaced by a quite sensitive description of concrete places and things, such as ranches, wild horses, harvest time, wine, and the ostrich. The

---

[30] Ibid., pp. 184–185.
[31] Ibid., p. 187. Arrieta writes that these words were part of his encouragement to Martínez Estrada.

poet begins to be himself, and reality becomes the adequate instrument for expressing his feelings. He has found his vital themes, the
infinite forms of life and death situated—for the first time in his
writings—in the Argentine atmosphere. In the opinion of Ricardo
Rojas, Argentine literary historian, Martínez Estrada "geometrizes
and harmonizes in a single, extremely personal style the signs of the
Zodiac and the signs of the pampa."[32] I think that Rojas oversimplifies and distorts the case. Although there is still, as another critic
writing in the same journal maintains, a strong tendency to resist
confession,[33] the poet has freed himself—by the time he sets out to
write Part II of Argentina—from his prolonged imprisonment in those
peculiarly rigid heavenly spheres. The will to resist confession does
not, in his case, prevent confession. There is confession of an underlying sorrow, which translates itself into the landscape ("Mountains," "The Salt Fields," "The Ombú," "The Viscacha") and in the
lyric recollection of certain experiences and frustrations ("The Tea
Hour" [Mate], "San José de la Esquina" [the author's birthplace]).
The atmosphere of loneliness and frustration has become the author's
fixed environment. He will reproduce it in X-Ray of the Pampa and in
Death and Transfiguration of Martín Fierro, and in all his fiction. Of
the desolate salt fields he writes,

> Y es tan triste este desierto
> y esta tristeza tan muda
> que empiezo a sentir la duda
> de si me he quedado muerto (p. 185).[34]

"The whole atmosphere leans on the tired earth," he writes in the
same poem. Then, transferring himself philosophically as well as
emotionally into the symbol of the ombú tree (one of his favorite
and most often repeated symbols), he achieves one of his finest meditations, and in only six simple lines:

---

[32] "Una carta abierta a Martínez Estrada," Babel 8, no. 27 (Buenos Aires,
1928).
[33] Julio Fingerit, "La poesía de Martínez Estrada," Babel 8, no. 27 (Buenos
Aires, March 1928).
[34] "And this wilderness is so sad / and this sorrow so silent / that I begin to
wonder / if I have died."

La soledad te ha hecho
luchador por el tronco,
por las ramas artista,
por la raíz filosofo.
El arbol más potente
es el que está más solo (p. 190).[35]

The only critic to pay more than the most fleeting attention to
Argentina to date, Engenio Pucciarelli, endeavors to show how Part
I and Part II complement each other.[36] From the first part to the second he believes that "nature prolongs itself into civilization," a process of which, to be sure, Martínez Estrada himself seems to be repeatedly reminding us in *X-Ray of the Pampa*. Indeed, as Pucciarelli
says, Part I is in an exultant, though also quite remote way, nature-
centered. Part II is unmistakably man-centered and, significantly,
the theme of the machine as the main symbol of modern life here
enters his work for the first time: the oil drill, the steam-run wheat
thresher, the plow, and the guillotine blade that sacrifices the lamb.
But, inexplicably, Pucciarelli characterizes the whole work by its
"vital euphoria." He believes that *Argentina* demonstrates the author's "conformity with the present, his confidence in the future, his
admiration of the past."[37] The examples we have seen scarcely confirm such a judgment; nor, certainly, does the poem on the wheat
thresher ("Trilla"), in which—after a gay, impressionistic description of the steam boiler and the intricate movement of pulleys and
gears—the poet adds the human ingredient, "the lamentable note"
of the presence of man. Wherever he finds himself his hand "leaves
a trace of sadness and fatigue." His activity is "the rude labor of the
chain gang." His eyes cast "crooked glances," his laughter is "bes-
tial" (pp. 175–176). Then there is "Iberá" (pp. 180–181), a hallu-
cinatory vision of a tropical lake, an obvious symbol of maleficent
nature that comes directly from Baudelaire and Nietzsche:

[35] "Solitude has made you / a wrestler because of your trunk, / an artist in
your branches, / by your roots a philosopher. / The strongest tree / is that which
is most alone."
[36] "La imagen de la Argentina en la obra de Martínez Estrada," *Sur*, no. 295
(July–August 1965): 34–48.
[37] Ibid., p. 39.

Naturaleza intacta, reducto del imperio
del Caos primitivo, donde aun en el misterio
de lo libre y lo elemental
los amores terribles y las muertes clementes
cierran un ciclo hermético con flores y serpientes
más allá del bien y del mal (p. 181).[38]

Still less attention has been given to the Buenos Aires section—
twelve poems in all—of *Argentina*. Although it is not particularly
significant poetic creation, the description of the city is realistic and
suggestive of the author's future negative view of the Argentine
metropolis. The descriptions are generally pejorative: employees
trying in vain to catch up with a world that had "begun the race"
before they were born; hair lotion "that acts as caustic in the eye";
"music that suffers a syncopation of cramps"; "afternoons of fatigue
and boredom"; a ticket taker at the circus, "humiliating her old age
with cosmetics"; a visit to the main cemetery of the city, "the city in
miniature" (pp. 193–199). Right here, in this "euphoric" book of
poems, is where Martínez Estrada sets forth the fatalistic pattern of
his future works: Buenos Aires, a cemetery in motion; civilization,
original Chaos in its final phase.

In 1929 Martínez Estrada published two poetic works: *The Light-
Footed Marionettes*, in which the light-footed style of Lugones is
quite evident; and *Humoresque*, which was by far the most serious
and personal of the author's books up to then.

Deliberately artificial in conception and structure, *The Light-
Footed Marionettes* is a *commedia dell'arte* in verse. The four-
hundred-year-old puppets, notwithstanding the capricious descriptive style of their author, reflect directly his tragic sentiment of human existence. Imprisoned in their wooden bodies, they have nevertheless acquired human sensitivity and consciousness. All have experienced frustration; all are condemned to continue their aimless
existences. Colombina, the eternal woman, repeats her refrain of

---

[38] "Nature unaltered, condensation of the empire / of original Chaos, where
even in the mystery of the elemental and the free / monstrous loves and merci-
ful deaths / seal a hermetic cycle with flowers and serpents / beyond good and
evil."

(Nietzschean) eternal recurrence throughout the work. Outside the frame of their stage existences the puppets have tasted the frivolities, passions, and sorrows of real life. Now they prefer either a return to the stage or death to their present aimless lives. Pierrot, the innocent and faithful lover, has had a child with Colombina. The child has died, and Colombina has since been seduced by Arlequín, the cynical, attractive lover. Pantalón, the adventurer, who in his own way also appeals to Colombina, has returned from an "imaginary" Japan, "which is but an illusion / without geographical existence" (p. 243), and which anticipates the author's "imaginary" Argentina (the Argentina that Argentines have dreamed of since the landing of the first Spanish explorers) described in *X-Ray of the Pampa*. Only Polichinela, the deformed clown who refuses to take life seriously, seems to accept his fate. The play coincides with the reunion of all the puppets, each presenting the testimony of his failure. In the end, all except Pierrot decide to return to their normal vocation of entertaining children. Pierrot, who represents the poet through his more sensitive and sentimental nature, remains alone to sing of his despair. About halfway through the poem Marabú (a marabou, or stork-like bird) appears in a choral function similar to that of Poe's raven. After analyzing the illusions and vanities of each of the puppets, Marabú disappears, prophesying for each:

> larga vida de lágrimas, el pan ácimo y duro
> del artista, el peligro de la celebridad
> y esa vida en la muerte que es la inmortalidad.[39]

Beyond the musical light-heartedness of the descriptive verses, Martínez Estrada has written a miniature yet powerful tragedy designed to show that love leads irrevocably to unhappiness. The introspective turn that the poet began to take in the second part of *Argentina* continues here. Colombina's compassion, Pierrot's melancholy sensitivity, Arlequín's romantic solitude, and Pantalón's skepticism are Martínez Estrada's indirect self-portrait, the symbolic dramatization of his personal viewpoint as a poet and as a man.

---

[39] "A long life of tears, hard and unleavened bread / of the artist, the perils of celebrity / and that life in death which is immortality" (p. 235).

The closer he comes to his definitive poetry, a poet in many ways finds his situation to be more and more restrictive. As he perfects his style and deepens his vision of reality it becomes increasingly difficult for him to tread the precarious line between intimacy and dignity. Only true awareness of his function and an objective recognition of his problematical circumstance in life will permit him to produce work representative of his highest capacity. Martínez Estrada comes closest to that awareness and recognition in *Humoresque* and, once he has written it, decides that poetry is no longer the proper form for the fulfillment of his literary mission. For now the writer's thoughts begin to be long thoughts—as the predominance of long lines in most of the poems of *Humoresque* suggests—and he moves toward the new expansiveness that he will soon find in his meditative prose. The paragraph will always constitute a freer form than the stanza.

The strange, for the most part, unpoetic vocabulary of many of the earlier pieces is now happily absent. In *Argentina* we find *gimnosofistas, diprothomo, agropecuaria*; in *Heavenly motives, viviparidad, progrediente, hipodérmica, galvanoplastia*; in *Nefelibal, hipóstasis, simbiótico, glíptico, termocauterio, ginolatría, cantárida*; in *Gold and Stone, argiraspido, ambiope, filarmonía, demetérico, grímpola, corpúsculo, álgida, heptacéfala*. Some, like many of Lugones' neologisms and scientific terms, are inserted (as are a much greater number of exotic, learned, and mythological proper names) simply to display knowledge. Others are compounded or invented words. In most cases they constitute a stumbling block, and often a vain search through the dictionary, to comprehension.

Despite his later claim (ca. 1945) that he had always been a man "incapable of confession,"[40] *Humoresque* is an open revelation of his sentiments and doubts. "Humoresque," of course, a musical composition of capricious character, reminds us of Martínez Estrada's other "vocation": the violin. In fact, "Humoresque on Vocation" (pp. 291–296) is a Walter Mitty–style dream in which the poet imagines himself as the world's most famous virtuoso, comparable only to the

---

[40] "Carta a Victoria Ocampo," *Sur*, no. 295 (July–August 1965): 4.

great Sarasate, the monster of technique. It is the only truly capricious poem in the collection; in it the author presents himself not only as a memorable musician but as a notorious personality very much like Ramón del Valle Inclán's Marqués de Bradomín:

> Almorzaría con magnates y ministros,
> cenaría con sus esposas
> y dormiría con sus hijas.[41]

While it is true that Don Ezequiel took his own study of the violin very seriously, his stimulus for writing "Humoresque on Vocation" was not so much his enthusiasm for music as his growing dissatisfaction with his mission as a poet. His wild dreams of virtuosity and fame so playfully described in this piece are actually an intentional contrast with his subdued literary role. Although he expresses satisfaction in the last stanza at being happy though not famous (p. 296), the inner sense of his preoccupation is unmistakable: disillusionment and regret at being one of the least-read poets in the Spanish language. Winning in late 1932 the National Prize in Literature for the two books published in 1929 did not impress him so much as the violent and rancorous controversy that ensued.[42] The controversy confirmed in 1932 the obsessive fear that one can read between the lines of "Humoresque on Vocation": that even his best poetry—and there can be no doubt that *Humoresque* contained his best poetry—was not to find readers beyond the small intellectual circle of a few friends.

Other factors seem to have contributed to his conversion to essay writing, which was not, as I have already pointed out, sudden, but rather a gradual movement toward his deeper vocation—that of the poet in prose. First was the anguished moment in 1926 when he desperately confessed to Rafael Alberto Arrieta that he had lost his touch and would be unable to write more poetry. In 1927 the trip to Europe and in 1928 the beginning of the close intellectual friendship with Horacio Quiroga gave him new and more serious perspectives;

---

[41] "I would lunch with magnates and diplomats, / I would dine with their wives / and I would sleep with their daughters" (p. 295).
[42] See Chapter I of this study.

and the virtual death of Argentine politics with the coup d'état of
1930 brought him very directly to the reappraisal of national history
that would be the nucleus of his work from then on.
"Tis one of those odd tricks which sorrow shoots out of the mind."[43]
This is the epigraph of *Humoresque* and it adequately reflects the
somber inspiration of these sprightly compositions. The author sets
the tone in the first poem ("Ezequiel Martínez Estrada"), autobiographical in both its reminiscences and its speculation. His philosophical mood is succinctly stated in the sixth section ("La obra"):

> El inútil apremio de la hormiga atareada,
> y al fin de tanto esfuerzo, de tanto afán prolijo,
> n un gran libro, ni un árbol que dé sombra, ni un hijo.
> La tristeza, el trabajo y el amor para nada.[44]

Frustration, in a word. But as the three "Variations" on themes by
Baudelaire, Leopardi, and Valéry show, a life of fascinating visions
remains, and it is even possible that his life of mounting disillusionment has made those visions easier to achieve. Like Baudelaire, he
now sees "nothing but the infinite from every window,"[45] and his
greatest inspiration is the sense of nothingness he assimilates from the
three great poets.

Infinite space from Baudelaire; death symbolized in the extinct
worlds described by Leopardi; the nightmare-enchantment of un-
reality in Valéry. These are, one could say, the three components of
his solitude. In "Variations on a Theme from Baudelaire" life is not
the interminable succession of experiences, but an endless fall into a
bottomless pit, and the bottomless pit turns out to be the poet
himself (p. 280). The same feeling of isolation and futility is emphasized also by allusion to Nietzsche's doctrine of eternal recurrence:

---

[43] Shakespeare, *Antony and Cleopatra*, IV, 2.
[44] "The useless drudgery of the harried ant / and after so much effort such
painstaking dedication, / no great book, no shade-giving tree, no son either. /
Only sorrow, travail, and love for naught."
[45] "Je ne vois qu'infini par toutes les fenêtres" (from "Le Gouffre", a poem of
the "Spleen et Ideal" section of *Les Fleurs du mal*). The line is part of Martínez
Estrada's epigraph for "Variaciones sobre un tema de Baudelaire" (pp. 278–
281), and he writes, in the fifth section of the poem, that he "opened four
windows that opened out on nothing," soon to discover that the terrifying void
has hardened into a substance "more compact" than the wall itself (p. 279).

everything that can be experienced has already been experienced before we were born. Even our most intimate dreams have been dreamed by others (p. 281). Yet, such alienation is not just the perspective of the sensitized automaton, or the psychically displaced person. Like all poets, Martínez Estrada regards himself as the center of all things. It is the "objective" world that is displaced or, more precisely, absorbed by the hypersensitive self. In "Variations on a Theme from Leopardi" he imagines himself to be a spindle whirling at great speed. This represents the absolute concentration with which he views himself, and as the concentration intensifies, he finds himself reduced to a needle point. The "atmosphere of fever and dreams" that surrounds him is "the struggle without glory or objective" of the world; and the poet, reduced to a motionless and infinitesimal point, would like to become even smaller (p. 284).

The "Humoresques" are also, essentially, "variations" on themes and attitudes of admired writers—"Humoresca heineana" on Heinrich Heine (1797–1856); "Humoresca quiroguiana" on Horacio Quiroga. Irony is the predominant note. The sensitive and persecuted Jewish poet visited in Münster the "cages" in which his coreligionists had been imprisoned and the plaza in which a few of them had been burned, but Martínez Estrada advises all impressionable ladies to take heart:

> Jews burn on the outside, it seems,
> and do not feel the flames; their cries are only
> subterfuges to afflict with pity
> those who feed wood to the fire.[46]

The whole poem is in the romantic-ironic tone. ("What do we care about a wretched poet long dead?") In the twentieth century "neither the lark, nor a woman, nor the nightingale" customarily dies of love. If women would not respond to the lonely Heine's tender passion, he at least had the advantage of God's attention. Accordingly, the childless and wifeless poet "incubated in his sick-bed / the nineteen volumes of his Complete Works" (p. 302). Heine had "a sidereal

[46] Calderón de la Barca receives partial credit for this observation ("Al menos eso enseña algún Auto Sacramental de Calderón," p. 300).

and musical soul"[47] that was the envy of his Argentine admirer. As if to counterbalance the creative exuberance that made the German poet's life tolerable, Martínez Estrada stresses the weight of his frustrations: the ironies of the potentially passionate lover whom women nevertheless ignore; the political libertarian to whom the common reaction is persecution and censorship; the supreme lyric spirit whose music is destined, for the most part, to fall on deaf or indifferent ears.

Whereas the "Humoresca heineana" is an impressionistic and largely speculative biography of Heine as a spirit, "Humoresca quiroguiana" is a nearly surrealistic testimony of the author's friendship with the eccentric Uruguayan short-story writer. Although the two men had known each other only about a year when Martínez Estrada wrote the poem, it makes a perfect prologue to the reminiscent *Brother Quiroga* published in 1957; for Quiroga was already, by the end of 1928, the spiritual and intellectual "brother" of Martínez Estrada. Although Quiroga inculcated in his young friend much of the anti-industrial and anti-urban sentiment to be expressed later in *The Head of Goliath* and *The Marvelous World of William Henry Hudson*, the Uruguayan was nevertheless a staunch believer in the necessity, for every man, of self-sufficiency and productive work. "His mentor," recalls Don Ezequiel, "was—as he was for me—Thoreau. His formula—attend to your own problems first, then concern yourself with the world—was from Emerson."[48] In conjunction with an imagination that extended from grotesque descents into morbidity to the wildest adventures in the wilderness, Quiroga was also a mechanic, engineer, architect, and agriculturalist by inclination (if not by achievement), and most important of all, a would-be inventor. His plans included a device to liquidate ants and the manufacture of orange extract through dehydration (five thousand dehydrated oranges would produce up to ten liters of extract, efficient machinery would be constructed, and in almost no time Quiroga and his prospective partner Martínez Estrada would be millionaires).[49]

---

[47] "Su alma sidereal y musical / era capaz de una pasión universal" (p. 303).
[48] *El hermano Quiroga*, p. 79.
[49] Ibid., p. 50.

"Humoresca quiroguiana" contains a Quiroga-style fantasy. Martínez Estrada imagines a super-machine capable of extracting from a person his "double." As the invention of a Dr. Nerio Rojas portrayed in the poem, this machine is based on a principle frequently implied throughout Martínez Estrada's work: that man is an antipodal duality "with an angelic beginning and an animal ending" (p. 305). The author allows himself an entertaining excursion into science-fiction not only through the machine's capacity to create a person's double but also through its second unique function. By a mysterious electrolytic process "optic ladies of the cinema" are "defilmed" (p. 306). What was at first a mere visual image on the screen can be removed and reassembled into an atomic reality. Or, in another sense, the new physical reality has been *projected* from the optical—a reverse photographic process that appears to be analogous to the literary creative process (development from an idea or notion of a character into the character itself).

Animal and angel, man is a duality, a "centaur," a hybrid creature of "reality" and "poetry." This antipodal nature makes him uncomfortable; he cannot get along with himself, and life is nothing but frustration. So feeling and so thinking, Martínez Estrada submits himself to Dr. Rojas' machine. He has a sensation of giving birth to himself as the machine projects a psychedelic checkerboard pattern of light and shadow over his naked body. He feels a "centrifugal ecstasy, a mystic charm," as his other self begins to take form. When the milky cloud emanating from Martínez Estrada No. One is condensed into Martínez Estrada No. Two, Dr. Rojas discovers he has a residue in the machine—enough white-magic plasm to create a woman. What in the beginning was one man is now to be a human trinity, two brothers and their sister.

The meaning of the title, "Humoresca quiroguiana," becomes clearly evident in the third and final section of the poem, in which the characters of the two "brothers" are contrasted. The original Martínez Estrada portrays himself as "the more intelligent, the more sensible, without vices or agonies." The impulsive, volatile, and more imaginative one, the newly created brother, remains as a difficult and morose member of the little family for fifteen months; then, "opening the valves of his violent dreams," he sets out with almost no money to the wilds of northern Argentina, where he dies, the victim of a snakebite. Everything in the description of this personage in drawn directly from the life, stories, and letters of Horacio Quiroga. This is the sense in which it may be considered a prologue to the informal biography published twenty-eight years later.

As for the sister, she also disappears, becoming the heroine in a movie entitled "Yellow Fever." At this point, nearly at the end of the poem, the poet reveals that eight years before her birth by the supermachine he had seen an earlier version of the same picture and had been infatuated with its heroine. So, going back, "my sister was the movie star that I absorbed." She had originated as an image on a film, and now she would again become—after passing through the spirit of Martínez Estrada and being reborn in the machine—an image on a film.[50]

In a gloomier vein is "Leonor," a poem in three "movements," which concludes the volume. It is an elegy for a seventeen-year-old girl, reminiscent to some degree of Edgar Allan Poe's brief poem of the same name ("An anthem for the queenliest dead that ever died so young/A dirge for her the doubly dead that ever died so young"). But it is a deeper poem than Poe's, and death is more vividly present. As one of his lines suggests, Martínez Estrada's piece is a lyric study of "the art of death and its wisdom" (p. 318). He refers to the cadaverous aspects of his heroine more than to her extinguished beauty (a fleeting reference to worms, a speculation on the "vitreous and opaque" quality of the eyes beneath the violet-hued eyelids), but there is no more than a suggestion of the grotesque. The funeral is a contrast between the attitude of the stereotyped mourners and the intense sensitivity of the poet. The narrative of the death and burial

[50] Enrique Anderson-Imbert describes briefly a novel by the Peruvian Clemente Palma, XYZ (1934), as follows: "It tells of the invention of a process for projecting motion picture images on protoplasm, thus creating lives that repeat exactly those of Hollywood actresses" (Spanish American Literature: A History, p. 217). I have been unable to consult Palma's book directly, and it is difficult to know whether Palma got any ideas from "Humoresca Quiroguiana." Martínez Estrada's poetry in book form reached painfully few readers. However, "Humoresca Quiroguiana" was first published in 1928 in the Sunday supplement of La Nación.

is interspersed with delicate recollections of the relationship—a suggestion of Tristram and Isolde—between the poet and the girl. He remembers how in the last days she spoke with the simple gravity of the saint and the sage, how she *lived* her death a long time before it took place. The superiority of this poem to Poe's "Leonore" (and, in fact, to most of Poe's death poetry) is mostly due, however, to the sincere revelation of the poet's own inner experience. Poe, by comparison, loses himself in his artifact; he is the great sculptor at work on his lyric statue. In the "Leonor" of Martínez Estrada everything is subjoined to the poet because of his all-pervading emotional vibration. Furthermore, his sense of fatality is intensified by the resignation of the heroine and by an extremely sensitive presentation of the *process* of death. Her death is all death, the "invisible forces" that Martínez Estrada feels and describes in *X-Ray of the Pampa*, the forces that lead hopeful men into the wilderness, make them age in body and mind, and, in the momentary glare of destructive reason, dissipate their dreams.

"Otros caminos de penitencia . . ."

In spirit, Martínez Estrada maintained his lyric vocation, and there are passages of lyric strength and beauty in his prose from 1930 on. Evaluations of his poetry are far from unanimous. As late as 1941 Borges referred to "the limpid and complex stanzas of our best contemporary poet."[51] H. A. Murena, the Argentine who comes closest to being a disciple of Martínez Estrada, writes off the latter's poetry as useless, "bad poetry, decorative; bad, that is, to tell the truth without euphemisms."[52] Murena sees the transition to prose, Don Ezequiel's definitive medium, as the result of one crucial psychological experience. It was, Murena says, the moment at which Martínez Estrada discovered himself alone, "with empty hands." He then saw that "the *rubenismo* [the style of Rubén Darío], culture, and the innovations of free verse were merely borrowed clothes." The frightening notion that not only he (Martínez Estrada) but all Argentines

[51] Prologue to *Antología poética argentina* (with the collaboration of S. Ocampo and A. Bioy Casares), p. 8.
[52] "La lección de los desposeídos," in *El pecado original de América*, p. 114.

and all Hispanic Americans were members of a historically "dispossessed" race was the most poignant motivation for a deepening of
his preoccupations and a sharpening of his prophetic sense. The substance of Murena's analysis is true; but he is erroneous in his timing.
It is clear from the preceding observations about *Argentina, The
Light-Footed Marionettes,* and *Humoresque* that there was no sudden moment at which the young poet made his luminous discovery of
emptiness, that even in isolated pieces in the earlier books one can
find the darkest of premonitions, that as early as 1920, Nietzsche
and Schopenhauer meant much more to the future prophet than
Darío. It should also be clear to the tolerant but discerning reader
that there is a considerable body of good poetry in *Humoresque,*
and that in that book Martínez Estrada is free of his former addiction to expressing his Olympian view of the universe in every other
stanza.

By late 1928, the same year in which the author of *X-Ray of the
Pampa* arrived at his fundamental conclusion ("sooner or later one
learns that the life process is an error that compounds itself"),[53]
friends convinced him that he had reached the end of his first literary
phase, and that he should follow his "new roads of penitence" in the
form of prose.[54]

I think the whole answer to the problem of how Martínez Estrada
became a serious and prophetic writer is found in a change in stylistic conviction—from creative writing based on metaphor to creative
writing based on paradox. His own consciousness of this change is
evident in the previously mentioned lecture of June 1934, "The Sense
of Paradox."[55] For a long time, he observes, metaphor and paradox
were nearly indistinguishable and coexisted in harmony. But in his
time, and ours, in the age of disbelief, it was no longer possible to
reveal the truth through simple imagery and metaphor—that is,
through "the poetic" in its superficially representational forms. Thus

[53] "Reflexiones acerca del error," *Síntesis,* no. 14 (Buenos Aires, July 1928),
p. 192.
[54] The influential friends were Enrique Espinoza and Horacio Quiroga. See *El
hermano Quiroga,* pp. 37–38.
[55] "Sentido de la paradoja," in *Anuario del Instituto Popular de Conferencias
de "La Prensa",* pp. 45–61.

considered, he tells us, the poetic is something "inherent in form," whereas "the paradoxical" is inherent in "the assertive," of life itself. In our time paradox is the only valid form of revelation, for it is only paradox—in its seeming self-contradiction—that dramatizes and clarifies the difference between appearance and reality, and that gives adequate expression to the mysteries of the subconscious and the "hidden forces" that purportedly surround us. Whereas the metaphor simplifies, the paradox shows complexity.

One might say that paradox does not materialize in a well illuminated part of an alert consciousness, but rather in some region on the frontier of the dark forces of divination and the lifeblood.

In what zone of the soul is paradox produced? What is its climate? Partly in the zone of the instincts, partly in the zone of passion.

We could find it in that place where the soul feels itself surrounded by the concealed, on the frontiers of all that has been conscientiously explored, with the testimony of ancestral and personal experience, on the borderline of the known and the unknown. Or, we might say, in that region where reason is still intuition, insecurity and anxiety.[56]

These are not the words of a man who has forsaken the lyric vocation. What he calls "the paradoxical" turns out to be more poetic than what he calls "the poetic."

The little poetry that Martínez Estrada wrote after 1929 was pure paradox: *Blindman's Songs* (1959) and *Other Blindman's Songs* (1968).[57] The songs ("coplas") are mere two, three, and four-line stanzas. In the two editions there are a total of 150. Some are simply capricious:

> Desnudábase una joven
> e iba plegando la ropa
> cuando advirtió que se hallaba
> en la plaza y no en su alcoba.[58]

Some are moralistic:

---

[56] Ibid., p. 46.
[57] *Coplas de ciego*, 59 pp.; *Coplas de ciego y otras coplas de ciego*, 88 pp.
[58] "A girl was undressing / and carefully folding her clothes / when suddenly she discovered she was / in a public square and not in her room" (*Otras coplas*, XLIV, p. 60. Subsequent references are to this edition).

Reinaron en armonía
la fuerza de la costumbre
y el poder de la mentira.[59]

Others are philosophical:

No hubiera sido posible
vivir en la verdad;
era preciso engañarse
y aceptar la realidad.[60]

Still others are religious:

Kierkegaard tiene razón:
son los mejores cristianos
aquellos que no lo son.[61]

All are imbued with the same somber humor and skeptical resignation. The writer wanted desperately to preserve his art of the paradox through both extended thought and these brief, spiritual calis-
thenics. Possibly his poetic legacy is best expressed—as well as in
many passages of the major essays—in three brief poems ("Three
Poems at Eventide") published in *La Prensa* in 1955. It is a monologue or inner dialogue between the poet and his soul. The three
poems are entitled "Alone," "Dusk," and "Cold." Each represents successive stages within the disillusionment preceding death. The poet
has lived sacrificially, rejecting "love, fortune and glory" for the bitter
wine of knowledge. "Y ahora, al final de tu camino,/buscas a Dios
que sabes que no existe."[62]

Solitude, he writes in the last of the three poems, surrounds the
soul and contracts slowly until the moment of death. The quest for
knowledge may be, in the end, as vain as the most frivolous existence. But virtue, suffice it to say, is nearly as indefinable as truth,

[59] "Ruling in harmony / were the force of custom / and the power of the lie"
(XLV, p. 33).
[60] "It would not have been possible / to live in truth; / he had to deceive himself / and accept reality" (XCVIII, p. 87).
[61] "Kierkegaard was right: / the best Christians / are those who are not"
(LXXV, p. 76).
[62] "And now, at the end of your journey, you search for God, knowing He
does not exist."

and no man is the proper judge of another man's proportion of good-
ness and vanity. As an artist, and as an artist he must be judged,
Martínez Estrada developed great dramatic tension between his
intelligence and his sensitivity. For this reason, the fine vibrant prose
he wrote from 1930 to the year of his death was not the rejection but
rather the expansion of what for several years he already felt as a
poet. For him, prose was the better weapon with which to face life,
that ominous "error that compounds itself." And writing prose seems
to have been the only way to change—if only in sporadic moments
of illumination—the landscape of a world that he had described in
his poem to Leonor as "the tired earth, now sterile to all miracles."

Epilogue

The theme and structure of the work of Ezequiel Martínez Estrada was progressive disillusionment, hardly a unique phenomenon in modern literature. Reading him is usually an uncomfortable experience. An analytic passion dominates his creations from the first poetry to the latest autobiographical laments, and a kind of cruel self-indulgence is clear in his forebodings. But Martínez Estrada was honest with himself, always the first prerequisite for an honest confrontation with the realities of a hostile world, and there is true satisfaction for the reader in watching that confrontation take place. Having lived in the most systematically murderous of all centuries, we are familiar with most of the historical background that led Martínez Estrada to his conclusions. We have shared his disenchantment, for the symbolic world he described has taken on more and more similarity with the real world. In the hands of an important writer words become important symbols. As such, they are insights into the true nature of existence up to now, and premonitions of what is to come. Martínez Estrada had this symbolic power and he became, like his biblical namesake, a prophet.

Both the physical and the abstract worlds abound in fantasy. Of Jorge Luis Borges, John Barth has written, "His artistic victory, if you like, is that he confronts an intellectual dead end and employs it against itself to accomplish new human work."[1] The reference is to Borges' interest in the persistent impact of certain works of literature of the past—the idea, for example, that an imaginary French poet of the nineteenth century, Pierre Menard, could compose strictly from his own imagination writings identical to several chapters of *Don Quixote*. Whereas Borges concerns himself with the unfathomable and often monstrous elements of the abstract realms of philosophy and literature, Martínez Estrada attacks the illusory distortions of the real, particularly as found in the perpetuation of historical myth and in stereotyped ways of accepting tradition. Both Borges and Martínez Estrada, the former through ironic skepticism, the latter by indignant involvement in the most adverse social and political questions, scorn the role of men in material history, for both believe that in most cases history is little more than a comic mask with which the unimaginative and the pompous cover up complex human idiosyncracies. Borges and Martínez Estrada are two sides of the Argentine intellectual coin: Borges strives to intellectualize life, forcing it into the abstract; Martínez Estrada attempts to vitalize intellectuality, forcing it into the concrete. Each man does this through his own interpretation of an essentially tragic sentiment. It is not now my proper function to evaluate in a comparative way the contributions of these two giants of twentieth-century Argentine literature. But I could appropriately remark that Martínez Estrada's critical spirit, which expressed itself through an experience of involvement, means more to the young intelligentsia of Hispanic America than does Borges' more artistic critical spirit, which has expressed itself most

[1] "The Literature of Exhaustion," *Atlantic Monthly* 222, no. 2 (August 1967): 31.

often through an experience of withdrawal into mental mysteries. If for both "the world is too much with us," only Martínez Estrada develops in his work the great struggle between utopian desire and tragic vision. Only he waged continuous verbal war against the oppressive "powers of money, arms and religious doctrine," and formulated his literary work in terms of that struggle.

The significance of this tormented writer resides ultimately in his homelessness. He could never find his place in the existent ideological and material schemes of things, and he wrote everything from the standpoint of spiritual exile. He had heroes—Nietzsche, Martí, Hudson, Quiroga—but they too traveled the roads of practical failure. He had positive political and social ideals, but they retained their definitive character only in the light of the impossibility of their application. In *X-Ray of the Pampa* and *Death and Transfiguration of Martín Fierro* he showed that bitterness and strong lyric subjectivity do not necessarily preclude historical perceptiveness, but few of his own generation were willing to heed his grim protestations. Widespread interest in his work began only in the 1950's. H. A. Murena, among a few others, discovered the vital sense in which Martínez Estrada had become a teacher to the generation that began to write in the 1940's. Murena's testimony appears in an essay, "A Lesson for the Dispossessed: Martínez Estrada."[2] The lesson, according to Murena, was Martínez Estrada's realization that to be a Latin American was to be a "pariah," and a rootless being born in a state of historical original sin, that is, without a history.

Europe, full of traditions, legends, and landmarks, still held together its cultural children in a family relationship; but the child of America was a cultural orphan, the offspring of obscure racial origins, "the dispossessed." This was an indispensable point of departure in the twentieth century, the beginning of a psychoanalytic liberation from nationalistic self-delusion that the intelligentsia needed. Martínez Estrada is the first to assert the problem in a conclusive way. Murena in Argentina and Octavio Paz in Mexico (*Labyrinth of Solitude*) follow him up, reminding the hopeful generation of the 1950's

[2] "La lección a los desposeídos: Martínez Estrada," in *El pecado original de América*, pp. 107–129.

that they would have to be both more realistic and more idealistic than the two or three preceding generations.

We can situate Martínez Estrada's restless view of contemporary man somewhere between Thomas Mann's search beyond the morbid and W. H. Hudson's exaltation of the living earth—basic fascinations, certainly, of the existential present and the romantic past. Our writer was attracted toward the morbid at the same time that he felt the remote enchantments of an *imagined* nature of the past. The progressive disillusionment that I have identified as the theme and structure of his work evolves amidst these two personal obsessions: the experience of death and a continuing lament on the lost paradise he might have had but never did.

The dark attractions of autobiography have been an increasingly noticeable feature of Western literature from Emerson to Sartre; "dark" because more and more the educated mind delves into the abysmal regions of the self and the subconscious. The outcome has been a new kind of understanding of the total context of human problems. What was thought of well into the nineteenth century as almost purely ideological and moral (the questions of justice and injustice, deceit and honesty, the nature of love and aggression) is now considered inseparable from the organic functions and the pathological aspects of human existence. Against this inevitable background Martínez Estrada describes a world reflected in the mirror of himself, the shadows of the past, and the bleak horizon of the future. The grim affinity that one may (or may not) feel toward him on reading his essays depends on the degree to which one is able to share his role of symbolic victim—the victim, that is, of just about every circumstance of contemporary life. He was the disciple of three basic masters: Spengler, Schopenhauer, and Freud. Spengler's interpretation of history as a process of decline, Schopenhauer's view of the universal revelation of adversity, Freud's psychoanalysis of suffering as the creation of hidden monsters in the subconscious. These were Martínez Estrada's main perspectives of discontent.

The attentive reader will quickly discern in his writings the nebulous line between critical acumen and heated indignation, but he will probably also realize that at a time when the persecution of the individual has reached an unprecedented level of sophistication we seriously need Martínez Estrada's kind of candor.

He has made an indirect offering of cultural history through the great gift of his poetic insight. Fleetingly he seizes upon one theoretician after another—historians, sociologists, philosophers, cultural anthropologists—to aid him in expounding on his passion for the moral well-being of his country. But they neither diminish his power nor do they add very much to his thought. Rather, he reads them with the symbolic preconceptions of the poet and prophet. The interesting thing is the broad fable of his own experience and his attempt, through the examples and symbols of history, to cure us of our illusions in an atmosphere of vanishing freedoms and initiatives. In the United States Daniel J. Boorstin has noted the same "extravagant expectations" and the recurring "feat of national hypnosis" that Martínez Estrada discovered in Argentina nearly three decades before. Boorstin's assessment of the American dilemma turns out to be a paraphrase of the basic conclusion of X-Ray of the Pampa:

> Nowadays everybody tells us that what we need is more belief, a stronger and deeper and more encompassing faith. A faith in America and in what we are doing. That may be true in the long run. What we need first and now is to disillusion ourselves. What ails us most is not what we have done with America, but what we have substituted for America. We suffer primarily not from our vices or our weaknesses, but from our illusions. We are haunted, not by reality, but by those images we have put in place of reality.[3]

Nihilistic radicals, vengeful patriots, and, even more, the Silent Majority partake of the will to self-deception that the nation as a whole has come to regard as sacred. It has been the unspoken tradition in both Argentina and the United States for most of this century.

---

[3] Daniel J. Boorstin, The Image: A Guide to Pseudo-Events in America, p. 6.

BIBLIOGRAPHY

I. Books by Martínez Estrada

Análisis funcional de la cultura (1960). Buenos Aires: Centro Editor de América Latina, 1967. 119 pp.

Antología. Mexico City: Fondo de Cultura Económica, 1964. 394 pp.

La cabeza de Goliat (1940). 3rd ed. Buenos Aires: Editorial Nova, 1957. 320 pp.

Coplas de ciego. Buenos Aires: Editorial Sur, 1959. 59 pp. 2nd ed., 1968, 88 pp. [The second edition contains *Otras coplas de ciego,* pp. 37–88.]

Cuadrante del pampero. Buenos Aires: Editorial Deucalión, 1956. 303 pp.

Diferencias y semejanzas entre los países de la América Latina. Mexico City: Universidad Nacional Autónoma de México, 1962. 594 pp.

En torno a Kafka y otros ensayos. Barcelona: Editorial Seix Barral, 1967. 271 pp.

Exhortaciones. Buenos Aires: Burnichon Editor, 1957. 91 pp.

Heraldos de la verdad: Montigne-Balzac-Nietzsche. Buenos Aires: Editorial Nova, 1958. 265 pp.

El hermano Quiroga. Montevideo: Instituto Nacional de Investigaciones, 1957. 92 pp. 3rd ed., 1968, 166 pp. [The third edition contains forty letters from Horacio Quiroga to Martínez Estrada previously published in *Cartas inéditas de Horacio Quiroga,* collected by Arturo Sergio Visca.]

Las 40. Buenos Aires: Ediciones Gure, 1957. 109 pp.

Leer y escribir. Mexico City: Joaquín Mortiz, 1969. 156 pp.

Leopoldo Lugones: Retrato sin retocar. Buenos Aires: Emecé Editores, 1968. 160 pp.

Marta Riquelme ("Marta Riquelme" and "Examen sin conciencia," 1949) Buenos Aires: Editorial Nova, 1956. 99 pp.

Martí: El héroe y su acción revolucionaria. Mexico City: Siglo XXI Editores, 1966. 266 pp. [The third and last part of the work entitled *Marti, revolucionario.*]

Martí, revolucionario. Vol. I. Havana: Casa de las Américas, 1967. xvi and 618 pp.

Meditaciones sarmientinas. Santiago, Chile: Editorial Universitaria, 1968. 172 pp.

Mi experiencia cubana: En Cuba y al servicio de la revolución cubana. Montevideo: El Siglo Illustrado, 1965. 219 pp.

Muerte y transfiguración de Martín Fierro. 2 vols. Mexico City and Buenos Aires: Fondo de Cultura Económica, 1948. 453 pp. 2nd, rev. ed., 1958, 473 pp.

El mundo maravilloso de Guillermo Enrique Hudson. Mexico City: Fondo de Cultura Económica, 1951. 342 pp.

Panorama de las literaturas. Buenos Aires: Editorial Claridad, 1946. 383 pp. and index.

Para una revisión de las letras argentinas. Buenos Aires: Editorial Losada, 1967. 204 pp.

Poesía (*Oro y piedra,* 1918; *Nefelibal,* 1922; *Motivos del cielo,* 1924; *Argentina,* 1927; *Títeres de pies* and *Humoresca,* 1929.) Buenos Aires: Argos, 1947. 331 pp.

La poesía afrocubana de Nicolás Guillén. Montevideo: Editorial Arca, 1966. 92 pp.

¿Qué es esto? Buenos Aires: Editorial Lautaro, 1956. 313 pp.

Radiografía de la pampa (1933). 5th ed. Buenos Aires: Editorial Losada, 1961. 350 pp.

Realidad y fantasía en Balzac. Bahía Blanca: Universidad Nacional del Sur, 1964. 894 pp.

Sábado de gloria ("Sábado de gloria," 1944; "Juan Florido, padre e hijo, minervistas," 1955). Buenos Aires: Editorial Nova, 1956. 123 pp.

Sarmiento. Buenos Aires: Biblioteca Argos, 1946. 207 pp.

La tos y otros entretenimientos. Buenos Aires: Editorial Futuro, 1957. 143 pp. [Thirteen short stories, including "La Tos."]

Tres cuentos sin amor ("La inundación," 1941; "Viudez," 1945; "La cosecha," 1948). Buenos Aires: Goyanarte, 1956. 138 pp.

Tres dramas (*Lo que no vemos morir* and *Sombras,* 1941; *Cazadores,* 1951). Buenos Aires: Ediciones Losange, 1957. 158 pp.

El verdadero cuento del tío Sam. Illustrated by "Sine." Havana: Casa de las Américas, 1963. 114 pp. and 12 unnumbered pp. [Text in Spanish, English, and French.]

II. Articles by Martínez Estrada

"25 aniversario de *Radiografía de la Pampa*." *La Gaceta* 5, no. 53 (Mexico City, Jan. 1959). [An address delivered Dec. 3, 1958, to the Sociedad Argentina de Escritores, Buenos Aires.]

"A Waldo Frank" (poem, 1929). In *Waldo Frank en América Hispana*, edited by M. J. Benardete, pp. 236–237. New York, 1930.

"Bahía Blanca es de Hecho la Capital de Media República." *El Atlántico* (Bahía Blanca), Dec. 21, 1955. [Includes a long open letter to Gen. Aramburu, then president of Argentina.]

"Carta a Victoria Ocampo" (1945). *Sur*, no. 295 (Buenos Aires, July–Aug. 1965): 3–7. [Reproduced in *Leer y escribir*, pp. 115–120.]

"Cepa de literatura ríoplatense." *Diógenes* 10, no. 43 (Buenos Aires, July–Sept. 1963):61–74.

"De los hombres libres: Henry David Thoreau." *La Prensa* (Buenos Aires), June 16, 1957.

"Doce de octubre." *La Vida Literaria* 3, no. 25 (Buenos Aires, Nov. 1930). [Reproduced in *Leer y escribir*, pp. 70–72.]

"Drama y comedia de la juventud." *La Vida Literaria* 4, no. 30 (Buenos Aires, April 1931). [Reproduced in *Leer y escribir*, pp. 73–81.]

"Energías anónimas." *Nosotros* 28, no. 106 (Buenos Aires, Feb. 1918): 225–233. [Reproduced in *Leer y escribir*, pp. 34–44.]

"Un ensayo sobre filosofía del ajedrez" (Parts I–IV). *La Nación* (Buenos Aires), Mar. 23, 1924. (Parts V–IX), *La Nación*, Mar. 30, 1924.

"El escritor argentino en funciones ancilares." *La Gaceta* 6, no. 66 (Mexico City, Feb. 1960).

"Estética y filosofía de Guillermo Enrique Hudson" (1941). In Angélica Mendoza, et al., *Guillermo Enrique Hudson: Vida y obra, bibliografía, antología.* New York: Hispanic Institute, 1946.

"El estimulo de vivir." *Nosotros* 27, no. 104 (Buenos Aires, Dec. 1917): 457–466. [Reproduced in *Leer y escribir*, pp. 22–33.]

"Estío serrano" (poems). *Nosotros* 36, no. 211 (Buenos Aires, Dec. 1926): 468–478.

"Familia de Martí." Cuadernos de la Casa de las Américas. Havana: Editorial Nacional de Cuba, 1962. 47 pp.

"El Fondo [de Cultura Económica], instituto editorial de instrucción superior y popular." *La Gaceta* 5, no. 61 (Mexico City, Sept. 1959).

"George Orwell: *Mil novecientos ochenta y cuatro*." *Sur*, nos. 192–194 (Buenos Aires, Oct.–Dec. 1950):308–309.

"Horacio Quiroga" ("Palabras pronunciadas por Ezequiel Martínez Estrada frente al cuerpo de Horacio Quiroga"). *Sur*, no. 29 (Buenos Aires, Feb. 1937):108–111.

"Informe sin objecto." *La Vida Literaria* 4, no. 32 (Buenos Aires, June 1931).

"La inmortalidad de Facundo." *Cuadernos Americanos* 4, no. 5 (Mexico City, Sept.–Oct. 1945):207–220.

"Los invariantes históricos en el *Facundo*" (Conferencias pronunciadas en la librería Viau en agosto de 1947). Buenos Aires: Viau, 1947. 39 pp.

"Leer y escribir." *La Vida Literaria* 3, no. 25 (Buenos Aires, Aug. 1930). [Reproduced in *Leer y escribir*, pp. 63–66.]

Letters to Manuel Pedro González (June 11, 1960, and Jan. 8, 1963). In *Casa de las Américas* 5, no. 33 (Havana, Nov.–Dec. 1965):61–62.

"Lo gauchesco." *Realidad* 1, no. 1 (Buenos Aires, Jan.–Feb. 1947):28–48.

"Las manos de Paganini." *La Nación* (Buenos Aires), Aug. 30 and Sept. 6, 1942.

"Mensaje a los escritores." Bahía Blanca: Editorial Pampa-Mar, 1959. 32 pp.

"Mester de juglaría." *La Vida Literaria* 1, no. 1 (Buenos Aires, July 1928). [Reproduced in *Leer y escribir*, pp. 67–69.]

"Nicolò Paganini en su epistolario." *La Prensa* (Buenos Aires), May 19, 1957.

"Nietzsche, filósofo dionisíaco." *La Nación* (Buenos Aires), Oct. 15, 1944. [Also the title of the 106-page essay in Martínez Estrada's *Heraldos de la verdad.*]

"Nietzsche, o del estilo." *Humanidades* 30 (University of La Plata, 1944–1945):37–50.

"Norteamérica, la hacendosa." *Sur*, nos. 192–194 (Buenos Aires, Oct.–Dec. 1950):156–159.

"Otra vez sobre las lentejas." *La Nación* (Guayaquil, Ecuador), Oct. 29, 1961. [Reply to an unsigned article in *La Nación* (Buenos Aires) on July 16, 1961, on Martínez Estrada's alleged acceptance of Cuban citizenship.]

"Palabras pronunciadas en el sepelio de Pedro Henríquez Ureña." *Sur*, no. 141 (Buenos Aires, July 1946):7–10. [Reproduced as "Homenaje a Pedro Henríquez Ureña" in *Leer y escribir*, pp. 143–146.]

"La pampa." *El Hogar* (Buenos Aires). Sept. 28, 1934, pp. 116–118.

"Placa de una *Radiografía*." *Revista do Livro*, no. 10 (Rio de Janeiro, June 1958):201–203.

Prologue to *Martín Fierro* by José Hernández. Buenos Aires: W. M. Jackson, 1938.

"Reflexiones acerca del error." *Síntesis*, no. 14 (Buenos Aires, July 1928): 187–192. [Reproduced in *Leer y escribir*, pp. 53–60.]

"Regreso a los padres." *Propósitos* 5, no. 99 (Buenos Aires, Sept. 1955).

"Sarmiento a los 120 años." *La Vida Literaria* 4, no. 28 (Buenos Aires, Feb. 1931). [Reproduced in *Leer y escribir*, pp. 82–90.]

"Sarmiento, escritor" (1950). In Rafael Alberto Arrieta, ed., *Historia de la literatura argentina*. Vol. II, pp. 371–434. Buenos Aires: Ediciones Peuser, 1958.

"Sarmiento y los Estados Unidos." *Cuadernos Americanos* 11, no. 3 (Mexico City, May–June 1952):186–204.

"Sarmiento y Martí." *Cuadernos Americanos* 5, no. 4 (Mexico City, July–Aug. 1946):197–214.

"Sentido de la paradoja." *Anuario del Instituto Popular de Conferencias de la Prensa* (Buenos Aires), June 1, 1934, pp. 45–61.

"Tesoros velados." *Nosotros* 27, no. 102 (Buenos Aires, Oct. 1917):193–199. [Reproduced in *Leer y escribir*, pp. 13–21.]

"Tres poemas del amanecer" ("Solo," "Vísperas," "Frío"). *La Prensa* (Buenos Aires), Feb. 5, 1956.

"La voz del violín en Paganini." *La Nación* (Buenos Aires), July 27, 1941.

III. Critical and Related Writings

Adam, Carlos. *Bibliografía y documentos de Ezequiel Martínez Estrada*. Universidad Nacional de la Plata, 1968. [The only extensive bibliography to date; twenty-five letters from Martínez Estrada and critical commentary by eleven authors are added.]

Alberdi, Juan Bautista. "La República Argentina, 37 años después de la Revolución de Mayo." In *Obras completas*, vol. III. Buenos Aires: La Tribuna Nacional, 1886.

Anderson-Imbert, Enrique. "Martínez Estrada en 1926." *Sur*, no. 295 (July–Aug. 1965):49–54. Also in *Casa de las Américas* 5, no. 33 (Nov.–Dec. 1965):50–54.

———. *Spanish American Literature*. Translated by John V. Falconieri. Detroit: Wayne State University Press, 1963.

Ara, Guillermo. *Los argentinos y la literatura nacional*. Buenos Aires: Huemil, 1966.

Arguedas, Alcides. *Pueblo enfermo* (1909). 3rd edition. Santiago, Chile: Editorial Ercilla, 1937. [The third edition contains a new preface and

an additional chapter, in which (pp. 255–256) Arguedas supports his
anticommunist argument with extensive quotations from Günther
Gründel, "teorizante excelso del nacismo," and Hitler's *Mein Kampf*
(pp. 264–265). In *Mein Kampf* Arguedas finds support for his own
theory of racial purity for Bolivia.]

Armani, Horacio. "La poesía de Martínez Estrada." *La Nación*, April 27,
1969.

Arrieta, Rafael Alberto. "Esteban Echeverría y el romanticismo en el
Plata." In vol. II of *Historia de la literatura argentina*, edited by Rafael
Alberto Arrieta. Buenos Aires: Ediciones Peuser, 1958.

———. "Ezequiel Martínez Estrada o la amistad discontinua." In *Lejano
ayer*, pp. 179–196. Buenos Aires: Ediciones Culturales Argentinas, 1966.

Astigueta, Fernando Diego. "La mentalidad argentina en el tango y sus
modismos." *Journal of Inter-American Studies* 7, no. 1 (Jan. 1965):
67–94.

Atlántida 43, no. 1123 (Buenos Aires, Sept. 1960):22–28. [Contains "Los
escritores frente a una actitud. Martínez Estrada y el país." Fourteen
commentaries on Martínez Estrada preceded by a speech by him.]

Barletta, Leónidas. Prologue to Martínez Estrada's *Mi experiencia cubana*,
pp. 7–22. Montevideo: Arca, 1965.

———. "Testimonio." *Casa de las Américas* 5, no. 33 (Nov.–Dec. 1965):
32–33.

———. See *Atlántida*, Sept. 1960.

Bates, Marston. "Man and the Balance of Nature." In *The Fate of Man*,
edited by Crane Brinton, pp. 482–490. New York: George Braziller,
1961. [See especially pp. 487–488 on Hispanic indifference to nature.]

Bergson, Henri. "L'Intelligence et l'instinct." In *L'Evolution créatrice*, pp.
147–164. 4th edition. Paris: Félix Alcan Editeur, 1908.

Bermann, Gregorio. Letter to Manuel Galich (Nov. 5, 1964) on the occasion of Martínez Estrada's death. *Casa de las Américas* 5, no. 33
(Nov.–Dec. 1965):36.

Billard, Jules B. "Buenos Aires, Argentina's Melting-Pot Metropolis." *National Geographic* 132, no. 5 (Nov. 1967).

Boorstin, Daniel J. *The Image: A Guide to Pseudo-Events in America*. New
York: Harper Colophon Books, 1961.

Borello, Rodolfo A. "Dos aspectos esenciales de la *Radiografía de la
pampa*." *Ciudad*, no 1 (Buenos Aires, Jan. 1955):24–27.

Borges, Jorge Luis. "Una efusión de Ezequiel Martínez Estrada." *Sur*, no.

242 (Sept.–Oct. 1956):52–53. [Borges defends Aramburu's regime against Martínez Estrada's criticism.]

———. "El escritor argentino y la tradición." *Sur*, no. 222 (Jan.–Feb. 1955): 3–8.

———. "El escritor argentino y la tradición." *Buho*, no. 4 (Buenos Aires, May, 1963):2, 6, 23–24.[Additional thoughts on 1955 article of the same name.]

———. "*Radiografía de la pampa* por Ezequiel Martínez Estrada." *Crítica* 1, no. 6 (Buenos Aires, Sept. 16, 1933):5. [Reproduced in *Bibliografía y documentos de Ezequiel Martínez Estrada,* by Carlos Adam, p. 220.]

———. See *Atlántida*, Sept. 1960.

———, with the collaboration of S. Ocampo and A. Bioy Casares. *Antología poética argentina*. Buenos Aires: Editorial Sudamericana, 1941.

Brown, Norman O. *Life against Death: The Psychoanalytical Meaning of History*. New York: Random House, 1959.

Bullrich, Silvina. See *Atlántida*, Sept. 1960.

Bunkley, Allison Williams. *The Life of Sarmiento*. Princeton: Princeton University Press, 1952.

Canal Feijoo, Bernardo. "Los enfermos de la patria." *Sur*, no. 295 (July–Aug. 1965):20–25.

———. "Radiografías fatídacas." *Sur*, no. 37 (Oct. 1937):63–77. [The most negative criticism of *Radiografía de la pampa*.]

Carballo, Emmanuel. "Tres radiografías de Martínez Estrada" (1959, 1960, 1962). *Casa de las Américas* 5, no. 33 (Nov.–Dec. 1965):38–49. [Three interviews with Martínez Estrada, tape-recorded in Mexico City at the beginning and at the end of a one-year stay in Mexico, and after a two-year stay in Cuba.]

Carrió de la Vandera, Alonso ("Concolorcorvo"). *A Guide for Inexperienced Travelers between Buenos Aires and Lima*. Bloomington: Indiana University Press, 1965.

Casa de las Américas 5, no. 33 (Havana, Nov.–Dec. 1965). "Homenaje a Ezequiel Martínez Estrada." [Critical commentaries and testimonies by sixteen authors and six texts by Martínez Estrada.]

Castagnino, Raúl H. *El teatro en Buenos Aires durante la época de Rosas* (1830–1852). Buenos Aires: Comisión Nacional de Cultura, 1944.

Chávez, Fermín. "Civilización y barbarie en la cultura argentina. *Estudios Americanos* 10, no. 49 (Seville, Oct. 1955):409–431.

Ciocchini, Héctor. "Notas sin orden, para la contribución a una imagen de

Ezequiel Martínez Estrada." In *Homenaje a Ezequiel Martínez Estrada,* pp. 51–62. Bahía Blanca: Universidad Nacional del Sur, 1968.

Ciudad, no. 1 (Buenos Aires, 1955). [Contains brief articles on Martínez Estrada (pp. 30–34) and a bibliography (pp. 35–38) compiled by Héctor Grossi.]

Clemente, José Edmundo. *El ensayo.* Buenos Aires: Ediciones Culturales Argentinas, 1961.

Collingwood, R. G. "The Historical Imagination." In *The Philosophy of History in Our Time,* edited by Hans Meyerhoff, pp. 66–84. New York: Doubleday Anchor Books, 1959.

Commoner, Barry. *Science and Survival,* New York: Viking Press, 1967.

Contorno, no. 4 (Buenos Aires, Dec. 1954). [Special issue on Martínez Estrada.]

Cossío del Pomar, Felipe. "Sudamérica al encuentro de su estilo." *Cuadernos Americanos* 19, no. 2 (March–April 1960):219–227.

Cúneo, Dardo. "Martínez Estrada, Martín Fierro y la Argentina." *Cuadernos Americanos* 8, no. 4 (July–Aug. 1949):210–217.

———. "Sobre Ezequiel Martínez Estrada." In *Aventura y letra de América Latina,* pp. 125–149. Buenos Aires: Ediciones Pleamar, 1964.

Darwin, Charles. *Charles Darwin's Diary of the Voyage of H.M.S. Beagle.* Edited by Nora Barlow. Cambridge, 1934.

El Diario (Buenos Aires), Nov. 23, 1932. [Contains an unsigned article on the National Prize for Literature awarded to Martínez Estrada.]

Diccionario de la literatura argentina. Vol 4 (Argentina), pp. 332–335. Washington, D.C.: Unión Panamericana, 1960. [Contains biographical, critical, and bibliographical material by Alfredo A. Roggiano.]

Durant, Will and Ariel. *The Age of Voltaire.* Vol. 9 of *The Story of Civilization.* New York: Simon and Schuster, 1965.

Earle, Peter G. "Espacio y soledad en la literatura argentina." *Sur,* no. 279 (Nov.–Dec. 1962):30–40.

———. "Función de la poesía en Martínez Estrada." In *Memorias del XIII Congreso Internacional de Literatura Iberoamericana,* in press.

———. "El perspectivismo narrativo de Martínez Estrada." *La Nación,* July 6, 1969.

———. "William Henry Guillermo Enrique Hudson." *Razón y Fábula,* no. 12 (Bogotá, March–April 1969):65–67.

"En la reunión realizada ayer." *La Prensa,* June 2, 1934. [Unsigned article on Martínez Estrada's lecture of June 1, 1934, "Sentido de la paradoja."]

Erro, Carlos Alberto. "Un Sarmiento ahistórico." *Realidad* 1, no. 2 (Buenos Aires, March–April 1947):267–275.

Espinoza, Enrique [pseud. of Samuel Glusberg]. *Tres clásicos ingleses de la pampa.* Santiago, Chile: Babel, 1951. [Essays of F. B. Head, W. H. Hudson, and R. B. Cunninghame Graham.]

"Las exequias de Martínez Estrada." *El Sureño,* Nov. 5, 1964.

"Ezequiel Martínez Estrada falleció en Bahía Blanca." *La Nación,* Nov. 5, 1964.

"Ezequiel Martínez Estrada murió en Bahía Blanca." *La Prensa,* Nov. 5, 1964.

Ferguson, Wallace K. *The Rennaissance in Historical Thought.* New York: Houghton Mifflin Co., 1948.

Fernández Retamar, Roberto. "Ramón de homenaje." *Casa de las Américas* 5, no. 3 (Nov.–Dec. 1965):5–14.

Fingerit, Julio. "La poesía de Ezequiel Martínez Estrada." *Babel* 8, no. 27 (Buenos Aires, March 1928).

Frank, Waldo. *South American Journey.* New York: Duell, Sloan and Pearce, 1943.

Galsworthy, John. Foreword to William Henry Hudson's *Green Mansions,* pp. v–x. New York: Carlton House, n.d.

Gálvez, Manuel. Correspondence with Miguel de Unamuno, in the chapter "El novelista argentino Manuel Gálvez," in *América y Unamuno,* by Manuel García Blanco, pp. 31–52. Madrid: Editorial Gredoa, 1964.

———. Letters to Carlos Obligado and Jorge Max Rohde. *La Fronda* (Buenos Aires), Nov. 25, 1932. [In these letters Gálvez objects to the National Prize in Literature awarded to Martínez Estrada.]

———. See *Atlántida,* Sept. 1960.

Grossi, Héctor. See *Ciudad,* no. 1.

Garasa, Delfin Leocadio. "Como somos los argentinos." *Journal of Inter-American Studies* 7, no. 3 (Gainesville, Fla., July 1965):363–374.

García, Germán. "El Sarmiento de Ezequiel Martínez Estrada." *Cursos y Conferencias* 17, nos. 199–200 (Buenos Aires, Oct.–Dec. 1948):38–51.

García Blanco, Manuel. *América y Unamuno.* Madrid: Editorial Gredos, 1964. [Correspondence between Unamuno and Gálvez, pp. 31–52; correspondence between Unamuno and Rojas, pp. 247–340.]

Gerbi, Antonello. *La disputa del nuovo mondo* (1955). Spanish translation by Antonio Alatorre. Mexico City: Fondo de Cultura Económica, 1960.

Ghiano, Juan Carlos. "Advertencia preliminar." In *Bibliografía y documentos de Ezequiel Martínez Estrada*, by Carlos Adam, pp. 7–10.

———. "Martínez Estrada, narrador." *Ficción*, no. 4 (Buenos Aires, Nov.-Dec. 1956):139–148.

———. *Poesía argentina del siglo XX*, pp. 76–82. Mexico City: Fondo de Cultura Económica, 1957.

———. "Política y literatura argentinas." *La Prensa*, April 6, 1958. [A review of *La tos y otros entretenimientos*.]

Gigli, Adelaida. "La poesía de Ezequiel Martínez Estrada: Oro y piedra siempre." *Contorno*, no. 4 (Dec. 1954):17–19.

González Tuñón, Raúl. Criticism of the National Prize in Literature awards. *La Acción* (Buenos Aires), Nov. 25, 1932.

Green, Otis H. "Gálvez's *La sombra del convento* and its Relation to *El diario de Gabriel Quiroga*." *Hispanic Review* 12, no. 3 (Philadelphia, July 1944):196–210.

———. "Manuel Gálvez, *Gabriel Quiroga*, and *La maestra normal*." *Hispanic Review* 11, no. 3 (Philadelphia, July 1943):221–252.

———. "Manuel Gálvez, *Gabriel Quiroga* and *El mal metafísico*." *Hispanic Review* 11, no. 4 (Philadelphia, Oct. 1943):314–327.

Guido, Beatriz. Interview published in *Confirmado*, no. 56 (Buenos Aires, July 1966). [Miss Guido accuses Martínez Estrada of opposing Lisandro de la Torre, leader of the Progressive Democrats, and of attempting to renounce his Argentine citizenship. She is answered by Pablo Lejarraga, q.v.]

Güiraldes, Ricardo. *Don Segundo Sombra* (1926). Buenos Aires: Editorial Losada, 1955. English translation by Harriet de Onís. London: Penguin Books, 1948.

Hanke, Lewis. *The Spanish Struggle for Justice in the Conquest of America*. Boston: Little, Brown and Co., 1965.

———. *South America*. Princeton: Van Nostrand Co., 1959.

Hernández, José. *Martín Fierro*. Edited by Eleutero F. Tiscornia. Buenos Aires: Editorial Losada, 1963. Bilingual edition translated by C. E. Ward. Albany: State University of New York Press, 1967.

Hernández, Juan José. "Ezequiel Martínez Estrada, poeta." In *Poesía de Ezequiel Martínez Estrada* (anthology), pp. 5–9. Buenos Aires: Ediciones de la Universidad de Buenos Aires, 1965.

"El hombre [Martínez Estrada] que soslaya la muerte." *Primera Plana 2*, no. 91 (Buenos Aires, Aug. 1964):36–38.

Homenaje a Ezequiel Martínez Estrada. Bahía Blanca: Universidad Nacional del Sur, 1968. [Four essays on Martínez Estrada.]

Hudson, William Henry. *Far Away and Long Ago: A History of My Early Life* (1918). Introduction by R. B. Cunninghame Graham. New York: E. P. Dutton & Co., 1959.

————. *A Hind in Richmond Park* (1922). London and Toronto: J. M. Dent and Sons, 1923.

————. *Idle Days in Patagonia* (1893). London and Toronto: J. M. Dent and Sons, 1923.

————. *The Purple Land* (1885). Introduction by William McFee. New York: Modern Library, n.d. [Originally titled *The Purple Land That England Lost*.]

————. *Tales of the Pampas*. New York: Alfred A. Knopf, 1916. [Includes *El Ombú* (1902).]

Ingenieros, José. "Nacionalismo e indianismo." *Revista de América* 2 (Paris, May–Aug. 1913).185–194.

Ivanissevich Machado, Ludovico. "El puritanismo en Martínez Estrada." *Ciudad* 1 (Buenos Aires, 1955):20–23.

Jung, Carl Gustav. "Psychology and Literature." In *The Creative Process*, edited by Brewster Ghiselin, pp. 208–223. New York: Mentor Books, 1955.

Kafka, Franz. *The Diaries of Franz Kafka*, vol. 11 (1914–1923). Edited by Max Brod, translated by Martin Greenberg and Hannah Arendt. New York: Schocken Books, 1949.

Kaufmann, Walter, ed. *Existentialism from Dostoevsky to Sartre*. New York: Meridian Books, 1959.

Keyserling, Hermann. *Méditations Sud-américaines*. Translated by Albert Béguin. Paris: Librairie Stock, 1932. [Martínez Estrada's private library contained a heavily annotated copy of this edition.]

————. *South American Meditations*. Translated by Theresa Duerr. New York and London: Harper and Brothers, 1932.

Kohn, Hans. "Nationalism." In *Nationalism: Its Meaning and History*, rev. ed., pp. 9–91. Princeton: Van Nostrand, 1965.

Kusch, Rodolfo. "Lo superficial y lo profundo en Martínez Estrada." *Contorno*, no. 4 (Dec. 1954):5–8.

Lancelotti, Mario A. "Martínez Estrada cuentista." *Sur*, no. 295 (July–Aug. 1965):55–59.

Le Bon, Gustave. *Lois psychologiques de l'évolution des peuples*. Paris: Alcan, 1895.

Lejarraga, Berta. "Aproximaciones a Ezequiel Martínez Estrada, poeta."
Cuadernos del Sur, nos. 8–9 (Bahía Blanca, July 1967–June 1968):
89–96.

Lejarraga, Pablo. Letter on Martínez Estrada's last years, especially those
spent in Cuba. Confirmado 2, no. 59 (Buenos Aires, Aug. 1966):73.
[Reply to Beatriz Guido, q.v.]

Liacho, Lázaro. "Ezequiel Martínez Estrada." Davar 34 (May–June
1951):40–60.

Lida, Raimundo. "Sarmiento y Herder." In Memoria del Segundo Congreso Internacional de Literatura Iberoamericana, pp. 155–171. Berkeley and Los Angeles: University of California Press, 1941.

López, Lucio V. La gran aldea (1884). Edited by Teresita Frugoni. Buenos Aires: Plus Ultra, 1965.

López Merino, Francisco. "Argentina." Síntesis 1, no. 7 (Buenos Aires,
Dec. 1927):114–115. [On Martínez Estradas's Argentina.]

Lugones, Leopoldo. Article on the controversy between Martínez Estrada
and Manuel Gálvez over the National Prize for Literature. La Fronda
(Buenos Aires), Nov. 25, 1932.

———. "Brindis jovial" (Dec. 9, 1932). On front jacket of Martínez Estrada's Poesía. Buenos Aires: Argos, 1947.

———. "Laureado del gay mester." La Nación, Nov. 25, 1932.

———. El payador (1916). In Obras en prosa. Mexico City: Aguilar,
1962.

Mafud, Julio. El desarraigo argentino. Buenos Aires: Editorial Américalee,
1959.

Mallea, Eduardo. Fiesta en noviembre (1938). 2nd ed. Buenos Aires: Losada, 1949.

———. Historia de una pasión argentina (1937). 3rd ed. Buenos Aires:
Espasa-Calpe, 1944.

Mansilla, Lucio V. Rozas: Ensayo histórico-psicológico. Buenos Aires: La
Cultura Argentina, 1923.

Matteis, Emilio de. La abulia mental en Latinoamérica. Buenos Aires: Editorial La Mandrágora, 1963.

———. Análisis de la vida argentina. Buenos Aires: Américalee, 1962.

Menéndez Pidal, Ramón. The Spaniards in Their History. Translated with
an introduction by Walter Starkie. New York: Norton and Co., 1966.

Morris, Desmond. The Naked Ape. New York: McGraw-Hill Book Co.,
1967.

Mosquera, Ricardo. "Martínez Estrada en la lucha por una Argentina contemporánea." In *Homenaje a Ezequiel Martínez Estrada*, pp. 5–29. Bahía Blanca: Universidad Nacional del Sur, 1968.

Mumford, Lewis. *The City in History*. New York: Harcourt, Brace, and World, 1961.

Murena, H. A. "El acoso de la soledad" and "La lección de los desposeídos: Martínez Estrada." In *El pecado original de América*, pp. 43–65 and 105–129. Buenos Aires: Editorial Sur, 1954.

——. *Homo Atomicus*. Buenos Aires: Editorial Sur, 1961.

Nietzsche, Friedrich. *The Genealogy of Morals*. Translated by Horace B. Samuel. New York: Modern Library, n.d. [Includes an appendix, "Peoples and Countries," intended by Nietzsche to form a supplement to Chapter 8 of *Beyond Good and Evil*.]

Ocampo, Victoria. "Cortina de alas." *Sur*, no. 295 (July–Aug. 1965):1–2.

——. See *Atlántida*, Sept. 1960.

Orfila Reynal, Arnaldo. "Nada más que un recuerdo." *Casa de las Américas* 5, no. 33 (Nov.–Dec. 1965):17–24.

Ortega y Gasset, José. *España invertebrada* (1921). Madrid: Revista de occidente, 1959.

——. "Historia y geografía" (1922). In *Obras completas* II, 371–373. Madrid: Revista de Occidente, 1957.

——. "La pampa . . . promesas" and "El hombre a la defensiva" (1929). In *Obras completas*, II, 635–643 and 643–666.

——. *La rebelión de las masas* (1929). 36th ed. Madrid: Revista de Occidente, 1962.

Otero, Lisandro. Prologue to Martínez Estrada's *El verdadero cuento del Tío Sam*, pp. 5–8. Havana, 1963.

Palcos, Alberto. *Sarmiento: La vida, la obra, las ideas, el genio*. Buenos Aires: El Ateneo, 1938.

"La paradoja, prejuicio gramatical." *La Razón*, June 1, 1934. [Unsigned article on Martínez Estrada's lecture of June 1, 1934. "Sentido de la paradoja."]

Paz, Octavio. *Labyrinth of Solitude*. Translated by Lysander Kemp. New York: Grove Press, 1962.

Pendle, George. *Argentina*. 2nd ed. London: Oxford University Press, 1961.

Pucciarelli, Eugenio. "La imagen de la Argentina en la obra de Ezequiel Martínez Estrada." *Sur*, no. 295 (July–Aug. 1965):34–48.

Quiroga, Horacio. *Cartas inéditas de Horacio Quiroga*. Collected by Arturo Sergio Visca. I, 77–149. Montevideo: Instituto Nacional de Investigaciones y Archivos Literarios, 1959. [Forty letters from Quiroga to Martínez Estrada, also reproduced in Martínez Estrada's *El hermano Quiroga*, q.v.]

————. *El desierto*. Buenos Aires: Babel, 1924.

Ramos, Samuel. *Profile of Man and Culture in Mexico*. Translated by Peter G. Earle. Austin: University of Texas Press, 1962. [See especially Chapter 3, pp. 54–72, "Psychological Analysis of the Mexican."]

Randall, John Herman, Jr. *The Making of the Modern Mind*. Rev. ed. New York: Houghton Mifflin, 1940. [See especially Chapter 19, "The Science of Man in the Growing World."]

"Regresó de la Unión un escritor argentino." *La Nación*, Sept. 3, 1942. [Unsigned article on Martínez Estrada.]

Rest, Jaime. *Cuatro hipótesis de la Argentina*. Bahía Blanca: Universidad Nacional del Sur, 1961.

————. "Evocación de Martínez Estrada." *Sur*, no. 295 (July–Aug. 1965): 69–72.

————. "Trayectoria de Martínez Estrada." In *Homenaje a Ezequiel Martínez Estrada*, pp. 46–51. Bahía Blanca: Universidad Nacional del Sur, 1968.

Rivera Indarte, ————. *Tablas de sangre de la administración de Rozas*. Quoted by Lucio V. Mansilla in *Rozas: Ensayo histórico-psicológico*, p. 193. Buenos Aires: La Cultura Argentina, 1923.

Rodríguez Monegal, Emir. "Crónica de Libros." *Marcha*, no. 638 (Sept. 5, 1952):14–15. [Includes a review of *El mundo maravilloso de Guillermo Enrique Hudson*.]

————. "Martínez Estrada o la toma de conciencia." In *El juicio de los parricidas*, pp. 13–28. Buenos Aires: Editorial Deucalión.

————. "Panorama de las literaturas." *Marcha*, no. 372 (Montevideo, March 21, 1947):14. [Review of Martínez Estrada's *Panorama de los literaturas*.]

Roggiano, Alfredo A. See *Diccionario de la literatura argentina*.

Rojas, Ricardo. "Una carta abierta a Ezequiel Martínez Estrada." *Babel* 8, no. 27 (Buenos Aires, March 1928).

————. *Eurindia*. In *Obras*, vol. 5. Buenos Aires: Librería "La Facultad." 1924.

————. *El profeta de la pampa* [Sarmiento]. Buenos Aires: Losada, 1945.

Romero, José Luis. "Martínez Estrada: Un renovador de la exégesis sarmienta." *Cuadernos Americanos* 6, no. 3 (May–June 1947):197–204.

Reproduced in *Argentina: Imágenes y perspectivas*, pp. 99–107. Buenos Aires: Editorial Raigal, 1956.

Sánchez Albornoz, Claudio. "La edad media y la empresa de América." In *España y el Islam*, pp. 181–199. Buenos Aires, 1943.

Sánchez Garrido, Amelia. "Un cuentista en su laberinto: Notas sobre la narrativa de Martínez Estrada." In *Homenaje a Ezequiel Martínez Estrada*, pp. 29–46. Bahía Blanca: Universidad Nacional del Sur, 1968.

Sarmiento, Domingo F. *Facundo*. Edited by Emma Susana Speratti Piñero. Mexico City: Universidad Nacional Autónoma de México, 1957.

Scalabrini Ortiz, Raúl. *El hombre que está solo y espera*. 10th ed. Buenos Aires: Plus Ultra, 1964.

Schlesinger, Arthur M., Jr. "On the Writing of Contemporary History." *Atlantic Monthly* 129, no. 3 (March 1967):69–74.

Schopenhauer, Arthur. *The World as Will and Idea*. Translated by R. B. Haldane and J. Kemp. New York: Dolphin Books, 1961.

Schultz de Mantovani, Fryda. "Martínez Estrada" (Lecture, Nov. 23, 1965, at Hotel Provincial, La Plata). In *Bibliografía y documentos de Ezequiel Martínez Estrada*, by Carlos Adam, pp. 235–241. Universidad Nacional de La Plata, 1968.

Sebreli, Juan José. *Martínez Estrada: Una rebelión inútil*. Buenos Aires: Editorial Palestra, 1960.

———. "Vida de un pequeño burgués." *Confirmado* 2, no. 59 (Buenos Aires, Aug. 4, 1966):41–43.

Silvert, K. H. "The Costs of Anti-Nationalism: Argentina." In *Expectant Peoples*, edited by K. H. Silvert, pp. 347–372. New York: Vintage Books, 1967.

Simmel, Georg. *Schopenhauer y Nietzsche*. Translated by Francisco Ayala. Buenos Aires: Editorial Schapire, 1944.

Soto, Luis Emilio. "Análisis espectral de la pampa" (1934) and "Arbitraje espiritual." In *Crítica y estimación*, pp. 109–124 and 125–135. Buenos Aires: Editorial Sur, 1938. [Both essays deal with *Radiografía de la pampa*.]

Spengler, Oswald. *The Decline of the West* (1918). Translated by Charles Francis Atkinson. 2 vols. New York: Alfred A. Knopf, 1950. [See especially "The Idea of Destiny and the Principle of Casuality," I, 117–160; and "The Symbolism of the World-Picture and the Space-Problem," I, 163–180.]

Stabb, Martin S. "Ezequiel Martínez Estrada: The Formative Writings." *Hispania* 49, no. 1 (Amherst, Mass., March 1966):54–60.

————. In Quest of Identity: Patterns in the Spanish American Essay of Ideas, 1890–1960. Chapel Hill: University of North Carolina Press, 1967.

————. "Martínez Estrada frente a la critica." Revista Iberoamericana 32, no. 61 (Pittsburgh, Jan.–June 1966):77–84.

Torchia Estrada, Juan Carlos. La filosofía en la Argentina. Washington, D.C.: Unión Panamericana, 1961.

Torres Ríoseco, Arturo. New World Literature. Berkeley and Los Angeles: University of California Press, 1949.

Unamuno, Miguel de. "Martín Fierro." In Obras completas, VIII, 47–63. Barcelona: Vergara, 1958.

Undurraga, Antonio. "Encuesta sobra la literatura hispanoamericana, argentina y chilena." Ciudad, nos. 2–3 (Buenos Aires, 1955):69–70.

Ustinov, Peter. "Politics and the Arts." Atlantic Monthly 218, no. 1 (July 1966):44–48.

Veiravé, Alfredo. "La poesía de Ezequiel Martínez Estrada." Lecture given Aug. 2, 1966, at the Sociedad Argentina de Escritores, Buenos Aires.

Vera Ocampo, Raúl. "El Sarmiento de Martínez Estrada: Un ensayo de autobiografía." Sur, no. 295 (July–Aug. 1965):60–68.

Viñas, David. "La historia excluída: Ubicación de Martínez Estrada." Contorno, no. 4 (Buenos Aires, Dec. 1954):10–16.

Viñas, Ismael. "Reflexión sobre Martínez Estrada." Contorno, no. 4 (Buenos Aires, Dec. 1954):2–4.

Weckmann, Luis. "The Middle Ages in the Conquest of America." Speculum 26, no. 1 (Cambridge, Mass., Jan. 1951):130–141.

Weil, Simone, L'Enracinement. Paris: Librairie Gallimard, 1949.

Whitaker, Arthur P. Argentina. Englewood Cliffs, N. J.: Prentice-Hall, 1964.

White, Lynn, Jr. "The Legacy of the Middle Ages in the American Wild West." Speculum 40, no. 2 (April 1965):191–202.

Zum Felde, Alberto. Indice crítico de la literatura hispanoamericana. Mexico City: Editorial Guaranía, 1954.

INDEX